T0064433

End Time Scenario

End Time Scenario

The Picture Is Getting Clearer

MOSES L.H. TAY

PARTRIDGE
A Penguin Random House Company

ISBN: Softcover 978-1-4828-3280-8
eBook 978-1-4828-3281-5

Print information available on the last page.

To order additional copies of this book, contact
Toll Free 800 101 2657 (Singapore)
Toll Free 1 800 81 7340 (Malaysia)
orders.singapore@partridgepublishing.com

www.partridgepublishing.com/singapore

To Yeshua,

The Beloved of the Father, to You He had committed all things. As the heir apparent, You must shortly bring all things under Your feet. Lord Jesus, come for the Church, Your Bride that You have been preparing these many years.

Contents

Acknowledgments ix

Introduction xi

Part 1 The Beginning of Sorrows 1

Chapter 1 Opening Of The Seals 3

Chapter 2 The Four Horses Of The Apocalypse 9

Chapter 3 Living Between The Seals 25

Chapter 4 The Jews 40

Chapter 5 Have The Christians Replaced The Jews? (Replacement Theology) 60

Chapter 6 Jewish Global Influence 87

Chapter 7 The Shemitah 105

Chapter 8 The Blood Moon 118

Chapter 9 America 125

Chapter 10 Moral Decline & Changing Of God's Law 135

Chapter 11 Economic Decline & Collapse Of The Usd 153

Part 2 Some Major Events Leading To The Second Coming Of Christ 161

Chapter 12 Coming Judgment Of America 163

Chapter 13 Coming Russian Invasion Of Israel 179

Chapter 14 Rapture 188

Chapter 15 70Th Week Of Daniel 207

Chapter 16 7 Years Reign Of The Antichrist 221

Chapter 17 7 Trumpets And 7 Bowls Judgment 238

Chapter 18 Second Coming Of Christ 242

NOTES 247

ACKNOWLEDGMENTS

I want to express my appreciation to the following persons for their permission to quote from the visions and dreams that God had given them. Without their contributions, this book could not be written.

First, I want to thank Michael Boldea, on behalf of his late grandfather Dumitru Duduman, for the revelation that the Bible does mention or do have references to America. It came to my knowledge many years ago as an answer to a major puzzle in my understanding of eschatology.

I want to thank Prophet David Edward Owour for the realization that the countdown has begun with the release of the four horses of the apocalypse. It put to rest the confusion that arises from conflicting opinions concerning the opening of the Seven Seals. With the inauguration of the Seals, the runway is now cleared, and we are finally on the way to taking off.

My thanks go to Pastor T D Hale. To you the Lord had shown America has a President, who will commit the final abomination. Moreover, he did just that a couple of weeks ago, working through the U.S. Supreme Court. This development should quell any remaining hope that the nation could turn around from its moral decline.

Thank you, Pastor Shane Warren, for the vision God gave you of the coming collapse of the USD followed by a major earthquake to hit the nation. It is a comforting thought that God cares and has informed His people to prepare. The Church will arise like a giant to face the challenging times.

Last but not least, I want to thank David Jones and Dr. Mary K. Baxter for the certainty that the rapture will take place soon. By showing them the Rapture in visions, God seeks to encourage the faithful who are eagerly waiting for the coming of the Lord.

INTRODUCTION

God has a big redemptive plan for mankind, and the program is broken up into several phases. Each stage has a starting point and an end. We are presently in the phase that coincided with the Seven Seals mentioned in the Book of Revelation. This period starts in the year 2001, and will close sometime in the next few years.

There is much talk about end times these days. End times does not mean the world is about to come to an end. The truth is; the world is not ready to stop anytime soon. The Bible says the earth will be made new one day, and it will carry on existing for an eternity. However, end times is upon us, time in which God brings to a close the current phase of His dealing with mankind. The present phase is an important one, although not the last. After that, He will initiate the next stage that will culminate with the second coming of Christ to set up His Millennium kingdom.

Humanity needs compass and direction. The God, who created us, has revealed His plans and purposes so that they may be a guide for us. It behooves the people of this generation to find out what the Most High has prepared, and that we may seek to flow along with His plan. God place the inhabitants of the earth into three groups: the general populace, the Jews, and His Church. Irrespective of which group one may currently belong, He is calling everyone to turn to Him in repentance, and to live holy lives as proof of one's repentance. Turn to Him while there is still time.

However, not everyone will turn to Him. If we do not put our faith in His redemptive plan, we resist Him. Even nations are rebelling. America, the world superpower is going down the path of defiance. With recent development in that country, what will become of her? Who can effectively resist Him and get away with it? Prophet Daniel of old said to King Nebuchadnezzar of Babylon that God had allowed certain matters to happen to his life so that he (Nebuchadnezzar) may know "...that the Most High rules in the kingdom of men and gives it to whomever He chooses" (Daniel 4:25). It is God who establishes a nation, and it is Him who can bring it down. History has shown that nations rise, nations fall, and kingdom rise and kingdom falls—all these happened with His approval.

When powerful nations rise or fall it creates tremendous upheaval in the world. It is so when accompanied by a global war. In the next few years, the world will witness the fall of America and the rise of Russia. Shortly after that, it will be Russia's demise and the ascension of the Antichrist kingdom (European Union). Eventually, the Antichrist kingdom will collapse when Christ returns to install His eternal kingdom on the earth.

From the current vantage point, all these events are still in the future. Regarding what lies ahead, there is a cacophony of man's opinions that are not in line with the Bible. However, God wants to make plain what He had written in there. For this reason, He has spoken through His present day servants, prophets and ministers of the gospel. He is doing this to clear out confusion from man's interference, and mishandling of His word. With regards to the subject of end times, He has been releasing bits of information here and there through visions and dreams. Each bit is a piece of information that when put together collectively will form one big jigsaw puzzle. In this book, we seek to bring as many pieces of information together, and by God's grace, attempt to put each piece in its proper place. A clear picture would emerge after that.

PART ONE

The Beginning of Sorrows

Chapter 1

OPENING OF THE SEALS

> And he said, "Go your way, Daniel, for the words are closed up and sealed till the time of the end. Many shall be purified, made white, and refined, but the wicked shall do wickedly; and none of the wicked shall understand, but the wise shall understand."
>
> [Daniel 12:9-10]

We commence with the Book of Revelation, the last book in the Bible. It contains visions and revelation of Jesus Christ given to His servant the Apostle John. Elderly by then, the Romans banished him to the island of Patmos c.AD 95. What were shown to John were events that had already taken place and those in the process of unfolding in his day. That is not all; he also saw prophetic events, that is, events that would be happening hundreds, even thousands, of years into the future.

In Chapter 4, we read that John heard a voice saying, "Come up here, and I will show you things that must take place after this" (Revelation 4:1). Immediately he was caught up in the spirit to heaven before the throne of God. He saw the appearance of God, four living creatures and twenty-four elders sitting on their thrones. Added to his amazement, he witnessed an assemblage of millions of angels worshipping God before His throne.

On the right hand of God was a scroll or book sealed with seven seals. An angel proclaimed with a loud voice saying, "Who is worthy to open the scroll and to release its seals?" At first it seemed no one was worthy. John was greatly comforted when Jesus Christ the Lamb of God, stepped forward, He who was the only one worthy to open it and to loose the seven seals (Revelation 5:4-7).

What is inside the scroll or book sealed with seven seals? It contains God's program that He had prepared for the Church and the world. When the Lamb of God opened them one by one, the program will be launched, assisted by His holy angels.

What is the program all about? The program comprises two parts. The first part is to prepare and bring His people home to heaven. The second part is to judge and to pour out His wrath on the inhabitants of the world for their rejection of Christ and mistreatment of His people. The first six seals covers the first part of the program. The remaining seventh seal covers the second part of the program.

The true Church is His Bride, and He is preparing to bring her home to heaven. The Lamb of God is the Bridegroom, and He is ready to come to lead her to her eternal home. The situation on the earth is being prepared for that glorious day.

The mass exit of God's people from the earth resembles the mass departure of the children of Israel from ancient Egypt, an event the Bible called the Exodus (Exodus 3-14). Following their exodus from Egypt, the children of Israel journeyed into the land of Canaan, the promised land (Joshua 1-4). In this generation, the world shall soon witness God's people exiting the earth and making their journey to heaven, their eternal abode that God had promised. This event of the mass departure from the earth is called the Rapture (See Chapter 14). However, it could not take place until the situation "on the ground" has been prepared.

The Scroll contains God's program. First part of the program is to bring the bride of Christ home to heaven

Up till the time of the Exodus, the children of Israel dwelled in Egypt for 430 years. In the early years of their sojourned they were welcomed and well-treated by Pharaoh and the Egyptians. In those days, Joseph was appointed the Prime Minister of Egypt by the Pharaoh. However, with each new Pharaoh, who inherited the throne, the attitude began to change from favoring them to mistreating them. The day came when the children of Israel were treated as slaves by the Egyptians under the cruel rule and control of the Pharaoh. As slaves, they had lost their civil rights. They were forced to make bricks from straws given to them. They were expected to meet a certain quota of bricks each day. The heavy burden exerted on them caused them to cry out to their God; the God of Abraham, Isaac and Jacob. In response to their pathetic cry, God Almighty sent Moses to tell Pharaoh to "let MY people go" that they may hold feasts to worship Him in the wilderness. Instead of relenting at Moses's initial request, he refused and hardened his heart. He even demanded the children of Israel to fulfill their daily quota of bricks without supplying them the needed straws (Exodus 5:6-14). Obviously, Pharaoh was unwilling to let the children of Israel go because they could make bricks, using them as a form of cheap labor.

It was dangerous to resist God the way Pharaoh did. Since he was adamant, and God knew he would continue to be adamant, the Bible said God hardened his (Pharaoh) heart. Would Almighty God harden Pharaoh's heart if he had an iota of humility towards God and respect for His people? He had said, "Who is the Lord that I should obey His voice to let Israel go? I do not know the Lord, nor will I let Israel go" (Exodus 5:2). Callous disregard for the wishes of the God of Israel firmly set his heart. He had no intention to back down. God began to initiate judgment on the land of Egypt with the first plague by turning river water into blood, killing all fishes in them. With more plagues following, Pharaoh showed a little remorse but was not truly genuine. His heart secret intention was exposed completely by the time the ten plagues judgment ended.

God's judgment on Pharaoh's kingdom wrecked his royal household and the subservient Egyptians. Taking on the attitude of their king, the Egyptians ratcheted up their mistreatment of the children of Israel as hard taskmasters. The more Pharaoh hardened his heart; the more the Egyptians hardened their hearts, increasing the oppression of the children of Israel. As the ten plagues judgment fell one after another, the tension between the Egyptians and the children of Israel reached a critical point. On unleashing the tenth plague where all the firstborn sons of Egyptian families died, the grip held by Egyptians over the children of Israel had broken finally.

Although the children of Israel were being treated as slaves by the Egyptians, the former were not at all ready to give up their homes, farmlands and businesses to travel to an unknown land introduced to them by Moses. Among the over two million men, women and children who left Egypt, many would have decided not to leave their familiar surroundings. At the end, the unbearable situation with the Egyptians disrupted their comfort zone. Finally, they have no choice but to leave Egypt.

Today, the Church of Jesus Christ is being prepared together with the world for the mass exodus of the faithful believers, the Bride of Christ. Judgment is upon the world, on the modern "Pharaohs and the Egyptians." The resultant side-effect is the oppression and persecution of the Church. Apparently, the Church needs to be loosed from the grip of the world. Scripture has said the Church is *in* the world but is not *of* the world. In fact, the Church which is the body of Christ comprised believers who are called out from the world. If called out then, she should not return to be re-entangled. Carnality has rendered the Church earth-bound. For this reason, the Church will be led through a short period of persecution. It will be the great tribulation when the fifth and sixth seals are opened (See Chapter 3). Through tribulation, the Church will be purified. Those willing to submit to cleansing will be set apart as the Bride of Christ ready to exit the earth in the event of the rapture.

When will the seals be opened? Throughout the lengthy period of Church history, many have studied and enquired as to its timing. Evidently, it remains the prerogative of the Lamb of God to announce its opening when the time is right.

Indeed, the time is right now as He had already announced the opening of the seals to one of His servants, Prophet David Edward Owour.[1]

Who is Prophet David Edward Owour?

It would be beneficial to know a little about the person whom the Lamb of God had entrusted with the announcement of the opening of the seals.

Dr. Owour is a Kenyan whom the Lord called in 1996 while he was pursuing his doctorate in Israel.[2] One night a glory cloud appeared to him in his room, and he heard his name called out three times. At the time, he did not respond to the ministry calling to follow and serve God. After his graduation as a scientist, he went to work in the United States. While pursuing his career there, the Lord reminded him about the call but he tried again to run away from the Lord by moving from city to city.

In the third city where he lived and worked, the Lord finally caught up with him on July 3, 2003. He saw a vision of these two verses of the Bible projected on the wall, in this sequence:

Isaiah 43:11
I, even I, am the Lord, and besides Me there is no Savior.

Isaiah 43:1
But now, thus says the Lord, who created you, O Jacob, and He who formed you, O Israel; "Fear not, for I have redeemed you; I have called you by your name; you are Mine.

The Scripture verses were a revelation of Who God is, and who he (Owour) is to God. Convinced, he surrendered his career and life to answer the call of God.

Soon, in one of the many visions God gave him, he was shown Moses and Daniel on one side of the Ark of the Covenant, and Elijah and himself (Owour) on the other side. He heard a voice said, "Now I've My four prophets." Also he heard, "Power has been given unto you."

The Lord commissioned him to preach to the Church the message of repentance and holiness because the Church is in dire straits and is not ready for the coming of the Messiah. The Church is experiencing decay: messages are adulterated, the presence of sexual sins, rampant falsehood and general lack of holiness.

In a vision on April 2, 2004, he saw the throne of God. John the Baptist came and spoke to him and said, "Go and prepare these people for the coming of the Messiah." In another vision on November 1, 2006, he saw two wedding rings appeared in the sky. The message is the Marriage Supper of the Lamb is ready but is the Bride of Christ ready?

So far, God showed him over sixty earthquakes, tsunami and other judgments fallen on the earth before they occur. Many of these prophesied events had already come to pass while some are still pending. Below are some major earthquakes, tsunami and powerful storms that devastated our planet in the recent past:

- Indian Ocean Tsunami prophesied on November 24, 2004, which was fulfilled on December 26, 2004. This tsunami, generated by a powerful earthquake registered 9.2 on the Richter Scale, resulted in the death of 230,000 people from fourteen countries, mainly Indonesia, Sri Lanka, India, Thailand, and Malaysia.

- Hurricane Katrina prophesied on July 20, 2005, which was fulfilled on August 29, 2005. It was a Category 5 hurricane but weakened to Category 3 when it made landfall in southeast Louisiana, USA. Nevertheless, it was one of the deadliest hurricanes in the nation's history which resulted in at least 1,833 deaths and the costliest in terms of property loss.

- Kenyan post-election violence prophesied on February 12, 2006, fulfilled in January 2008. The crisis erupted after the incumbent President Mwai Kibaki was declared the winner of the presidential election held on December 27, 2007. The violence unleashed by groups along political and ethnic lines. Eight hundred to 1,500 people were believed killed, and 180,000 to 600,000 people displaced.

- Haiti earthquake prophesied on November 28, 2009, fulfilled on January 12, 2010. The earthquake registered a magnitude of 7.0 on the Richter Scale, resulted in deaths estimated at between 100,000 to 160,000 people.

- A massive flood in Austria prophesied on July 9, 2012, which was fulfilled on June 1, 2013. After several days of incessant rain in Central Europe, many areas were inundated with flood waters. Not only Austria but at least six other European nations were affected, resulted in total estimated loss of €12bn, albeit with a low fatality rate.

Will the Church and the world-at-large wake-up and take heed of the message of El Elyon before it is too late?

Chapter 2

THE FOUR HORSES OF THE APOCALYPSE

Jesus Christ, the Lamb of God, is the only one worthy to open the seven seals. At this point (early 2015), the first four seals are already opened. When the seals opened, one after the other, the four horses representing each seal proceeded from the presence of God in heaven and made their way down to the earth.

Of the seven seals, the first four seals were represented by four colored horses. In chronological order, the horses are colored white, red, black and pale and are known as the four horses of the apocalypse.[1]

There are similar colored horses mentioned elsewhere in the Bible. If we take a look at these other references, it will help our understanding to know who they are. Are these horses the spirits from the kingdom of darkness or spirits from the kingdom of heaven? Who are the riders? Are they demons or angels?

Now, similar colored horses were shown to Prophet Zechariah. It happened one day when the Jewish remnant had returned from the Babylonian exile. It was in the days of the rebuilding of the second Temple in Jerusalem.

> **Zechariah 1:8-11**
> **8** I saw by night and behold, a man riding on a red horse, and it stood among the myrtle trees in the hollow, and behind him were *horses: red, sorrel, and white.* **9** Then I said, "My lord, *what are these*?" So the angel who talked with me said to me, "I will show you what they are." **10** And the man who stood among the myrtle trees answered and said, "*These are the ones whom the*

> *Lord has sent to walk to and fro throughout the earth.*" **11** So they answered the Angel of the Lord, who stood among the myrtle trees, and said, "We have walked to and fro throughout the earth, and behold, all the earth is resting quietly." (Emphasis added)
>
> **Zechariah 6:1-8**
>
> **1** Then I turned and raised my eyes and looked, and behold, four chariots were coming from between two mountains and the mountains were mountains of bronze. **2** With the *first chariot were red horses, with the second chariot black horses, **3** with the third chariot white horses, and with the fourth chariot dappled horses--strong steeds.* **4** Then I answered and said to the angel who talked with me, "*What are these*, my lord?" **5** And the angel answered and said to me, "These are *four spirits of heaven*, who go out from their station before the Lord of all the earth. **6** The one with the black horses is going to the North country, the white are going after them, and the dappled are going toward the south country." **7** Then the strong steeds went out, eager to go, that they might walk to and fro throughout the earth. And He said, "Go, walk to and fro throughout the earth." So they walked to and fro throughout the earth. **8** And He called to me and spoke to me, saying, "See, those who go toward the North country have given rest to My Spirit in the north country." (Emphasis added)

Notice that Zechariah was having a conversation with the rider on one of those horses, and the identification of the rider is that he was an angel. We believe all the riders on the colored horses that Zechariah saw were angels. Those angels riding on those horses (spirits of heaven) walked to and fro throughout the whole earth surveying the regional situation and keeping watched over the people of God.

Based on what Prophet Zechariah saw, we believe the "he" or "him" (Revelation 6:2,4, 5, 8) in the Apostle John's vision were angels riding on those horses. They were not human beings or demons as some have mistaken them to be. They were sent out from heaven, as there are no demons found in heaven.

The angels on their respective horses were sent out on missions to execute God's plan for the earth. At this critical period, God's plan involves executing judgment on the inhabitants of the earth. With sobriety, we acknowledged that God's judgment will always be tempered with His mercy unlike the case with His wrath. Upon being warned that God will judge sins, the one who repents will receive mercy and experience redemption. The one who refuses to repent will be hardened.

Now in the following few pages, we shall first look into the description of each of the horses, and what their respective missions are on earth. We shall make reference to the time of their release as shown to God's servant. Finally, we shall determine what the outcomes or evidence of the angels' activities were as far as we can determine, since the time they were released.

First Seal: Angel on the White Horse

Beginning in the Book of Revelation Chapter 6, verses 1-2, we read that when the first seal opened, the white horse[2] was released to the earth. The angel who sat on it had a bow, and a crown was given to him, and he went out conquering and to conquer.

The bow in the angel's hand refers to an ancient projectile weapon. Normally an arrow or a spear is mentioned together with the bow as in "bow and arrow" or "bow and spear." In this instance, only the bow was cited. Is this peculiar and has a hidden meaning? Or is it just a shortened form of expression? We shall take our cue from a passage of scripture in Genesis 49:22-26.

According to the passage, Jacob (Israel) was advanced in age. Before he passed away, he called all his twelve sons to appear before him. One by one, he prophesied over them, foretelling what will become of their lives and their descendants commencing with Reuben, the eldest son. When it came to Joseph's turn, his eleventh son, this was what Jacob said:

> **Genesis 49:22-26**
> **22** "Joseph is a fruitful bough, A fruitful bough by a well; His branches run over the wall. **23** The archers have bitterly grieved him, Shot at him and hated him. **24** *But his bow remained in strength, And the arms of his hands were made strong* By the hands of the Mighty God of Jacob (From there is the Shepherd, the Stone of Israel), **25** By the God of your father who will help you, And by the Almighty who will bless you With blessings of heaven above, Blessings of the deep that lies beneath, Blessings of the breasts and of the womb. **26** The blessings of your father have excelled the blessings of my ancestors, Up to the utmost bound of the everlasting hills. They shall be on the head of Joseph, And *on the crown of the head of him* who was separate from his brothers. (Emphasis added)

Joseph was the favorite son of Jacob. The prophetic word Jacob gave to Joseph and his descendants was a good one and very positive. Joseph would be fruitful and his fruitfulness, overflowing. However, Joseph would have many enemies who hated him and grieved him. His enemies would be like archers shooting arrows at him with intent to kill. Nevertheless, he would be strong and be able to stand and defend himself as his "bow remained in strength." God would strengthen his hands. Moreover, with great blessings from the God of his fathers, Joseph would indeed be prosperous and be victorious over his enemies. The abundant overflowing blessings would be seen settling "on the crown of his head."

We reiterate here that Joseph's "bow remained in strength" was a phrase that suggested his weapon was still intact after having used it to repulse his enemies attack. Furthermore, his hands that held the weapon were being strengthened by God. The conclusion then is this; the mentioned of the bow without mentioning the arrow or spear along with it was not something peculiar. There is no hidden meaning attached to it. Simply, it was just a shorter form of an expression.

Resuming, we note that the angel with a bow in hand went out conquering and to conquer. His mission was to execute God's judgment on the people of the earth. He encountered opposition from the enemies of God. From

God's perspective, the enemies were the forces of darkness colluding with wicked men opposing God and the Church. However, the angel is assured of victory. The crown on his head indicates that outcome because a crown is an object that symbolizes victory. The forces of darkness led by Satan operate a devious system of control over mankind. Originating from the spiritual realm, it entwines itself around the political, economic, religious and other human systems in the world. God must expose Satan's power. The particular mission of the angel on the white horse is to expose and defeat it.

Released of the Angel on the White Horse

The angel on the white horse was believed released in the year 2001. What significant event took place in that year? The world was shocked to learn on the morning of September 11 that great destruction came upon the World Trade Center buildings in New York City, USA. The group of buildings included not only the North and South Twin Towers but also Building Number 7 (WTC7). Apart from these, the Pentagon building located in Arlington County, Virginia was also hit. Together, the event saw the death of nearly 3,000 people.

These buildings are the pride of the United States of America. They represent the political, economic and military powers of America. So what does this mean? All these are the judgment of God on America. Remember, the mission of the four horses of the apocalypse is to execute God's judgment on the inhabitants of the earth. Specifically, the mission of the Angel on the white horse is to confront the enemies of God and to expose their secret intent. How does this relate to the alleged terrorist attack on the World Trade Centre? Despite the "nineteen Arab terrorists" could not possibly have the ability to carry out such a complicated operation, the powers that be running America wants the world to believe they did it. It was to be an excuse to launch the "war on terror."

Why could not the "nineteen Arab terrorists" carry out the attack? Consider these few observations and evidence:

a. Two airplanes hit the North and South Twin Towers of the World Trade Centre (WTC) around 9 am, and they collapsed. Another building, the 47-story WTC Building No.7 also collapsed at 5 pm, despite not being hit by any airplane.

b. The airplanes could not have caused the Twin Towers to collapse because:

   i) The towers were built to withstand multiple hits by large airplanes
   ii) Jet fuel burning at the maximum heat of 400°C (750°F) could not melt steel at the core of the buildings that could only melt at 1,300°C (2,400°F).

c. Collapsed of all three buildings were in a "free fall" manner. It means the fall did not encounter any resistance (Newton's Third Law: "For every action there is an equal and opposite reaction" did not seem to be at work at the time). It must indicate it was a controlled demolition rather than a structural weakness that cause the buildings to collapse.

d. The sound of explosions heard by over 100 witnesses, some heard it while they were still inside the buildings. Some explosion was heard coming from the basement floors.

e. What caused the explosions? Scientists, examining the molten steel and ashes left behind at Ground Zero, found the presence of nano-thermite, an advanced type of explosives which can burn up to 2,400°C (4,500°F). Only the military has possession of this kind of explosives.

f. September 11 was a Tuesday. A few days earlier, there was a power-down on Saturday and Sunday (September 8 and 9) meaning electrical power was completely shut off in those buildings. Security personnel testified they saw people brought into the buildings boxes of materials during the power-down period.

g. The attack on the Pentagon. We were told Flight 77 a Boeing 757-200 plane hit the Pentagon building. The plane of that size should have created a much larger hole in the wall. Instead, a security camera located nearby captured a missile hitting the building.

h. Over 2,300 architects and engineers put their reputation on the line expressing their doubt 9/11 attack was carried out by Arab terrorists. They disputed the official government reports:

   i) The 9/11 Commission Report issued by the 9/11 Commission
   ii) The NIST Report published by the National Institute of Standards and Technology (commonly known as NIST).[3]

It is not the purpose here to delve into too much detail. Suffice to say that the destruction of the buildings on September 11 was not due to an attack by the Arab terrorists but rather was an inside job. The people who carried out that operation had unwittingly made themselves visible. Remember, the precise mission of the angel on the white horse is to conquer the forces of darkness through exposing their secret agenda. These people are globalists, an international cabal, with their New World Order agenda. Since they do not pledge allegiance to any country nor any religion but Lucifer, using America or any other country for their egocentric purpose is considered their inalienable rights. Their agenda for a global government did not preclude them from using any means, whether inhumane or not, to subjugate nations under their dominance. Apparently, they are using the U.S. military and NATO (North Atlantic Treaty Organization) to threaten or to attack countries whether justified or not. The "war on terror" is just one of the many examples. Using international financial leverage to lend and get nations into debt. As the saying goes, "the borrower is a servant to the lender," through massive debt creation, countries become servitude. Controlling the international mass media and using it to disseminate information favorable to them.

The presence of such a group of people was not noticeable to the world-at-large earlier on, although they have been in existence for decades. They hid behind smoke screens and carried out false flag operations around the world undetected. However, their existence and secret plan are slowly coming to light as a result of the landmark event of September 11. More and more people around the world are waking up to their presence in our society. They are now being exposed as the modern-day Pharaohs. It is one of the successes of the angel on the white horse whose mission is not over yet. Together with the other three colored horses, their work will continue until the Church is being set free from these tyrants.

Second Seal: Angel on the Red Horse

When the Lamb of God opened the second seal, the Apostle John saw a fiery red horse proceeded from the presence of God, and it made its way to the earth. God granted authority to the angel to take peace from the earth, and that people should kill one another, and there was given to him a great sword (Revelation 6:3-4).

Very clearly, the mission of the angel on the red horse was to take away or remove peace from the earth that invariably would result in tension and conflict arising among peoples and nations. We were told the angel carried a great sword with him, and men began killing one another on the earth.

Released of the Angel on the Red Horse

Prophet David Edward Owour received the knowledge of the opening of this second seal. It was through a vision God gave him on April 2, 2004.[4] Bear in mind that this happened just nine months after the day he responded to the call of God to serve Him in the ministry. The date was on July 3, 2003.

As he related his experience, in the vision he was caught up in the spirit into the presence of God in heaven. Suddenly, appeared above the throne of God was the moon. The moon began to turn red, gradually at first but finally became completely reddish. He then saw the red moon cast its shadow on the earth below. He was made to understand that conflicts were about to break out among some nations of the earth.

Since that day, numerous religious, ethnic and ideological conflicts had indeed broken out. A few of them listed below:

- Israel – Gaza Conflicts in 2004, 2007, 2008 and most recently 2014
- Israel – Hezbollah War in 2006
- Central African Republic Bush War 2004-2007
- Shia insurgency in Yemen in 2004 – present (2014)
- Ukraine 2014

Third Seal: Angel on the Black Horse

When the Lamb of God opened the third seal, the Apostle John saw a black horse. The angel who rode on it held a pair of scales in his hand. In addition, John heard a voice uttered by one of the four living creatures. The living creature says, "A quart of wheat for a denarius and three quarts of barley for a denarius, and do not harm the oil and the wine" (Revelation 6:5-6).

The pair of scales is an instrument for weighing things — two trays hung from each end of a balance beam. A quart of wheat would be the estimated amount of food for one's daily consumption and sustenance. However, it would require a denarius to buy that. A denarius is an ancient Roman silver coin representing a typical day's wage for an ordinary laborer. Similarly, it would require a denarius to purchase three quarts of barley, the amount of food perhaps just enough for the daily sustenance of a small family. The idiom "living from hand to mouth" is a very apt description of these circumstances.

The dire situation depicted above was either the result of shortages of food or the effect of hyperinflation, that is, the rapid loss of real value in one's money. The former could be the direct consequence of war and other conditions such as severe drought that would curtail food production while the latter could be the direct fallout of financial and economic slump due to unsustainable debt. Whatever the reason, the Angel was instructed not to harm the oil and the wine. Is the oil here referring to cooking oil or crude oil, or both? Whichever it may be, there will not be any shortages. There will be an abundant supply of both oil and wine which would mean that these two commodities will be cheap in prices.

Released of the Angel on the Black Horse

A few days before his revival crusade in Nakuru, Kenya, on August 19, 2008, Prophet Owour had a vision. He was before the throne of God. In front of him appeared a glory cloud, and out of that cloud came forth a black horse.[5] It galloped towards him and stopped momentarily directly in front of him. It neighed, and its mane flapped like a flag. Then it turned and went down to the earth.

During the revival crusade that followed the vision, he told the crowd what he saw. He announced that the coming global economic crisis was going to hit the world. Within weeks of that announcement, the world felt jittery by the collapsed of Lehman Brothers, the fourth- largest investment bank in United States. Lehman Brothers filed for bankruptcy protection on September 15, 2008. To date, it remains the largest bankruptcy filing in U.S. history with the company's holding of USD639b.

The U.S. Congress debated on a bill submitted by the Treasury Secretary on September 21, 2008, asking Congress to approve USD700b bailout package to buy mortgage-backed securities from ailing financial institutions that were in danger of defaulting. The goal was to instill confidence in the functioning of the global banking system, which had narrowly avoided collapse. Congress stalled on passing that bill. Traders lost confidence on hearing the bad news. It created a panic that saw the collapsed of the Dow Jones Industrial Average (DJIA) in the New York Stock Exchange (NYSE) on September 29, 2008.

The panic wave that was not contained in the United States began to spread across the Atlantic Ocean to the European continent causing massive bank runs there. Many European financial institutions suffered huge losses and even faced bankruptcy, requiring massive public funding or government bailouts.

Fourth Seal: Angel on the Pale Horse

When the Lamb of God opened the fourth seal, the Apostle John saw a pale horse. The angel who rode on the horse was named Death and accompanied him was another angel called Hades. They received power over a fourth of the earth to kill with sword, with hunger, with death and by the beasts of the earth (Revelation 6:7-8).

The word pale comes from the Greek word *chloros,* meaning "pale green," the color of corpses. The angels were named Death and Hades, and the word Hades means the abode of the dead. It might be difficult for some to accept God's holy angels called by these names. God created angels to serve Him, and He had created different types of angels. There are angels with wings and some without wings. There are messenger angels, the ones who proclaim or make announcements. There are worshipping angels, the ones who worship God day and night and do nothing else. Another category is the warrior angel, the ones who carry out punishment and enforce the wrath of God.[6] It is to this third group that the Angels of Death and Hades belong.

Notice the different ways the angels execute God's judgment: kill with sword, with hunger, with death and by the beasts (or pestilences) of the earth, the whole gamut of it. It should compel us to be in a ruminative mood reflecting on what has been happening in our world today. Frequent occurrences of earthquakes, tsunamis, and volcanic eruptions, and powerful storms, asteroids plummeting to the earth, famines, droughts, incurable diseases, and wars are not coincidental. Neither should we accepts them as purely natural disasters. The truth of the matter is God is speaking to mankind through them. It is a wake-up call.

It is a wake-up call, indeed. Why? The reason is that the angels presently had a limited area of the world to execute their judgment from God. Their jurisdiction to operate is only over a fourth of the earth, not the entire earth. In case there is misunderstanding, the Scripture explicitly says "over a fourth of the earth" and not "over a fourth of mankind" or something to that effect. In other words, it is referring to the geographical area of the earth and not the population of the world.[7] The difference, of course, is enormous. If it were to apply to the population, then roughly 1.7 billion or a quarter of the global population of 7 billion people are currently under the judgment of God. We have to thank God for His patience and longsuffering, giving mankind time to repent. People not yet under the judgment of God should contemplate and reflect on how they live their lives. Gloomy news of what is happening to the one-quarter of the world keeps coming in unabated.

Released of the Angel on the Pale Horse

On July 29, 2009, Prophet Owour was at an airport in South Africa in transit. While resting in the waiting area, to his astonishment, a pale horse suddenly appeared moving towards him.[8] The horse came right next to him and lowered its head to an arms-length distance from him. Prophet Owour observed that the horse mane around the crest area, that is, the area between the head and shoulder is white in color. Consciously or unconsciously he did not say, he reached out his hand to touch the muzzle of the horse. Then, the horse flapped its mane like a flag and then flew away.

Following the vision, he began to tell the world that he had seen the release of the pale horse. He made this announcement not only in Kenya but also in Venezuela, South Korea, and Australia. Approximately a year and a half into the broadcast, protests, riots, demonstrations, and civil war began to break out in the North African and the Middle Eastern countries. It started in Tunisia in December 2010. People were demonstrating against the authority due to high unemployment and corruption. It soon led to the overthrow of the Tunisian government.

Like a ferocious wildfire, the wave of protests spread to the neighboring country of Algeria. Then, it continued to Jordan, Mauritania, Sudan, Omen, Yemen, Saudi Arabia, Egypt, Djibouti, Morocco, Iraq, Bahrain, Iran, Libya, Western Sahara, and Syria. High unemployment and corruption levels were not the only reasons people took to the streets. In some of these countries, political suppression and human rights violation by dictatorial regimes had also led to the outbursts.

Commentators and bloggers writing in cyberspace about these happenings began to coin the term "Arab Spring" since these revolutionary waves of demonstration and protest occurred mostly among the Arab nations during the spring season.

The protests were not of the same intensity in all of these countries. Some were minor causing just a handful of the fatality and negligible damage to properties. For others, protests developed into major uprisings where intensity were severe such as in Yemen, Egypt and Libya (including Tunisia already mentioned) that saw the overthrow of their governments. In the case of Libya and Syria, damage to the nation's economy and physical infrastructure is incalculable, and will require years to restore and rebuild.

The "Arab Spring" protest was largely over by 2013, except in Libya, Syria and Iraq where the authorities are still fighting to subdue the various rebel groups out to topple the legitimate regimes. Human rights groups have been keeping track of reported deaths around the region since the start of the popular uprisings. However, due to the chaotic nature of each nation's conflict, many of the death tolls are rough estimates at best. They estimated the death toll at around 36,000.[9]

As pointed out earlier, the angels on the pale horse were given power over "a fourth of the earth." It refers to the geographical area of the earth to which they are to execute the judgment of God. Which part of the earth is this area? If we looked at the evidence of the angels' activities, which may include activities of the other three previous angels as well, it is a reasonably accurate observation to say that the area encompasses the following:

A fourth of the Earth (Revelation 6:8)
United States
Europe
Middle East
Northern Region of Africa

Let us review development in these regions of the earth since the opening of the seals:

- The United States. On the release of the angel on a white horse in 2001, the United States witnessed the judgment of God in the form of the destruction of the New York World Trade Center. The event was an excuse to launch the "war on terror" by the United States and the United Kingdom against the nation of Afghanistan in October of that year. Then, in March 2003, the "war on terror" was extended to the country of Iraq. There is no consensus on the exact number of war casualties from the decade-long war. However, estimates deaths in these two countries ranges from 80,000 to 1,200,000. A conservative estimate would be around 200,000 as reported by one European news website.[10]

  On the release of the angel on a black horse on August 19, 2008, the United States financial sector suffered convulsion from the collapsed of Lehman Brothers. It caused the Dow Jones Industrial Average to drop by 777.7 points, the largest drop in its history. These took place in September, a few weeks after the release of the black horse.

- Europe. Since the release of the angel on the black horse on August 19, 2008, some Eurozone member states have been suffering from debt crisis beginning late 2009. These states comprises Portugal, Ireland, Greece, Spain, and Cyprus. These nations were unable to repay or refinance their sovereign debt. They were bailed out by the European Financial Stability Facilities (EFSF), European Central Bank (ECB) and the International Monetary Fund (IMF), collectively known as the Troika (a Russian word meaning a group of three). The Troika extended the financial lifelines of these nations on condition that they had to implement stringent austerity measures. It led to a series of mass protests on the streets of these countries.

  Also, evidence of the activities of the angel on the pale horse could be seen when conflict broke out in Ukraine in February 2014. Ukraine, a former Soviet state flanking the southern border with Russia, became divided when three Eastern oblasts or administrative regions declared their independence from the central government as a consequence of the Euro-maidan Revolution. Russia supported one side of the opposing parties while the European Union supported the other. The conflict is primarily economic in nature, and not military at this time. The European Union started to impose economic sanctions against Russia. In a tit for tat, Russia reciprocated by imposing sanctions on Europe. The people in this region are feeling the brunt of the sanctions as a result of the economic war.

- The Middle East. We have already mentioned about the United States "war on terror" in Afghanistan and Iraq, evidence of the work of the angel on the white horse.

  On August 19, 2008, the black horse was released. This horse was sighted flying over the sky of Jeddah, Saudi Arabia on November 26, 2014. A handful of witnesses saw the incident and had it recorded on their mobile phones.[11] Less than two weeks after the sighting, the crude oil price fell from USD100 to USD70 a barrel. The price continues to tumble to USD48 as at the middle of January 2015. The impact of low oil price is hurting oil exporting countries, both in OPEC (Organization of Petroleum Exporting Countries) and the non-OPEC countries. It drastically reduces revenue, forcing them to run a budget deficit. In the case of Saudi Arabia, the central player in OPEC, she could draw on her reserve and tolerate the situation for a few years. However, the overall situation remains shaky.

There is also evidence of the judgment brought about by the angel on the pale horse—the Arab Spring protests. The horse released on July 29, 2009 and sighted on April 6, 2011, was moving among the crowd of protesters in Tahrir Square in the center of Cairo, Egypt. The throng did not see the horse but show up in the video recording of an MSNBC cameraman.[12]

- North Africa. In 2002, the year after the release of the angel on the white horse, conflict broke out in the Horn of Africa. Then in 2010 the Arab Spring protests ignited, first in Tunisia and then spread to eight other nations in the North African region.

  In December 2013, the Ebola virus disease broke out in Guinea, a West African state that lies just to the south of the country of Mauritania. The virus transmitted to people from wild animals and spreads in the human population through human-to-human transmission. Recall that the angel on the pale horse was given the power to kill by the beasts of the earth (Revelation 6:8b). The beasts of the earth include pestilences or viruses originated from animals. The virus spread quickly to the neighboring countries of Liberia, Sierra Leone, Mali, and Senegal. There is still no known vaccine to cure the disease. The latest figure on the number of deaths caused by the disease stands at 8,429.[13]

What about the other regions, the other three-quarters of the earth? Are those areas spared from conflicts and wars, economic troubles, and the epidemic of diseases? Not so, although the situation is not as bad. During the corresponding period, minor conflicts did erupt in Northern Nigeria, South Thailand, Georgia, Uzbekistan, Pakistan, and a few others areas. However, these zones of conflict were far apart from each other, not in proximity to one another or clustered together as it should be expected.

With regards to economic issues, the rest of the world fared relatively better. There was robust economic growth in Asia, Africa, Latin America and also the Middle East. Real GDP (Gross Domestic Product) compound annual growth for the various regions compiled for the year 2000 to 2013 indicates performance was much higher than the global average. Below is the list[14] showing the GDP growth rates.

- Emerging Asia 7.8%
- Africa 4.9%
- The Middle East 4.6%
- Latin America 3.7%
- Central & Eastern Europe 3.5%
- World 2.8%
- Developed Economies 1.5%

Although the Middle East lies in the "fourth of the earth" region it seemingly also had real economic growth of 4.6%. However, the increase is mainly contributed by the sale of crude oil. Notice the growth performance of the Developed Economies, which included the United States, Southern Europe (Portugal, Spain, Italy, and the Balkan Nations) and Japan managed to grow at only 1.5%. These statistics confirmed the activities of the angel on the black horse which was to bring judgment on the economy of the said regions.

Chapter 3

LIVING BETWEEN THE SEALS

At the time of this writing, we are living between the fourth and the fifth seals. The four horses of the apocalypse are still carrying out their missions. They are executing God's judgment on the earth. They are at it simultaneously. The angel on the white horse is defeating the forces of darkness. The angels on the red, black and pale horses are bringing on the plagues of conflicts, wars, financial, economic, and health woe. The world is apprehensive of these plagues, but they are concentrated mainly in the transatlantic regions and the region around the Mediterranean Sea.

However, the situation will turn for the worst when the fifth seal opens.

When will the fifth seal open? Jesus, the Lamb of God, had chosen Prophet Owour to announce the opening of the previous seals. We believe He will continue to reveal to him the opening of the fifth, and the sixth seal at the appropriate time. We encourage readers to visit his website to find out about this.

We understand it is the Lord's prerogative to inform us through His servant when the time has arrived to open the fifth seal. Notwithstanding, is there any clue as to roughly when that will be? Let us make some observations about the opening of the first four seals. Let us jot down the dates when they were opened and find out the time lapse between each of the seals.

- First Seal opened in 2001

  The opening of the first seal is believed to be in 2001. Note that the Lord began to call Prophet Owour into the ministry in 1996, but he only responded to the call on July 3, 2003.

- Second Seal opened on April 2, 2004
  The opening of this second seal was shown to Prophet Owour just nine months after he responded to the Lord's call. The time lapse between the first and the second seal is about **3.3 years** (i.e. if we consider the first seal opened at the beginning of 2001).

- Third Seal opened on August 19, 2008
  The time lapse between the second and third seal is approximately **4.3 years**.

- Fourth Seal opened on July 29, 2009
  The interval between the third and the fourth seal is approximately **1 year**.

From the tabulation above, the time lapse between the four seals ranges from 1 to 4.3 years. At the date of this writing (early 2015), the time lapse from the opening of the fourth seal till now is about **5.5 years**. We do not know when the fifth seal will be opened, and the Lord could delay its opening even longer. While we wait, we do sense it could be soon taking into consideration what the fifth seal is about and what is currently happening in the world.

Musing over this matter, if we add the interval between the opening of the fourth seal and the present time i.e. 5.5 years to the tabulation above, it would total 14.1 years (3.3+4.3+1+5.5=14.1 years). Now if we divide the total 14.1 years by 4, this would be 3.5 years *average* for the time lapse between the seals. The timeline will look like this:

First Seal [3.5 years] Second Seal [3.5 years] Third Seal [3.5 years] Fourth Seal [3.5 years] Fifth Seal.

If the fifth seal indeed does open very soon from now, then the tabulation above will be significant. Should this be the case, could we further theorize that the interval between the fifth seal and sixth seal will also be 3.5 years on *average*? Moreover, the time lapse between the sixth seal and seventh seal also 3.5 years on *average*? Again, should this be the case, then, the total number of years would be 7 years between the opening of the fifth seal and the opening of the seventh seal. The seventh seal is a marker. It is post-rapture meaning when the seventh seal opens the event of the rapture would have taken place. What follows the seventh seal will be the outpouring of God's wrath upon the earth.

Fifth Seal: Martyrdom

When the Lamb of God opened the fifth seal, this was what the Apostle John saw, and we quote:

> **Revelation 6:9-11**
> **9** When He opened the fifth seal, I saw under the altar the souls of those who had been slain for the word of God and for the testimony which they held. **10** And they cried with a loud voice, saying, "How long, O Lord, holy and true until You judge and avenge our blood on those who dwell on the earth?" **11** Then a white robe was given to each of them; and it was said to them that they should rest a little while longer, until both the number of their fellow servants and their brethren, who would be killed as they were, was completed.

John saw martyred souls waiting in a holding area under the altar of God in heaven. They died for being Christians bearing the name of Christ. The Scripture did not say how many of them were there, but it could be in the millions. Also, there was no mention of when these martyrs died. Some are of the opinion they died during the duration of the opening of the first four seals. If this is the case, then they were there beneath the altar not too long ago. However, it is more likely they died since the days of the early Church as their cry may suggest. They asked the Lord in a mournful voice when He will revenge their brutal death, showing a tinge of impatient after having waited for a long time.

They were given white robes to wear and told they have to wait a little while longer until the pre-determined number of martyrs had been killed as they were. During the period of the fifth seal, this would be carried out in earnest by people who hate Christians. Christian martyrdom will become a frequent occurrence.

Martyrdom is a phenomenon that is not exclusive to Christianity. It happens to people of other faiths and ideologies. However, what do we understand by Christian martyrdom? Who is a Christian martyr? The English word 'martyr' derived from the Greek word *martys*, which means 'witness." So anyone who witness or testify to the name of Jesus Christ the Son of God is a martyr? Not so. Or what if that person is being persecuted for his witness — is he then a martyr? Not yet. The qualification is much higher than that. A true Christian martyr is one who, in the course of being a witness for Christ, suffered death. The death or termination of his life is forced upon him, and not due to say, old age, sickness or accident. He is compelled to die (of course not by himself for that would be suicide) by someone, a persecutor, who hates him because he is a Christian, a believer in Jesus Christ. And the persecutor can be an individual, group of people or the state authority. Below are some examples of martyrs from the early Church:

As Recorded in the Bible

- Jesus Christ Himself was martyred
- John the Baptist
  He was beheaded by Herod the tetrarch (Matthew 14:1-12)
- Stephen
  He was stoned to death by a Jewish mob (Acts 7:58-60)
- James, the son of Zebedee, elder brother of John
  He was killed by Herod Agrippa I, the first apostle of Jesus to be martyred (Acts 12:1-2)

As Mentioned by Hippolytus of Rome (170-235)[1]

- Simon Peter
  "Peter preached the Gospel in Pontus, and Galatia, and Cappadocia, and Betania, and Italy, and Asia, and was afterwards crucified by Nero in Rome with his head downward, as he had himself desired to suffer in that manner."
- Andrew
  "Andrew preached to the Scythians and Thracians and was crucified, suspended on an olive tree, at Patræ, *a town* of Achaia; and there too he was buried."

- Philip of Bethsaida
  "Philip preached in Phrygia, and was crucified in Hierapolis with his head downward in the time of Domitian, and was buried there."
- Bartholomew (Nathaniel)
  "Bartholomew again, *preached* to the Indians, to whom he also gave the Gospel according to Matthew, *and* was crucified with his head downward, and was buried in Allanum, *a town* of the great Armenia."
- Thomas (Didymus)
  "Thomas preached to the Parthians, Medes, Persians, Hyrcanians, Bactrians, and Margians, and was thrust through in the four members of his body with a pine spear at Calamene, the city of India, and was buried there."
- James the Lesser
  "James the son of Alphæus, when preaching in Jerusalem, was stoned to death by the Jews and was buried there beside the temple."
- Paul
  "Paul entered into the apostleship a year after the assumption of Christ, and beginning at Jerusalem, he advanced as far as Illyricum, and Italy and Spain preaching the Gospel for five-and-thirty years. And in the time of Nero he was beheaded at Rome and was buried there."

According to Hippolytus, the rest of the twelve apostles did not suffer martyrdom but died of natural death including John, Matthew, Simon the Zealot, Thaddaeus-Judas, and Matthias.[2]

As Mentioned in the Martyrdom of Polycarp[3]

- Polycarp, the Bishop of Smyrna, a disciple of Apostle John
  "When he had offered up the Amen and finished his prayer, the men in charge of the fire lit it. And as a mighty flame blazed up .....For we also perceived a very fragrant aroma, as if it were the scent of incense or some other precious spice."

There are Christian organizations that are keeping track of the number of Christian martyrs from the time of the early Church until the present time.

From their research, it seems the number of martyred Christians could be in the range of 60 to 70 million. According to them, the chief persecutor had been the state authority.[4]

When the fifth seal opened, we should see a spike in the number of Christians being martyred. Already, about every few days we are hearing news of Christians being killed for their faith. The most notorious region is in the Middle East, especially in the area north of Iraq and east of Syria. The persecutors of Christians comprised the rebel Islamist groups of IS (Islamic State) and Jabhat al-Nusra. They have committed horrendous acts of beheading believers and displaying their severed heads in the public square. The most recent case carried out by this group took place in Libya.[5] It involved the beheading of twenty-one Egyptian Coptic believers who were migrant workers. The incident took place on the beach near Tripoli, the capital of Libya. The execution was intentionally video recorded and shown in their organization website. After the act, the video showed the seawater nearby turned crimson.

Persecutors of Christians found elsewhere include such groups as the Al-Qaeda in Pakistan, Yemen, and Algeria; Al-Shabab in Somalia; and Boko Haram in northeast Nigeria. The Boko Haram are also active in Chad, Niger, and northern Cameroon.

Believers everywhere should brace for a time of considerable testing as Christian martyrdom will become a worldwide phenomenon during the fifth and sixth seals period.

Sixth Seal: Great Tribulation and Rapture

When the Lamb of God opened the sixth seal, this was the scene presented to the Apostle John:

> **Revelation 6:12-17**
> **12** I looked when He opened the sixth seal and behold, there
> was a great earthquake, and the sun became black as sackcloth
> of hair, and the moon became like blood. **13** And the stars of
> heaven fell to the earth, as a fig tree drops its late figs when

> it is shaken by a mighty wind. **14**Then the sky receded as a scroll when it is rolled up, and every mountain and island was moved out of its place. **15** And the kings of the earth, the great men, the rich men, the commanders, the mighty men, every slave and every free man, hid themselves in the caves and in the rocks of the mountains, **16** and said to the mountains and rocks, "Fall on us and hide us from the face of Him who sits on the throne and from the wrath of the Lamb! **17** For the great day of His wrath has come, and who is able to stand?"

In this vision, John saw six phenomena occurring in the sky and on the earth. They are:

i) A great earthquake.

A great earthquake will strike the earth. Where the mighty earthquake will strike is not clear, but the tremor will be registered high on the Richter magnitude scale.

ii) Sun became black as sackcloth of hair.

It is not a natural phenomenon. Meaning, it is not the result of total solar eclipse taking place in our solar system. Rather it is a supernatural sign, as the sun will temporary stop shining. This phenomenon also cited in Joel 2:30-32 and Matthew 24:29-31. In both these scriptures, the mentioned of this phenomenon is in the context of the coming of the Lord at the time of the rapture. In Joel's case, notice the encouraging word that "whoever calls on the name of the Lord shall be saved" (Joel 2:32). People everywhere should start calling upon the name of the Lord, to lay hold on the salvation God offers while there is still an opportunity. To those that response positively, it will be their time of redemption at the rapture.

In Matthew, when Christ comes in the rapture, the angels "will gather together His elect from the four winds, from one end of heaven to the other" (Matthew 24:31). Contrast this to His second coming at the end of the 7 years reign of the Antichrist, there will be no gathering of the elect because He Himself will set foot on the

Mount of Olives in Jerusalem. When the Lord returns in His second coming, there will be no more opportunity for repentance because He will return as a righteous judge.

iii) Moon became red as blood.
It is also a supernatural phenomenon when the moon temporary will not reflect sunlight but instead take on a reddish appearance. Hence, the term "blood moon." As stated, this occurs in conjunction with the sun became black as sackcloth of hair. This phenomenon is also cited in Joel 2:30-31 and Matthew 24:29-31.

iv) Stars of heaven fell to the earth.
Stars are incandescent bodies in space (heaven). The star that is located nearest to the earth is the sun. Not too long ago, astronomers discovered the smallest star known to man. Although this newly discovered star is the smallest, it is about the size of planet Jupiter in our solar system, and Jupiter is about 120 times the size of planet earth! So what does the Bible mean by "the stars" of heaven fell to the earth? Apparently, it is not referring to actual stars but astronomical objects such as asteroids, meteoroids or comets. Astronomers called these objects Near Earth Objects (NEOs). They may be small, relative to the size of the earth, but should one of them with a diameter of say, 1 km, hit the ground it will cause a massive catastrophe. It will be an Extinction Level Event (ELE) for the earth and mankind.

In recent years, scientists have recorded increasing number of these astronomical objects plunging to the earth. With just the size of fewer than 100 feet in diameter, these objects are producing 20-30 times more energy than the atom bomb dropped on Hiroshima. Fortunately, they were not creating massive death and destruction (yet) because they either exploded while still up in the air over the ocean or hit areas with a very tiny population.

When the sixth seal opened, we believe these objects will hit populated cities and oceans causing tsunami with an enormous number of fatalities and destruction.

v) Sky receded as a scroll when it is rolled up.
It is a strange scene that John witness. We know a scroll is an object that is rolled up, not folded. So, the sky (heaven) over the earth is rolled up. It would imply the sky or heaven is opening up, inferring that a passageway is being created. In the context, a passageway is created for the coming of the Lord in the rapture.

Here we must recall that Moses strike the Red Sea with the rod in his hand, and the sea opened up for the children of Israel to cross over on dry land:

Exodus 14:21-22
21 Then Moses stretched out his hand over the sea, and the Lord caused the sea to go back by a strong east wind all that night, and made the sea into dry land, and the waters were divided. **22** So the children of Israel went into the midst of the sea on the dry ground, and the waters were a wall to them on their right hand and on their left.

The Red Sea parted for the children of Israel to pass through on their journey to the promise land. Soon the sky (heaven) will be parted for the Bride of Christ to pass through to glory land. Hallelujah!

vi) Every mountain and island moved out of its place.
What could be the cause of this? Could it be the humongous shaking of the earth generated by the great earthquake? Or, could it be the colossal impact of the fallen stars (astronomical objects) on the surface of the earth? It could be. Then again, it could be something else. The power that shakes and moves the mountains and islands out of their place seems to be felt all over the world, and not just confined to a particular location.

There is no limit to God Almighty's power. There is no restriction to Him, who holds the universe in His hand, even in the way in which He will demonstrate His power. In all probability, this will be another supernatural act of Almighty God unleashing His power upon the earth at the time He comes to take His holy people home.

Residents on the planet in the days of the sixth seal period will witness the phenomena mentioned above. What will be their reaction to all these? The Scripture says people from all strata of society including kings, great men, rich men, commanders, mighty men, slaves and freemen (Revelation 6:15) will react with great fear. They will be driven to seek shelter in caves and mountains, even wanting the rocks to shut them off from the fearful presence of Almighty God. They will say to the rocks, "Fall on us and hide us from the face of Him, who sits on the throne and from the wrath of the Lamb. For the great day of His wrath has come....." (Revelation 6:16-17).

What impel them to utter those words? First, why do they address the One who sits on the throne? He who sits on the throne is Almighty God, the God of Abraham, Isaac and Jacob. He is the God of the Bible. They must have heard of Him and know who He is but refuses to acknowledge Him in the past. Second, they make reference to the Lamb of God. The Lamb of God is none other than the Lord Jesus Christ, the Son of God. Do they know who He is? Probably yes. They also know He is angry with them and about to pour out His wrath. They know He is angry with them because they see all these phenomena racking the earth. Third, but why do they utter those words at that time? What cause them to look up to heaven in one accord, in that manner? In all probability, they must have witness the event of the rapture, the great snatching away of God's people from the earth. This event cannot be in secret. It cannot be discreet or be silent. Multiple millions of believers from the four corners of the globe will disappear into the sky and taken to heaven. We believe they utter those words because they witness the rapture but are themselves left behind.

What follows after this? Continuing with the Scripture, we note that John was presented with more scenes. In Revelation Chapter 7 verses 1-8 he was shown a new scene in which he witness angels sealing the foreheads of 144,000 Jews of the twelve tribes of Israel. These will be God's Jewish ministers of the gospel during the 7-years reign of the Antichrist.

After this, his vision changed, and he was back at the throne of God. What he saw is described below:

Revelation 7:9-17

9 After these things I looked, and behold, a great multitude
which no one could number, of all nations, tribes, peoples,

> and tongues, standing before the throne and before the Lamb, clothed with white robes, with palm branches in their hands, **10** and crying out with a loud voice, saying, "Salvation belongs to our God who sits on the throne, and to the Lamb!" **11** All the angels stood around the throne and the elders and the four living creatures, and fell on their faces before the throne and worshiped God, **12** saying: "Amen! Blessing and glory and wisdom, Thanksgiving and honor and power and might, Be to our God forever and ever. Amen." **13** Then one of the elders answered, saying to me, "Who are these arrayed in white robes, and where did they come from?" **14** And I said to him, "Sir, you know." So he said to me, "These are the ones who come out of the great tribulation, and washed their robes and made them white in the blood of the Lamb. **15**Therefore they are before the throne of God and serve Him day and night in His temple. And He who sits on the throne will dwell among them. **16** They shall neither hunger anymore nor thirst anymore; the sun shall not strike them, nor any heat; **17** for the Lamb who is in the midst of the throne will shepherd them and lead them to living fountains of waters. And God will wipe away every tear from their eyes."

The Apostle John saw a great multitude of people "which no one could number," interpreting this to mean millions. They came from all nations, tribes, peoples and tongues; that is to say, of all nationality and ethnic groups on the earth. They were all wearing white robes and holding palm branches in their hands. Before the throne, they worship God and the Lamb, the Lord Jesus Christ. Millions of angels assembled around, joining in with these people to worship, adore, thank and bless God, who sits on the throne. The twenty-four elders and the four living creatures, which John first met when he arrived there at the throne, also join in the worship.

Then, one of the elders asked John, "Who are these arrayed in white robes, and where did they come from?" John did not know which prompted the elder to disclose saying, "These are the ones who come out of the great tribulation, …" (Revelation 7:14).

Note that this scene is still within the period of the sixth seal. The seventh seal is yet to open. The multitude in white robes came out of the great tribulation, as divulged by one of the elders. It means the great tribulation is during the sixth seal period. But we already know what would happen during the fifth seal period — it is a time of great persecution, the martyrdom of Christians. Thus, we can safely say that the great tribulation is a time that falls within the fifth seal and the sixth seal. The sequence of events will be like this:

Fifth Seal [great tribulation] Sixth Seal [great tribulation + rapture] Seventh Seal.

Great tribulation means severe trouble or suffering felt on a worldwide scale. Why is the great tribulation necessary? The elder said to Apostle John that these who came out of the great tribulation "washed their robes and made them white in the blood of the Lamb." Thus, tribulation is the process to purify the Church.

Seventh Seal: Seven Trumpets Judgment

When the Lamb of God opened the seventh seal, there was silence in heaven for about half an hour:

> **Revelation 8:1-7**
> **1** When He opened the seventh seal, there was silence
> in heaven for about half an hour. **2** And I saw the seven
> angels who stand before God, and to them were given seven
> trumpets. **3** Then another angel, having a golden censer,
> came and stood at the altar. He was given much incense
> that he should offer it with the prayers of all the saints upon
> the golden altar which was before the throne. **4** And the
> smoke of the incense, with the prayers of the saints, ascended
> before God from the angel's hand. **5** Then the angel took

> the censer, filled it with fire from the altar, and threw it to the earth. And there were noises, thundering, lightning, and an earthquake. **6** So the seven angels who had the seven trumpets prepared themselves to sound. **7** The first angel sounded: ....

> The Scroll contains God's program. The second part of the program is to pour out His wrath on the world for their rejection of Jesus Christ and the mistreatment of the Church

At this juncture, the Church the Bride of Christ is already in heaven. Hence, the first part of the program contained in the scroll is now accomplished. This signal the time to introduce the second part of the program. The second part involves the pouring out of God's wrath on the inhabitants of the earth for their rejection of Jesus Christ and the mistreatment of His Church. The people left behind themselves appropriately acknowledged that it was their due (Revelation 6:17).

There is an interlude, a silence in heaven for about half an hour. A solemn atmosphere pervades the entire heaven. We can imagine everyone, the four living creatures, the twenty-four elders, the myriad of angels and the redeemed, stood in silence. As time in heaven is unlike that on the earth, the half an hour is not exactly 30 minutes of earth time. Whatever the equivalent of earth time may be, it was time for preparation to commence pouring out God's wrath on the earth.

An angel with a golden censer offered incense on the golden altar before the throne. Incense gives out an aroma that pleases God. The scent mixed with the prayers of the saints. It is wonderful to know that the prayers of the saints are not in vain. They are being collected and preserved and are now brought out to be remembered by Him. It should be an encouragement to believers everywhere to persevere in their prayers to our faithful God. Further, smoke from the incense mingled with the prayers ascended to God. The aroma pleases Him, and the time has come for Him to answer those prayers, the prayers of His beloved people. Next, the angel took the golden censer, filled it with fire from the altar, and threw it to the earth, and there were noises, thundering, lightning, and an earthquake on the earth. What the angel is doing reveals that God is now ready to repay vengeance on behalf of His people. For

God's people are always instructed not to judge and not to take revenge, for vengeance belongs to Him. They are to commit to Him their unjust suffering in the hands of unreasonable people. He will repay on their behalf when the time is right (Romans 12:19-21). With fire from the altar thrown to the earth, the earth began to suffer convulsion, the initial sign of anguish.

Standing ready before the throne and in the midst of the angel with the golden censer are another seven angels with seven trumpets. The sounding of the trumpets starting with the first angel will see the wrath of God rain down on the earth in succession. When the last angel, the seventh angel sound his trumpet, there appears to be another interlude. Apparently, proceeding from the seventh trumpet are seven bowls of the wrath of God. These seven bowls are the seven last plagues of the wrath of God to be executed by the angels (Revelation 15:1). Understand that the pouring out of the wrath of God beginning from the first trumpet to the seventh bowl will correspond with the reign of the Antichrist. The reign of the Antichrist will last 7 years. We will describe the reign of the Antichrist, the seven trumpets, and the seven bowls wrath with greater detail later.

The Seventh Seal is a marker. It is post-rapture. Its time frame encompasses the 7 years reign of the Antichrist

From what is described so far about the seven seals, it becomes palpable that the seventh seal is a marker. It is post-rapture. When it opened, the rapture would have already taken place. Also, the time frame of the execution of the wrath of God within the seventh seal is during the reign of the Antichrist.

The Four Horses Executing Judgment on Modern "Pharaoh & the Egyptians" in Preparation for the Rapture of the Saints

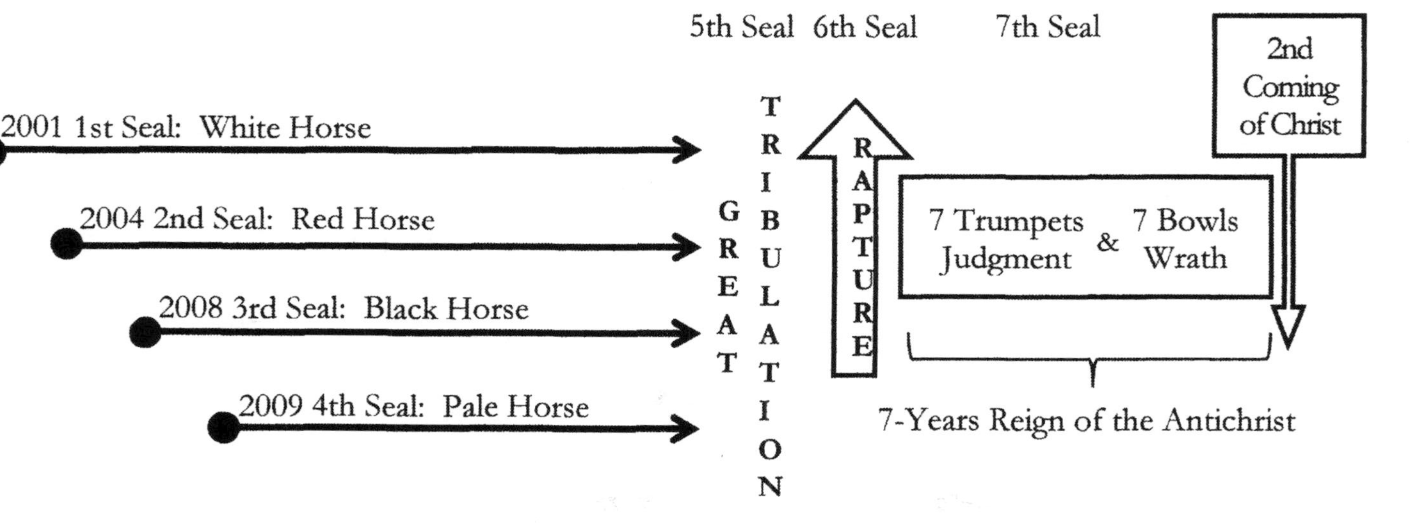

Chapter 4

THE JEWS

Thus far, we had gleaned over the seven seals in the Book of Revelation, one of the sixty-six books of the Bible canon. Within those books can be found records of hundreds of visions, dreams and prophecies of the future or related to future events. Men and women received them by the inspiration of God. Many of these are being fulfilled already. Those not yet fulfilled will, without a shadow of a doubt, be brought to pass on schedule. They led us to affirm that the Bible is a prophetic book.

Not only that, but the Bible is an authentic historical book. Except one or the most two of the books written by Gentiles, the rest of it were written by the Hebrew people, better known in the present epoch as the Jews. The overall content of those books is mainly about the Jews themselves. Within it are historical records of the founding of the Hebrew-speaking people. Its formation into a nation called Israel, its expansion into a glorious kingdom, its decline, and subsequent dispersion of the Jews into the four corners of the earth. Were the records be the end of the story, the Jews would have suffered similar fate befallen all, if not most nations of the earth. But the Jews are a peculiar people. The race[1] and the nation of Israel have a different destiny than others. The Bible has much to say about their future course. There are powerful prophetic words that seem to make trumpeting call for world attention. Take note for she is destined to be restored and ultimately attained her place as the leader among the nations of the world in the end times. Needless to say, the Jews and the nation of Israel are playing and will continue to play a very significant role in our world.

Brief History: Old Testament Period

The ancient history of the Jews traces back to a man called Abram (his name later changed to Abraham). He was born in about 2000 BC in Ur in the land of Chaldea, the area that lies in the southeastern part of present-day Iraq. While still a young adult, with his immediate family, he moved northwest to the city of Haran and settled there. Haran is located in present day Syria. Thus, the Bible disclosed that Abraham was a Syrian or Aramean (Deuteronomy 26:5).

One day, God appeared to him and called him to go to the land of Canaan which God promised he and his descendants would possess. He believed and obeyed, together with his wife and nephew Lot made the long journey south to the land of Canaan which is today called the land of Israel. God also promised to make him highly regarded, that he will be the father of many nations. Through him, all the families of the earth will be blessed.

Abraham and his wife Sarai (her name later changed to Sarah), had Isaac, who in turn had Jacob. Jacob (his name later changed to Israel) had twelve sons. In the midst of a severe famine that ravaged the region, they were forced to migrate to Egypt for survival because there was food there. Jacob, together with his extensive family of seventy people, made the move to Egypt and settled there until the time of their exodus out of Egypt. They were there for four hundred and thirty years (1830-1400 BC), and by then, their number had grown to between two to three million men, women, and children. Thus, they had morphed from being just a family to becoming a young nation. Moses led them out of Egypt on a journey to the promise land but because of fear and disbelief, they remained stranded, wandering in the Sinai wilderness for 40 years.

During their time in the wilderness, God instructed Moses to build Him a Tabernacle or "tent" (which would later be replaced by the Temple). He was given the system of laws comprising the Ten Commandments, Mosaic laws and the Levitical Priesthood laws to accompany the Tabernacle. It was a sacred place where God chose to meet with His people. The worship of God in the Tabernacle was instituted as the center of their national life. The young nation had beautifully found her place in God, and God had delightfully acknowledged them as His special people (Deuteronomy 26:18).

In time Joshua, Moses's assistant finally led them across the Jordan River from the east side into the land of Canaan. Fear began to grip the inhabitants of the territory when they heard the children of Israel had come, for they had heard stories of God performing awesome signs and wonders on their behalf. In the course of taking possession of the land God promised to Abraham, they managed to defeat over forty tribal kings, drive out the native peoples, built towns and cities and cultivate the land.

For the first three hundred years (approximately 1400-1100 BC) of living in the promise land, the Hebrew nation had no strong central authority. They were a confederacy of twelve independent tribes, with no unifying force, except their God. The form of government the people had in those days is known as Theocracy— God Himself was supposed to be the direct ruler of the nation. However, the people did not take their God very seriously and were continually falling away into idolatry. In a state of anarchy, off and on, and harassed at times by civil war among themselves. Enemies surrounded them who made attempt after attempt to exterminate them. The Hebrew nation was struggling to be strong and cohesive. Again and again, God provided for them judges to lead them in battles against their enemies, sending them deliverance from enemy oppression. When the judges were alive, the judges were the moral compass for them. When there were no judges, the people played the harlot after the idols.

The period of the judges came to an end with the appearance of Samuel the prophet. There were prophets before him, but Samuel was the founder of a regular order of prophets with schools for prophets set up in several cities in the land. These schools act as a sort of moral check on the people including the priests in the light of the priesthood becoming quite degenerate. Clearly then, the form of administration under the judges had been a sort of failure. So God raised up Samuel to unify the nation under a king.

Up to this time, the people were under theocratic rule. In a predatory world, what was recognized was the law of the jungle. A nation needs to be strong to survive. God accommodating Himself to their wishes permitted the Hebrew nation to unify under a king as the surrounding nations did. Saul was the first king to be installed, but he was a dismal failure due to his persistent disobedient to the will of God. With the installation of Saul as king, the form of government had changed from Theocracy to Monarchy—the nation was no longer rule directly under God but via an earthly king.

After the death of Saul, David was appointed king (1000 BC). He was a man after God's heart. Being a skillful military man, he won many battles and succeeded in expanding his kingdom to great heights. The extent of David's kingdom was more or less, what God had promised Abraham. And again, the family of David was singled out to be the channel through whom the blessings for the nations will come, in fulfillment of the other part of God's promise to Abraham. A descendant of David shall one day sit on his throne. The reign of that future King will have no end. He will bless all the nations of the earth.

Solomon ascended the throne following the departure of David his father (960 BC). He was given the privilege to build the Temple for God in Jerusalem. God prospered him even more with power, wealth and wisdom. The period of his reign is view as the golden age in the nation's history. However, he committed very grave sins in the sight of God by having 700 wives and 300 concubines, most of whom were idolatrous Gentiles. They influenced him to worshiped idols. The judgment of God fell upon his kingdom immediately after his death. It split into two parts; the Northern and Southern Kingdom.

The Northern Kingdom called Israel comprised ten tribes. All the nineteen kings of Israel were evil kings serving the Calf and Baal. The kingdom lasted from 933-721 BC. They finally fell and led into captivity by the Assyrian. They never returned to their land. Bible historians called them the ten lost tribes. As to the kingdom in the south, it was called the Kingdom of Judah which included the tribe of Benjamin. Twenty kings ruled it, and they were mostly bad ones. The kingdom lasted from 933-606 BC. The Babylonians invaded it and took many captives back to Babylon. Included among the prisoners were Prophets Daniel and Ezekiel. Before they left, the invaders destroyed the Temple and the city of Jerusalem.

Prophet Jeremiah was the resident prophet in Judah and Jerusalem in the years leading to the Babylonian invasion and captivity. He lived to see many of the inhabitants exiled to Babylon. They were there for seventy years. After overrun by Persia, the Persian kings allowed some Jews to return to rebuild the Temple and the city walls. Among them were Zerubbabel, Joshua, Ezra, and Nehemiah. The population in Judah did increase a little, to probably not more than 30,000, and that of Jerusalem to no more than 1,500. Judah remained a Persian province throughout the period of the Persian rule that lasted from 539-331 BC. It marked the close of the Old Testament period.

For the next 350 years or so, what happened to the Jews, to Judah and Jerusalem were not recorded in the Bible. Information of the period comes from the Apocrypha, books included in the canon of the Orthodox and Roman Catholic traditions. The other sources include the writings of Josephus, the Jewish historian, and Philo of Alexandria, the Jewish Philosopher.[2]

Inter-Testaments Period

Up to this time, the great powers of the world had been in Asia. After Persia had fallen to the Greek, world empires passed from Asia to Europe. In 331 BC, Alexander the Great invaded Palestine. He showed great consideration to the Jews.[3] He spared Jerusalem and offered immunities to the Jews to settle in Alexandria, Egypt. After his death, his empire split into four sections, each in control by his four generals. The two eastern parts of his empires, Syria and Egypt were under Seleucus and Ptolemy, respectively. Palestine, lying between Syria and Egypt, was first under Syrian control but later went under Egypt's rule (301 BC). It remained under the control of Egypt until 198 BC.

Under the kings of Egypt, called the "Ptolemies," the condition of the Jews was mainly peaceful. Those living in Egypt built synagogues in all their settlements. Alexandria became an influential center of Judaism.

Antiochus the Great reconquered Palestine (198 BC), and it passed back to the kings of Syria called the "Seleucids."

Antiochus Epiphanes (175-164 BC) was violently bitter against the Jews.[4] He was determined to exterminate them and their religion. He devastated Jerusalem (168 BC), defiled the Temple, and offered a sow on its altar. He erected an altar to Jupiter, prohibited Temple worship and forbade circumcision on the pain of death. He sold thousands of Jewish families into slavery, destroyed all copies of Scriptures found and slaughtered everyone discovered in possession of them. He resorted to every conceivable torture to force Jews to renounce their religion. It led to the Maccabean Revolt, one of the most heroic feats in Jewish history.

Matthias, a priest, infuriated by Antiochus Epiphanes attempt to destroy the Jews and their religion, gathered a band of loyal Jews and raised the standard of revolt. He had five heroic sons; Judas, Jonathan, Simon, John, and Eleazar. Matthias died in 166 BC. His mantle fell on his third son Judas, who managed to win many battles against unbelievable and impossible odds. He reconquered Jerusalem in 165 BC, and purified and rededicated the Temple.

The Feast of Dedication or Hanukkah had its origin with this event.[5] Judas united the priestly and civil authority under him, and thus established the line of Asmonean priest-rulers who for the following 100 years governed as independent Judea (167-63 BC).

In the year 63 BC, Palestine was conquered by the Romans under Pompey. Antipater, an Idumean (Edomite, descendant of Esau), was appointed the ruler of Judea. His son Herod the Great, who was king of Judea (37-3 BC) succeeded him. To obtain the favor of the Jews, Herod rebuilt the Temple with great splendor. But he was a brutal, cruel man. It was this Herod, who ruled Judea when Jesus was born. It was he who slew the children of Ramah near Bethlehem after the wise men did not return to inform him they had found the baby Jesus (Matthew 2).

Brief History: New Testament Period

The New Testament period began with the first coming of the Jewish Messiah, the Lord Jesus Christ. He was the central figure during this era of Jewish history. The manner of His conception was unusual. Angel Gabriel had appeared to Mary a virgin engaged to a man called Joseph and announced to her that she had been chosen to bear a Child. She was told, "...you will conceive in your womb and bring forth a Son, and shall call His name Jesus. He will be great, and will be called the Son of the Highest; the Lord God will give Him the throne of His father, David" (Luke 1:31-32). She asked the angel how this could be since she is not married. To show the way out of her predicament, the angel said, "The Holy Spirit will come upon you, and the power of the Highest will overshadow you ..." (Luke 1:35). Thus, Jesus's conception was by a supernatural act of God.

Joseph and Mary were in Bethlehem, the city of David when the time for Jesus to be born had arrived. As there was no available room in the inn, He was born in a stable. The first group of people notified was the Jewish shepherds while they were in the field, keeping watch over their flock by night. Following the angel's announcement to them, they quickly located the Baby to pay their homage. About a year later, the first group of Gentiles was informed. They were magi or wise men (astronomers) from the East, possibly Persia, that is, present- day Iran. An unusual bright star guided them to Bethlehem. They gladly came and presented gifts to Him: gold, frankincense, and myrrh.

Jesus grew and increased in wisdom and stature, and in favor with God and men. At age thirty, He began His public ministry of preaching and teaching. With His twelve disciples with Him, He traveled to many cities in Israel healing all manner of sicknesses and diseases and setting the demon possessed free. His fame spread rapidly and caught the attention of the religious leaders in the nation, comprised mainly of the Scribes, Pharisees, and the Sadducees. Out of jealousy and hardness of heart, refusing to acknowledge that Jesus is the promised Messiah foretold by the prophets, they plotted to have Him killed. These conspirators had found someone akin to a "fifth column" among Jesus disciple —Judas Iscariot.

The Roman soldiers put Jesus to death on the cross of Calvary. Who gave the order for this to be done was the Sanhedrin. The Sanhedrin was the supreme council, or court, at the time. It comprised seventy-one men made up of Rabbis and elders, and prescribed over by the high priest or the President (Hebrew *nasi*). The Sanhedrin had its police force that could arrest people, as they did Jesus Christ. While the Sanhedrin heard both civil and criminal cases and could impose the death penalty, in New Testament times it did not have the authority to execute convicted criminals. Only the Romans had that power. It explains the crucifixion of Jesus, a Roman punishment, rather than being stoned to dead according to the Mosaic Law.

The rejection of Jesus Christ as their Messiah was a national decision, as represented by the Sanhedrin. Jesus had said they will not see His face again until they say, "Blessed is He who comes in the name of the Lord!" (Matthew 23:39). In the near future, as a nation, Israel have to repent and utter these words to have Jesus Christ restored as their Messiah.

After His resurrection, Jesus appeared to over five hundred of His disciples over a span of forty days. His disciples and followers carried the gospel message to the then known world. Embarking from Jerusalem, it spread to Judea, Samaria, Galilee, and the utmost parts of the earth. Initially, the people who embraced the message were Jews. As time passed, there were more Gentiles than Jews who believed in Him.

For continuation of this topic, go to the next Chapter: Have the Christians Replaced the Jews? (Replacement Theology).

Why are the Jews God's Special People?

El Elyon — the Most High God has so chosen the Jews among the many different races or ethnic groups on the earth to be His peculiar people (Deuteronomy 7:6; 26:18-19). The choice was not due to their large size for they are indeed one of the smallest in number, since the ancient times as it is today. They were favored not because of the color of their skin, nor for their inherent persona. Plainly, it was not on any merits they possess but is purely of God's sovereign choice. They derived significance from their association with God.

Sin had tinted and weakened every race and ethnic groups in the earth. The Jews are no exception. They are not perfect nor will they ever attain perfection here in this dispensation. But God could still work with them to achieve His purpose for mankind. He has a great plan.

Their Right Standing with God through the Abrahamic Covenant

God had established a covenant with patriarch Abraham, the father of the Jewish race. A covenant is an agreement or a contract made between two parties. Covenants are common, but the Abrahamic Covenant is unique and paramount for the redemption of the human race. God was the initiator of this covenant where He appeared to Abraham in Haran and invited him to migrate to a new country. At that instant, God made him a promise (Genesis 12:1-3) that He later confirmed and amplified it (Genesis 13:14-17; 15:1-7; and 17:1-18). Summarizing the content of the promise, we note, there are three aspects to the covenant promise:

I. Abraham's descendants would possess the land on which he set his foot on

   [This aspect of the promise has to do with the *land*. It is being called the Palestinian Covenant promise land]

II. God will make Abraham himself great, and his descendants will be a great nation
[This aspect of the promise has to do with the *seed.* It is being called the Davidic Covenant promise seed]

III. "All the families of the earth," that is, the Gentiles will be blessed by Abraham's descendants
[This aspect of the promise has to do with the *blessings.* It is being called the New Covenant promise blessings]

We further note the promise is made to three parties, not just to Abraham alone, but to his descendants and the Gentiles at large. Fulfillment of these promises must be literal. It should not be spiritualized away, as some people attempt to do. Take the case of Abraham, the promise that applied to him. God said He will bless him and make him great. Promises fulfilled literally in the life of Abraham are as follows:

a. Abraham had a son even in old age (Genesis 21:1-5)
b. He was blessed with land (Genesis 13:14, 15, 17)
c. He had a lot of servants (Genesis 14:14)
d. He had much cattle, silver, and gold (Genesis 13:2; 24:34-35)
e. He was blessed spiritually as God was with him constantly (Genesis 21:22)
f. He had a great name and reputation (Genesis 23:5-6).

While the Abrahamic Covenant remains the primary covenant, God had also initiated amplified covenants with Abraham's descendants to reveal more details of what He had promised their forefather Abraham. The purpose was also to cajole them to co-operate with Him to ensure the fulfillment of the covenant. It was necessary as they lived in the different era, separated by many generations. Now, there are four such amplified covenants— the Mosaic Covenant, the Palestinian Covenant, the Davidic Covenant and the New Covenant.

We learned there were two kinds of covenants God had made with His people: revocable covenant and irrevocable covenant. The Mosaic Covenant is a revocable covenant. It means cancelation is possible. Should the receiver of the covenant (the Jews) fail to live up to its obligations, the covenant will cease. Indeed, this was what happened to the Mosaic Covenant. The Jews did not fulfill the requirements expected of them, and God had disregarded the covenant (Hebrews 8:7-9, 13). Another factor was that it had inherent weaknesses within it such as the use of animal blood. As animal blood is imperfect, it could only atone or cover up the people sins, much like sweeping the dirt under the carpet. Their sins remained with them, although covered up. The people could be sincerely sorry, but their consciences continue to prick. What was needed was the efficient removal of sins, having them cast into the deep blue sea, never to be remembered by both themselves and God. It is what the Bible called remission of sins. Application of the blood of Christ will remit the people sins, and clears the conscience. God had planned to have the imperfect animal blood sacrifice replaced with the perfect and eternal blood of His Son Jesus Christ, the Lamb of God.

The other three amplified covenants, the Palestinian Covenant, the Davidic Covenant and the New Covenant are irrevocable. By irrevocable, it is implied that God will not cancel the covenant even if the receiving party (the Jews) failed to fulfill the terms. No, they will not be easily laid off. Severe punishment will be meted out. They will be forced out of the promise land, and their blessings withheld from them. But the covenant will still retain its validity. Once they repent, change their ways, and return to God in faith and humility, God will restore to them what is rightfully theirs. It should be clearly understood by all, that as the initiator of the covenant, God will ensure and do His utmost to remove any obstacles that hinder the receiver from receiving from Him. He commits irrevocably to see the fulfillment of the covenant. What He plans to achieve by the covenant will indeed be achieved.

Now, as the primary covenant, the Abrahamic Covenant is also an irrevocable covenant.

When God made the promise to Abraham, he believed it. His faith in God accounted to him for righteousness. To prove it to and to encourage Abraham, God instructed him to offer as sacrifice a three- year-old heifer, a three-year-old female goat, a three-year-old ram, a turtledove and a young pigeon. The animals were cut up and laid on the make-shift altar. After it was done, a burning torch from the Lord passed through and burned those sacrifices, sealing the covenant with blood from those animals (Genesis 15:7-18). God, who initiated this act, sealed the covenant while Abraham fell asleep! It was a bit humorous like God was saying to Abraham, "You go to sleep, don't stay up too late. And don't worry, I'll handle everything."

Still, why was there a need to shed blood? The issue at hand was not about God's power to perform, but it was because of the sin barrier coming from Abraham. The Bible informs that the life of the flesh is in the blood (Leviticus 17:11). Abraham was a fallen man, and there was a need to atone for his sins. God accepted blood shed on the altar as atonement for his soul. The animal blood sacrifice that Abraham offered had atoned for his sins. It was a temporary arrangement until Christ came to make propitiation for sins. Christ eternal blood, not restricted by time, points to the future and also to the past, effectively remitting the sins of Abraham.

I. Promise that Abraham's Descendants would possess the Promise Land (Palestinian Covenant)

Ten different Gentile tribes formerly occupied the land of Canaan. The biggest of the tribes was the Canaanites; the others include the Kenites, the Kenezzites, the Kadmonites, the Hittites, the Perizzites, the Rephaim, the Amorites, the Girgashites, and the Jebusites. This piece of real estate belongs to God, the One, who created the heavens and the earth. Hence, it is His prerogative to give to whomever He chose, and He decided to hand this land to the descendants of Abraham. He had said, "To your descendants I have given this land, from the river of Egypt to the great river, the River Euphrates (Genesis 15:18-21).[6]

Moses was with the children of Israel for forty years in the Sinai wilderness. It came time for them to enter and take possession of the land of Canaan, the land promised to them. They made their way to the plains of Moab, on the East side of the Jordan River. Across the shallow waters of the Jordan River, to the West is the city of Jericho. There at the plains of Moab, God, commanded Moses to make this covenant with the children of Israel with these words:

> **Deuteronomy 30:1-10**
> **1** "Now it shall come to pass, when all these things come upon
> you, the blessing and the curse which I have set before you,

> and you call them to mind among all the nations where the Lord your God drives you, **2** and you return to the Lord, your God and obey His voice, according to all that I command you today, you and your children, with all your heart and with all your soul, **3** that the Lord, your God, will bring you back from captivity, and have compassion on you, and gather you again from all the nations where the Lord, your God, has scattered you. **4** If any of you are driven out to the farthest parts under heaven, from there, the Lord your God will gather you, and from there He will bring you. **5** Then the Lord your God will bring you to the land which your fathers possessed, and you shall possess it. He will prosper you and multiply you more than your fathers. **6** And the Lord, your God, will circumcise your heart and the heart of your descendants, to love the Lord your God with all your heart and with all your soul, that you may live. **7** Also the Lord your God will put all these curses on your enemies and on those who hate you, who persecuted you. **8** And you will again obey the voice of the Lord and do all His commandments which I command you today. **9** The Lord, your God will make you abound in all the work of your hand, in the fruit of your body, in the increase of your livestock, and in the produce of your land for good. For the Lord will again rejoice over you for good as He rejoiced over your fathers, **10** if you obey the voice of the Lord your God, to keep His commandments and His statutes which are written in this Book of the Law, and if you turn to the Lord your God with all your heart and with all your soul.

This amplified covenant is called the Palestinian Covenant. It forms an integral part of the main Covenant, the Abrahamic Covenant. This covenant would be the title deed to the land they are going in to possess. But why is it called the *Palestinian* Covenant? The Bible did not use this term then. There were a people known as the Philistines though. The Philistines were Phoenicians, a Semitic people who migrated to the strip of land along the Mediterranean coast which lies to the southwest of the land of Israel. Today this piece of land is called the Gaza Strip. The Philistines lived during the time of Abraham, and he had interaction with them (Genesis 21:22-34). Subsequently, over an extended period, there were wars between the children of Israel and the Philistines (e.g. 1 Samuel 14:52).

Around 450 BC, a Greek historian named Herodotus, who was a seasoned traveler, visited the area. In his book, *The Histories*, he called the area "Palastina." Then, during the British Mandate, and just before the Jewish State was formed in 1948, the Arabs from neighbor countries living in the territory adopted the name Palestine ("Falastin" in Arabic). Since then, there is serious contention between Israel and the Arabs as to who lives there first, who continuously occupies the land the longest, and who has the perpetual right to it. It is a long-standing issue, but it will surely be settled one day in the not-too-distant future.

Without deliberating further on this, should not the covenant be just called the Land Covenant? It should. However, the term has become entrenched and is commonly accepted by all. We may as well continue to use it.

In the covenant statement, the children of Israel were told that blessings and curses are hanging over their heads. Should they obey God's commandments they will be blessed, but should they disobey there will be curses. Further analysis of the terms of the covenant reveals the following:

a. The nation will be plucked off the land for her unfaithfulness (Deuteronomy 30:1-3).
b. There will be a future repentance of Israel (Deuteronomy 30:1-3)
c. Their Messiah will return (Deuteronomy 30:3-6)
d. Israel will be restored to the land (Deuteronomy 30:5)
e. Israel will be converted as a nation (Deuteronomy 30:4-8)
f. Israel's enemies will be judged (Deuteronomy 30:7)
g. The nation will then receive her full blessing (Deuteronomy 30:9)

As one survey the broad areas included in this one passage, which sets forth this covenant program, one is compelled to feel that God takes Israel's relation to the land as a matter of extreme importance. God not only guarantees its possession to them but obligates Himself to judge and remove all Israel's enemies. He foresees them losing the land because of their sins. That said, he plans to give the nation a new heart, a conversion they needed prior to placing them back in the land.

The confirmation of this same covenant appeared later in Israel's history. God made it known to Prophet Ezekiel, and it became a subject of his prophecy (Ezekiel 16:1-63). It was what God revealed to him. God affirmed His love for Israel at the time of her infancy (vs.1-7). He reminded her that she was chosen and related to Jehovah by marriage (vs.8-14), but she played the harlot (vs.15-34). Therefore, the punishment of dispersion was meted out to her (vs.35-52). It is not a final setting aside of Israel, for there will be a restoration (vs.53-63), and this it is based on the promise (vs.60-62).[7]

Thus, the Lord reaffirms the Palestinian Covenant and calls it an eternal covenant by which He bound Himself to it.

II. Promise that Abraham's Descendants will be a Great Nation (Davidic Covenant)

The first three hundred years in the promise land, the children of Israel were living under theocratic rule. They had no king. God provided judges to look after the various tribes, who led them into battles against their enemies, and be a sort of moral guide to the people. Desiring to be like the Gentile tribes who all had kings to look after their welfare, the children of Israel began pestering Samuel the prophet that he would ask God to give them a king. God acceded to their request and gave them Saul to be their first king. Later, David was anointed to replace Saul as the next king.

David's reign lasted forty years. He managed to subdue all the nations in and around Israel. He started by taking over Jerusalem; then he defeated the Philistines, the Moabites, the Ammonites and the Syrians. His kingdom reached great heights and glory. In the midst of his great victory and success, God sent Nathan the prophet to him with a great promise:

> **2 Samuel 7: 12-16**
> **12** "When your days are fulfilled, and you rest with your fathers, I will set up your *seed* after you, who will come from your body, and I will establish <u>his kingdom</u>. **13** He shall build a <u>house</u> for My name, and I will establish the <u>throne</u> of his

> kingdom forever. **14** I will be his Father, and he shall be My son. If he commits iniquity, I will chasten him with the rod of men and with the blows of the sons of men. **15** But My mercy shall not depart from him, as I took it from Saul, whom I removed from before you. **16** And *your house* and *your kingdom* shall be established forever before you. *Your throne* shall be established forever." (Emphasis added)

The promise amplified covenant is called the Davidic Covenant. The seed promise contained in the Abrahamic Covenant is now made the center of the Davidic Covenant. The seed promise in general and the seed line of David, in particular, with his kingdom, house, and throne, are amplified in this covenant.

Can we say that David now fulfills the promise that Abraham's descendants will be a great nation? The answer is yes, but it is only a partial and a temporal fulfillment, as the fulfillment did not last. The reason this is so is due to two factors:

a. God would not have promised David that his seed coming out from his body would inherit a throne and that his throne will endure forever if David had fully fulfilled that promise; and
b. Solomon was the seed of David (words underlined in above- quoted scriptures), yet his kingdom did not last but was broken up as a result of apostasy.

So, who then is the seed of David who will inherit David's kingdom, his house, and his throne (words in italic above)? This person is none other than Christ Jesus Himself. As angel Gabriel, who appeared to Mary, had said, "And behold you will conceive in your womb and bring forth a Son, and shall call His name Jesus. He shall be great, and will be called the Son of the Highest. The Lord God will give Him the *throne* of His father David, and He will reign over the *house* of Jacob forever, and of His *kingdom* there will be no end" (Luke 1:31-33). (Emphasis added)

It is pristinely clear to us that Christ, as the seed of David, has inherited the kingdom, house and throne of David. Through Him, Abraham's descendants will achieve greatness or be a great nation that will endure forever. On this point, everyone agrees. However, in some circle, the understanding is different on *how* and *when* this is working out. Some say the kingdom of David is replaced by the Church, the house of David is replaced by the household of faith (the Christians), and the throne of David is Christ's throne in heaven on the right hand of God. In other words, they view the Church, which is composed mainly of Gentile believers, as Abraham's descendants replacing the Jews and the nation of Israel. If one holds to this view, then the fulfillment has been spiritualized away. There is no more expectation of a literal fulfillment in which the Jews or the nation of Israel, as Abraham's descendants, will have any more relevant part to play to showcase her greatness. For a brief treatment of this issue, refer to the next Chapter, Have the Jews Been Replaced? (Replacement Theology)

How and when will Christ Jesus, the seed of David, who had already inherited the kingdom, house and throne of David, be seen to have done so? Where is the evidence? It requires the physical kingdom of David to be reinstalled or reestablished in the land of Israel so that all may witness it. For over 1,800 years, the Jewish people were dispersed and did not have a national homeland. During this long period, in whatever country they may be living, every Jew will pray this prayer at the annual Passover feast, "Next Year in Jerusalem!" Their heart cry was finally answered on May 14, 1948, when Israel became a sovereign state. The Jews have thus officially returned to possess the land promised to their forefather Abraham. They have come a long way though, but their journey has not yet ended. There is still the last mile to travel. In this last mile, two critical matters have to be resolved:

a. The kingdom boundary promised to Abraham is "from the river of Egypt to the great river, the River Euphrates." (Genesis 15:18). The current boundary of Israel is smaller than the promised made to them. The limit should include Lebanon and Syria in the north, the Negev Wilderness and the River of Egypt in the south; with the Mediterranean coast and the River Jordan bordering the west and east, respectively. The Arabs are currently occupying those territories, and they will never surrender them to Israel without a fight. Israel has to have it, for these belong to them. The situation appears insurmountable for Israel to overcome. The good news is, what is insurmountable to them is doable for God, for God all things are possible. In the end, God will ensure they owned all the land promised, but it will only happen when the Millennium reign of Christ begins (Revelation 20:6).

b. Christ Jesus must Himself return to earth bodily in order to reign over David's covenanted kingdom. But He will only return when Israel welcomes Him back. As a nation, they rejected Him as their Messiah, as expressed by the decision of the Sanhedrin, their highest religious authority. Hence, national repentance must be expected of them before Christ Jesus will return for them (Zechariah 12:10-14; Luke 13:34-35).

III. Promise that "All the Families of the Earth" would be Bless by Abraham's Descendants (New Covenant)

Jeremiah was the resident prophet in Jerusalem in the years leading to the Babylonian captivity. His prophetic ministry lasted for forty years during which time he witnessed the deterioration in the spiritual condition of his countrymen. He warned and pleaded with them to repent that the impending invasion from the north may be averted. He was not successful in his effort, and with the situation not checked, the judgment God had pronounced on the nation would have to take its predetermined course. The temple and the city would raze to the ground, and most of the people who did not die in the siege will be captives in Babylon. With this bleak prospect in view, how would the promise made to Abraham that Israel would be a blessing to "all the families of the earth" be fulfilled? Well, the promise can only be satisfactory fulfilled when Israel's spiritual condition changed first. It boils down to the state of the heart. Their hearts need to be converted. God had a plan in mind to bring about their conversion. Turning His thoughts to the future, God revealed to Jeremiah how His plan would work out for Israel. It was God's prophetic word to him:

Jeremiah 31:31-34

31 "Behold, the days are coming, says the Lord, when I will
make a new covenant with the house of Israel and with the

> house of Judah-- **32** not according to the covenant that I made with their fathers in the day that I took them by the hand to lead them out of the land of Egypt, My covenant which they broke, though I was a husband to them, says the Lord. **33** But this is the covenant that I will make with the house of Israel after those days, says the Lord: I will put My law in their minds, and write it on their hearts, and I will be their God, and they shall be My people. **34** No more shall every man teach his neighbor, and every man his brother, saying, "Know the Lord," for they all shall know Me, from the least of them to the greatest of them, says the Lord. For I will forgive their iniquity, and their sin I will remember no more."

God had to perform a new thing with Israel. A new covenant had to be drawn up. This covenant would replace the existing covenant that "I made with their fathers in the day that I took them by the hand to lead them out of the land of Egypt." The existing covenant God referred to was the Mosaic Covenant, which now was found to be faulty and ineffective (Hebrews 8 & 9). God revoked it. And in its place the operation of the New Covenant would open the way for the forgiveness of the sins of Israel. It is something not possible with the old system. It would be made effective by the eternal blood of Christ to, once and for all, bear away their sins and to cleanse their conscience from dead works to serve the living God. With His blood, He would enter the Holy Place in heaven to obtain eternal redemption, that Israel may call upon Him to receive their promised eternal inheritance.

It was with His disciples that Christ sealed the New Covenant. They were ordinary people, most of them were fishermen. They were neither the religious nor the political leaders of the nation. Nevertheless, God sees them as representing the nation of Israel. It is God's right as the initiator of the covenant. In His kingdom, He ruled the covenant He made with them as valid; and who dare question Him? As far as He is concerned, His authority is *de jure*.

On this matter, the religious leaders of Israel took a different stance. The chief priest declared in the presence of Pilate that they have no king but Caesar (John 19:15). He was the head of the Sanhedrin, a council of seventy-one priests and Rabbis. They should have accepted Christ as the promised King of Israel; for He had come to inherit the kingdom, house and throne of David, their forefather. Their rejection of Him means that they also reject the New Covenant. In consequence, the blessings of the New Covenant will be withheld from the nation of Israel—for Israel is joined to God in a national covenant. Be clear on this point, that though individual Jews could and would be able to enjoy the blessings of the New Covenant, as a nation they can't until there is national repentance.

We wish to restate here the New Covenant blessings applicable for the individuals:

Individual or Personal Blessings

a. Experience forgiveness of sins as "their iniquity, and their sin I will remember no more" (Jeremiah 31:34)
b. Experience regeneration of the heart as "I will put My law in their minds, and write it on their hearts" (Jeremiah 31:33)
c. Enjoy intimate relationship with God as "I will be their God, and they shall be My people" (Jeremiah 31:33)

Following Israel's rejection of the New Covenant, God turned His attention to the Gentiles, offering them these similar blessings (Matthew 21:43; Acts 13:46-48). The invitation to receive these benefits is presented in this manner:

- It is through the name of One person only.
  Acts 4:12 — Nor is there salvation in any other, for there is no other name under heaven given among men by which we must be saved.

- The need to call upon the Name
  Acts 2:21— And it shall come to pass that whoever calls on the name of the Lord shall be saved.

- Those who believe will be saved, and possibly their family also.

Acts 16:3:1— So they said, "Believe on the Lord Jesus Christ, and you will be saved, you and your household."

In retrospect, this excellent opportunity should have been seized by everyone, but most missed it. However, the invitation has not been withdrawn yet. There is still time for all who are alive today to receive their salvation. Take note that Christ second coming is drawing near, and when He comes it will be too late.

Chapter 5

HAVE THE CHRISTIANS REPLACED THE JEWS? (REPLACEMENT THEOLOGY)

What is Replacement Theology? It is a theological view among some Christian circles that the Church has replaced Israel in God's redemptive program. Another term for this view is Supersessionism—it comes from two Latin words *super* (on or upon) and *sedere* (to sit). It conveys an image of a person sitting on another person's seat thus, replacing the latter.

This view postulate that Christianity (comprises mainly Gentile Christians) continues where the Old Testament ends, in effect superseded Judaism as God's religious system of choice for His people. When the Jews rejected Christ as their Messiah; the response from God was to reject them conveniently in favor of the Christians, who have now become His special people. The blessings promised in the covenants are now categorically poured out on the Church while Israel receives the corresponding curses. Through the promised Holy Spirit and His abiding presence, the Church is empowered to live triumphantly "according to the Spirit" while Israel "according to the flesh" has been left vanquish to obscurity.

Historical Development

How did this erroneous view developed? It was not possible for this view to breed during the first century, at least not during the first forty years of the Church's existence. These were formative years, that is, from the birth of the Church at Pentecost till the destruction of the Jerusalem Temple in AD 69.

Since the formation of Israel as a nation, the Jews had their religion called Judaism. It began to splinter into various camps such as the Pharisees, the Sadducees, the Essenes, and the Zealots. The Church or Christianity was the new kid on the block, and it added to this list of parties,[1] as it too was birth out of Judaism. Initially, it was not called Christianity but Nazarenes, as Christians were followers of Jesus who was from the town of Nazareth. At the early stage, the Church was predominantly Jewish, as the focus of the Apostles and the disciples' evangelistic effort was on their fellow Jews. Their number grew within Israel, and many congregations established in the surrounding regions of Judea, Samaria and Galilee.

The Jerusalem Church by default had been the mother church, and from this base, missionary effort was stepped up to reach further the diaspora in the other territories of the Roman Empire. The Apostles continued to have their base in Jerusalem, but some of them, especially the Apostle Paul, spent most of his time and effort among the diaspora Jews. He would conscientiously, meet them in the synagogues to share the gospel with them in whichever town he went. Many turned to the Lord, but there was also strong opposition. In time, blasphemous reaction to the gospel message from some Jews forced him to turn to the Gentiles. Just as well, it was the Lord's specific calling in his life to reach the Gentiles (Acts 18:6; Galatians 2:7-8).

Paul who was the Apostle to the Gentiles, together with his missionary team was accredited to have planted the most number of Churches. It comprised mainly Gentile Christians. Being young and not yet well established, these Churches depended on their Jewish counterpart for teaching, leadership, and guidance. They could help themselves to the Septuagint, the Old Testament translated into Greek. Greek was the common language at the time. The other primary source was, of course, from Paul's personal attention and through his epistles; for he wrote over a dozen epistles. Other apostles also provided assistance, whether by personal communication or through writings. Apostles such as Matthew, Mark, and John, who wrote the Gospels; and Peter, James, John and Jude, who wrote the Epistles. Through these writings, communications, and leadership provided by the Jerusalem Church, the Gentile Christians have developed a very strong connection to Jewish or Hebraic roots.

The Jewish Christians in Israel were peace loving and law- abiding. There was placid tolerance of adherent of other religious and political parties in the land. Although, not exactly please living under foreign rule, they had no intention to rebel against Rome. There were occasional disturbances due to hostilities among the Jews themselves, and protests against Roman authorities but none as severe as the Zealots uprising against the Romans imposing taxation on the locals. The Romans responded by plundering the Jewish Temple and executing up to 6,000 Jews in Jerusalem, prompting a full-scale rebellion. It was the spring of the First Jewish Revolt lasting from AD 66-73.

By early AD 69, the Roman army led by General Titus had taken full control of Galilee, Samaria and the northern part of Judea and began besieging Jerusalem. Trapped within the city was a multitude of people, many coming from the surrounding regions including Perea and Decapolis (present-day Jordan) and other remote areas, to celebrate Passover in Jerusalem. Within a few months, the city succumbed to the Romans, after the Temple and part of the city was burned to the ground. When the siege was over, 1,100,000 Jews, including proselytes from other countries, died from either the fighting, fire or starvation; and 97,000 were captured alive by the Roman armies.[2]

Some Jewish Christians could have participated in the unsuccessful Revolt. There was no record indicating the majority of them did. Notwithstanding, it was believed a significant numbers of them had died in the Revolt, considering the difficulty to escape. Those who managed to flee did flee to Pella, a notable town in Perea[3] about 60 miles northeast of Jerusalem. Evidently Christ had forewarned them to do so. This particular warning was given by Christ, not less than thirty-five years earlier, when He was talking with His disciples on the Mount of Olives (Luke 21:5-24). During this Olivet discourse, His disciples asked Him about His remark on the Temple destroyed one day in which "not one stone shall be left upon another that shall not be thrown down." He cautioned them when they see Jerusalem surrounded by foreign armies they have to leave immediately everything behind. They were told that they must be prepared to "flee to the mountains, let those who are in the midst of her depart and let not those who are in the country enter her (Jerusalem)." We believe this prophetic word of warning was the key reason for their non-participation in the Revolt against Rome. Other likely reason could be the advice they have been given not to resist Caesar or governmental authorities (Matthew 22:17-21; 1 Peter 2:13:17).

The destruction of the Jerusalem Temple was a landmark event. Before its ruin, the Jewish Christians continued to visit the Temple for prayers while they also gathered in the synagogues and house churches (Acts 2:46; 3:1). How did they view the loss of the Temple? With great sorrow and distress, that is for sure. Emotion aside, they did have a different attitude towards the Temple. Unlike Jews who refused to believe Jesus as the Messiah and thus, continued to put their trust in Temple rites. Jewish Christians took comfort in the fact that the Herod Temple was no longer essential to their salvation experience. They came to know that Temple sacrifices were made redundant by Christ sacrificing Himself as the Lamb of God. In Chapter 9 of the book of Hebrews, Paul explained clearly to the Jewish Christians that the "first tabernacle" (Herod Temple) has been superseded by the "perfect tabernacle not made with hands," that is, heaven itself. Moreover, they had been taught to view the church as the spiritual temple of God (Hebrews 13:15-16; 1 Peter 2:5). This truth brought great relief to their sorrow and distress.

The Jews had to prod on without the Temple in the post-destruction era. They realized the need to consolidate the practice of their religion, especially on the matter of the Law. The Pharisees as the dominant party among them took the lead in reinterpreting Jewish concepts and practices in the absence of the Temple and for people in exile. It gave rise to a new party known as the Rabbinical Judaism, not surprisingly became the dominant form of the Jewish religion until the present time.

Beginning of the Schism

How did the Gentile Christians view the loss of the Temple? Earliest Christian sources seem to suggest they felt sorrow for what had happened to the Temple and Jerusalem. They were sympathetic towards their Jewish counterpart who had to go into exile. However, the cordial relationship that had existed for several decades, even after AD 69, became less friendly after the Second Jewish Revolt (AD 132-135).

In AD 132, a man named Simon Bar Kokhba, a Jewish Zealot, orchestrated the second revolt against Rome. The revolt erupted as a result of religious and political tensions in Judean province. Simon, the commander, was regarded by many of his compatriots as the Messiah, who would restore Israel sovereignty. His status was enhanced greatly by the support of Rabbi Akiva, a very influential Rabbi at the time. Initial victories from the Revolt established an independent territory over parts of Judea for over two years, but the Roman army led by Emperor Hadrian finally crushed it. This Revolt resulted in an extensive depopulation of Judean Jewish communities, even more than the First Revolt in AD 69 ever did.

To spite the Jews, Emperor Hadrian attempted rebuilding of Jerusalem into a Roman city, renaming it Aelia Capitolina after himself (Aelius was his family name). Moreover, he renamed the regions of Judea, Samaria and Galilee to be collectively called Syria Palestina. Following his death in AD 138, there was significant easing of persecution of the Jews. However, one policy of his continues to be in force after his death. The Romans continue to bar Jews from entering Jerusalem, except for attendance in Tisha B'Av, a day of remembrance of the Temple destruction. This prohibition applied to all Jews including Jewish Christians.

The after-effects of the Second Jewish Revolt caused schism to appear; first, between the Jews and the Jewish Christians. The latter were not in the position to help in the revolt against the Romans because they could not accept Simon Bar Kokhba as the Messiah. Their non-cooperative stances evoke resentment from the rebel camp. Second, the relationship between Jewish Christians and Gentile believers became less cordial. While the Gentiles were welcome and enjoyed free access to Aelia Capitolina, the Jewish Christians were denied entry. The restriction forced Gentile Christians to appoint their church leaders in the city from then on.

By this time, the Church had separated herself from Judaism in Jerusalem in particular, and in Palestine in general. Up to this time, the Jewish Christians had provided the linkage to Judaism, but the Gentile Christians now finds herself all on her own. The Jerusalem Church was no longer Jewish but had taken on a wholly Gentile appearance. A contemporary development of great significant was beginning to take place elsewhere — ecclesiastical power initially resided with the Church in Jerusalem began to decentralize having shifted to the Churches in Antioch, Alexandria, and Rome. Although, these cities have a large Jewish population with the significant number of Jewish Christians, it was the Gentile Christians who were taking the leadership role.

Another positive note is that decentralization added impetus to the growth of the Churches throughout the Roman Empire. As the prevailing trend, the Gentile Church experienced the numerical growth while the number of Jewish Christians was diminishing.

This trend reinforced the view among the Gentile Christians that God had abandoned the Jews and rejected Judaism. If God had rejected Judaism, it stands to reason that He must surely have rejected the nation Israel. In their fellowships, they began to discuss these questions. Has the Church replaced Israel? Has God now accepted the Christians as His special people in place of the Jews? Then, Christianity must have superseded Judaism?

In the meantime, the growth of Christianity created more and more friction with Judaism. It became a major concern to Rome. Under Roman law, Judaism was considered a legal religion, as it pre-dated Rome. Christianity post-dated Rome, and thus, was regarded as an illegal religion by the Romans. The practice of Christianity was a punishable offense. Hence, we read of Christians being persecuted during the first 200 years of her existence until the adoption of Christianity as the official religion of the Roman Empire. In an attempt to alleviate persecution, Christian apologists tried in vain to convince Rome that Christianity was an extension of Judaism. This effort still failed to convince Rome to change her stand. The resultant persecution of Christians caused them to develop ill-feeling towards the Jewish community, who were free to worship without persecution. Later, when Christianity became the official religion of the Empire, the Church helped to pass laws against the Jews in retribution.

The writings of the early Church Fathers reflected resentment against the Jews. Church Fathers who lived during the time of the Second Jewish Revolt till the close of the third century had expressed their misgiving on the standing of the Jews in God's eyes. We quote two examples here:

- Origen of Alexandria (AD 185-c.254)

  "Therefore we may see that after the advent of Jesus the Jews were altogether abandoned, and possess now none of what were considered their ancient glories, so that there is no indication of any Divinity abiding amongst them. For they have no longer prophets nor miracles, traces of which to a considerable extent are still found among Christians, and some of them more remarkable than any that existed among the Jews; and these we ourselves have witnessed, if our testimony may be received."[4]

- Cyprian of Carthage (AD 200-258), A student of Tertullian
  "A word this, moreover, which rebukes and condemns the Jews, who not only unbelievingly despised Christ, who had been announced to them by the prophets, and sent first to them, but also cruelly put Him to death; and these cannot now call God their Father ....In a repudiation of these, we Christians, when we pray, say Our Father; because He has begun to be ours and has ceased to be the Father of the Jews, who have forsaken Him. Nor can a sinful people be a son; but the name of sons is attributed to those to whom remission of sins is granted and to them immortality is promised anew, in the words of our Lord Himself: "Whosoever committeth sin is the servant of sin. And the servant abideth not in the house forever, but the son abideth ever." [5]

The Church Triumphant

The Gentile Church grew increasingly confident as she enters the new century. In AD 306, Emperor Constantine, became a new member of the Church, the first Roman Emperor to do so. As mentioned earlier, Judaism was a legal religion while Christianity was illegal throughout the empire. The Edict of Milan issued in AD 313 changed that, giving benevolent treatment to Christians while the Jews suffered further misfortune. Some people in the Church were seeking to restrict their movement and their interaction with Christians. Subsequent laws were passed which were discriminatory against them. For instance:

a. Judaism no longer enjoyed the right as an ancient religion in the Empire
b. They would be burned if found breaking the imperial laws
c. Rabbinical jurisdiction severely curtailed

d. Proselytism was prohibited and punishable by death
e. They were excluded from holding high office in the government or the military.

In AD 321, Emperor Constantine adopted Christianity as the official religion. From then on, Christian persecution gradually eased. It never entirely ceased though, as Christians continued to receive persecution in certain outlying provinces of the Empire. On the other hand, the fate of Jews gradually grew worst. In AD 325, Constantine convened a meeting of 250 Christian bishops in Nicaea, later known as the First Council of Nicaea. The Council deliberated some issues and adopted one of them regarding the rest day. Constantine decreed all businesses should cease on "the honored day of the sun." He made Sunday as the day of worship for Christians. The Jews felt slighted as Saturday was their Sabbath day of rest. The change in the attitude of the Imperial authority was influenced partly by the church clergy and partly due to prevailing political and religious environment. In that meeting, the moderator was Eusebius Pamphili (AD 265-340), Bishop of Caesarea. He was known as the "father of church history" for his effort in writing a ten-volume work on the history of the church. He wrote a good deal about the life and deeds of Constantine by way of celebrating the triumph of the church, of which Constantine was the standard-bearer.

Like the previous century, there were certain Church Fathers of the fourth century who also had negative views about Judaism, the Jews and their Synagogues. Church Fathers such as Hillary of Poitiers (AD 291-371), Gregory of Hyssa (AD 330-394), Saint Ambrose (AD 340-397), and St. Jerome (AD 347-407), had briefly expressed them in their writings. But there was one whose virulent criticism was voluminous. Not only that, his diatribe contained some extreme statements. He stood out like a sore thumb among the Church Fathers so far. He was none other than John Chrysostom (AD 349-407), Archbishop of Constantinople. The word *Chrysostomos* anglicized as Chrysostom, means "golden-mouthed" in Greek and was given because of his legendary eloquence.

He wrote a series of homilies. Among them, eight were directed against Judaizing Christians. In this context, Judaizing Christians would be a Gentile Christian, but who had an interest in observing certain Jewish customs or practices. His views and writings were considered by some to have had an impact on the development of Christian anti-Semitism. The following are selected extracts from his writings entitled "Eight Orations against Judaizing Christians," each accompanied by a short remark:

- Homily I. II. 1 [6]

  But do not be surprised that I called the Jews pitiable. They really are pitiable and miserable. When so many blessings from heaven came into their hands, they thrust them aside and were at great pains to reject them. The morning Sun of Justice arose for them, but they thrust aside its ray and still sit in darkness. We, who were nurtured by darkness, drew the light to ourselves and were freed from the gloom of their error. They were the *branches of that holy root, but those branches were broken. We had no share in the root, but we did reap the fruit of godliness.* From their childhood, they read the prophets, but they crucified Him whom the prophets had foretold. We did not hear the divine prophecies, but we did worship Him of whom they prophesied. And so they are pitiful because they rejected the blessings which were sent to them while others seized hold of these blessings and drew them to themselves. Although those Jews had been called to the adoption of sons, they fell to kinship with dogs; we who were dogs received the strength, through God's grace, to put aside the irrational nature which was ours and to rise to the honor of sons. How do I prove this? Christ said, "It is no fair to take the children's bread and cast it to the dogs." Christ was speaking to the Canaanite woman when He called the Jews children and the Gentile dogs. But see how thereafter the order was changed about: they became dogs, and we became the children. (Emphasis added)

Remarks: He admits the root from which the Jews exist is holy, and that Gentiles believers are reaping the benefit of godliness from that root. Due to their misfortune, the Jews now are dogs while the Gentile Christians are God's children. What he said is reasonably correct, but for two points. First, the Apostle Paul warned Gentile Christians not to be boastful against them since we depended wholly on the root and not the other way around (Romans

11:18-22). Second, the Jews can and will be restored back to their fortune when they repent (Romans 11:23-26).

- Homily I. III. 3 [7]

  If, then, the Jews fail to know the Father, if they crucified the Son, if they thrust off the help of the Spirit, who should not make bold to declare plainly that the synagogue is a dwelling of demons? God is not worshiped there. Heaven forbid! From now on it remains a place of idolatry. But still some people pay it honor as a holy place.

Remarks: If someone who, say, happened to be in a nightclub, gambling house or any such places, could he possibly be reached by the Spirit of God? If presented with the gospel or the Word of God, could he possibly be convicted by the Spirit in that place? We should not doubt he could, although this does not happen always. Now, surely the Synagogues would be a more sanctified place compare with those places mentioned!

- Homily I. IV. 7 [8]

  Do you see that demons dwell in their souls and that these demons are more dangerous than the ones of old? And this is very reasonable. In the old days the Jews acted impiously toward the prophets; now they outrage the Master of the prophets. Tell me this. Do you not shudder to come into the same place with men possessed, who have so many unclean spirits, who have been reared amid slaughter and bloodshed? Must you share a greeting with them and exchange a bare word? Must you not turn away from them since they are the common disgrace and infection of the whole world? Have they not come to every form of wickedness? Have not all the prophets spent themselves making many and long speeches of accusation against them? What tragedy, what manner of lawlessness have they not eclipsed by their blood-guiltiness? They sacrificed their own sons and daughters to demons. They refused to recognize nature, they forgot the pangs, of birth, they trod underfoot the rearing of their children, they overturned from their foundations the laws of kingship, they became more savage than any wild beast.

Remarks: John seems to imply ALL Jews are demon-possessed. To him, the demons in his days were more dangerous or wicked than those in the past. We should not greet them. Since we could not have a conversation with them, this must mean, they are beyond reach of the gospel message. It must mean, they are beyond repentance, totally hopeless. But did not Paul say they will one day repent? Again, John seems to think all Jews "sacrificed their sons and daughters to demons." In the distance past, such acts could have been carried out by their forebears. But to accuse them all of doing these things is fallacious. Are not these deeds done by some other race or ethnic groups in other parts of the world as well?

- Homily IV. III. 4 [9]

  But before I draw up my battle line against the Jews, I will be glad to talk to those who are members of our own body, those who seem to belong to our ranks although they observe the Jewish rites and make every effort to defend them. Because they do this, as I see it, they deserve a stronger condemnation than any Jew. Not only the wise and intelligent but even those with little reason and understanding would agree with me in this. I need no clever arguments, no rhetorical devices, and no prolix periodic sentences to prove this. It is enough to ask them a few simple questions and then trap them by their answers.

Remarks: According to the statement made here, there were some Gentile Christians who continued to have fellowship with Jews. Obviously, John was not happy about it. He planned to "trap them" by his cunning Q & A to prevent them from continuing. He was out to make them feel guilty about their supposed error, and their guilt must be worse than the Jews themselves!

- Homily V. IV. 1-3 [10]

  1.We have said enough to prove that the temple will never be rebuilt. But since the abundance of proofs which support this truth is so great, I shall turn from the gospels to the prophets because the Jews put their belief ill them before all others. And from the words of the prophets *I shall make it clear that the Jews will recover neither their city nor their temple in days to come.* And yet the need was not mine to prove that the temple will not be restored. This was not my obligation; the Jews have the obligation to prove the opposite, namely, that the temple will be rebuilt. For the years that have elapsed stand by my side in the combat and bear witness to the truth of my words.

2.Even though the outcome of events defeats them, even though they cannot prove in deeds what they maintain in words, even though they are simply making a rash boast, they have a right to present their testimony. The proof for my position is that the events of which I speak did actually occur: Jerusalem did fall and has not been restored after so many years. Their position rests on their unsupported words.

3.Yet the burden of proof was on them to show that the city would rise again. This is the procedure for giving proofs in courts of law. Suppose two people are in dispute over some matter, and the first party presents the claim for his position in writing while the second party attacks his statement. The second party must then bring forward witnesses or other proofs in refutation of what is said in the written deposition, but the plaintiff need not do so. This is what the Jews must now do. They must produce a prophet who says that by all means Jerusalem will be rebuilt. *For if there was going to be an end to the present captivity for you Jews, there was every need for the prophets to foretell this, as is clear to anyone who has even so much as glanced at the prophetic books.* For it was the custom of old among the Jews that under inspiration from above, their prophets would foretell the good or evil things which were going to befall the people. (Emphasis added)

Remarks: Well, John did not believe the Jews will one day returned to reclaim the Jerusalem city. He was wrong, of course. They did. First, they recovered back the land of Palestine from the Arabs when on May 14, 1948, Israel was declared a new sovereign nation under the United Nation Charter. At the time, they did not control the Old City of Jerusalem. Then, in the Six Day War in June 1967, they defeated the Arab armies and took control of the Old City. So, Jerusalem is today the Capital of the Nation of Israel. The challenge now for the Israeli is to retake the Temple Mount, located in the heart of the Old City. This site is still under Arab control. They must, and they will reclaim the site so that they could rebuild the Third Temple on it in fulfillment of prophecies.

John was mistaken to think there were no prophets foretelling the Jews will return to rebuild Jerusalem and the Temple. There are Scriptures such as Zechariah Chapters 12-14, where the prophet foretold the repentance of national Israel (12:10-11). There will be restoration, and the Lord, their Messiah, will return to meet them in the land of Israel (14:4). The Messiah will reign in His holy city of Jerusalem, and everyone who is alive at that time must go up to Jerusalem to the Feast of Tabernacle to worship Him. Those who don't obey will be punished (14:16-19).

Another Prophet is our Lord Himself. In the Olivet Discourse, the disciples asked Him about the destruction of the Herod Temple (Luke 21:5-7). He told them to watch. When they see a foreign army surround the city, they are to run to the hills. It came to pass about thirty-five years later when the Roman army invaded Jerusalem and destroyed the Temple. And Jesus foretold the rebuilding of Jerusalem, and the Temple (Luke 21:24).

- Homily VIII. VIII. 7-8 [11]

  7. But how will you go into the synagogue? If you make the sign of the cross on your forehead, the evil power that dwells in the synagogue immediately takes to flight. If you fail to sign your forehead, you have immediately thrown away your weapon at the doors. Then the devil will lay hold of you, naked and unarmed as you are, and he will overwhelm you with ten thousand terrible wounds.

  8. What need is there for me to say this? The way you act when you get to the synagogue makes it clear that you consider it a very serious sin to go to that wicked place. You are anxious that no one notice your arrival there; you urge your household, friends, and neighbors not to report you to the priests. If someone does report you, you fly into a rage. Would it not be height of folly to try to hide from men your bold and shameless when God, who is present everywhere, see it?

Remarks: According to John, it is certain there are demons in the synagogue, and one is protected by making a sign of the cross on one's forehead. Failure to do that, the demons will surely be able to overpower the person. Well, is that the way the Bible says we are to be protected? No. Our protection comes from being sure that we walk in the Spirit. Those who walk in the Spirit covers themselves with the blood of Christ, which provide actual protection against evil spirits.

Leaving John Chrysostom, we shall now turn to another Church Father, who was a contemporary of John although much older, St. Augustine of Hippo (AD 354-430). He is viewed as one of the most famous post-Nicene Church Fathers in Western Christianity for his outstanding works, that is, *The City of God* and *Confessions*.

In his days, the presence and continuous survival of the Jews called into question their belief that the Jews should have faded into obscurity. Contrary to their expectation, Judaism still maintained a significant presence and, in fact, managed to attract Christians to its fold. As the eminent theologian in his day, he wrote a sermon entitled "Against the Jews" in his attempt to explain the issue. His view was that the Jews have been kept alive by God to serve as a witness to the truth of Christianity. However, their status shall be lower than the Christians, serving as slaves and servants to the Church.

One of the areas the Jews could serve was as money-lenders. The loaning of money was essential in a growing economy. But this type of activity or profession was not suitable for Christians. Usury or the lending of money at high interest could endanger the souls of the believers. Why not get the Jews do this dirty job? After all, they are spiritually lost. With centuries of engaging in this business, this explains why the Jews today are well known for their financial acumen.

The Church in the Middle-Ages

The Church's attitude towards the Jews continues a downward trajectory going forward for the next one thousand years, roughly from AD 500 to 1500. It is a period known in European history as the Middle-Ages. The time is divided further into three periods: Early Middle-Ages (AD 500-1000), High Middle-Ages (AD 1000-1300), and Late Middle-Ages (AD 1300-1500). The Early period was relatively quiet. The High period was dominated by the event of the Crusades while the Late period saw the horrors of the Inquisition.

The Crusades

European Christians have been visiting or making pilgrims to the holy land from the late fourth century. Since 536, Jerusalem came under Muslim control but they continued to allow Christians to enter the city. By 1055, the Muslim Turks cut off the routes by which the pilgrims traveled to the holy land. They further disrupted Christian worship in Jerusalem. It prompted Pope Urban II to intervene. In 1096, he mobilized the First Crusade, in which he managed to garner 35,000 volunteers of peasants and artisans in France and Germany to set out for the holy land. Unable to control their explosion of fervor, they began to seek out the Muslims. Finding none, they lay their hands on the Jews as they considered them as infidels as much as the Muslims. Many were killed right there in France and Germany even before the journey began.

As the Crusaders marched through Europe en route to the holy land, they pillaged, plundered and raped Jewish communities. Thousands were killed. Many were forced to undergo Christian baptism, and be killed when refused to do so.

Three years later, the Crusaders finally arrived in Jerusalem on June 7, 1099. They besieged the city until July 15, 1099 when they finally broke through the walls. The Crusaders numbered 12,000 men, including 1,300 knights.[12] There were estimated 60,000 Muslim and Jews, excluding women and children held up in the city. Most of them were killed. Jerusalem, thus, came under Christian control. It would remain so until 1291 when the Muslim once again re-conquered the city. There were nine Crusades launched in the intervening years.

The Inquisition

The Inquisition was a Roman Catholic tribunal for discovery and punishment of heresy. Pope Innocent III (1198-1216) instituted it in Rome. Initially, the Inquisition dealt only with Christian heretics and did not interfere with the affairs of the Jews. In 1481, it was implemented in Spain, and it was there that the Jews were targeted. Thousands of Jews were baptized there by force. They were known as *Conversos* (New Christians) and expected to behave as Christians. They submitted themselves to this act so they could continue to stay in the country.

Most of the *Conversos* continued to practice Jewish customs such as abstaining from eating pork and observing the Feast Days, just to name two. There were over 35 Jewish traditions in all. According to the Inquisition Laws, anyone caught practicing any of the customs will be prosecuted. More than 13,000 *Conversos* were put on trial during the first twelve years of the Spanish Inquisition. The powers expelled the Jews in 1492 to eliminate ties between the Jewish community and the *Conversos*. By the time of the abolition of the Spanish Inquisition in 1821, thousands were burned to death at the stake.

The expulsion of the Jews from Spain forced thousands of them to flee to neighboring Portugal. But in 1536, the Inquisition was implemented there as well. Tribunals were set up in Lisbon and other cities to try offenders. The outcome there was not as terrible. Even so, roughly 40,000 cases were tried, and over a thousand burned to death. The Portuguese Inquisition was abolished finally in 1821.

The Church in the Modern Era

Leaving behind the Middle-Ages, which is also called the Dark Ages we enter into a period known as the Modern Era. This Era is broken up into two periods: the Early Modern Era (AD 1500-1800) and the Late Modern Era (AD 1800-present). Several milestone events mark the Early Modern Era. They include the Fall of Constantinople in 1453, the discovery of America by Christopher Columbus in 1492, and the discovery of the sea route to the East in 1498. It ended around the time of the French Revolution in 1789.

The Reformation

From the Protestant Church perspective, the Reformation was the most powerful thing that took place in the Early Modern Era. It was a movement for change; to rejuvenate the spiritual condition of the sluggish Church. The movement for change came about because of growing criticism against the Church of Rome. There were several people leading the Reformation movement, but Martin Luther played the most significant role. He was a German-born monk. Following his enlightenment, he took a stand against the Church teaching in the matter of selling indulgences, on the doctrine of purgatory, among others, which infuriated the Roman Church ecclesiastical body. In 1521, Pope Leo X issued the papal bull that excommunicated him from the Church.

The movement requires time to grow and mature. Similar to a growing crop that produce first the blade, then the head, after that the full grain in the head (Mark 4:28). One area that required much time is the status of the Jews. He had a favorable view of them at first. He wrote a pamphlet entitled "That Christ was born a Jew." It was his attempt to reach them with the Gospel whom he acknowledged as Christ's brothers in the flesh. He said, "I hope that if one deals with the Jews in a kindly way and instructs them carefully from Holy Scripture, many of them will become genuine Christians and turn to the faith of their fathers, the prophets, and patriarchs."

However, when they were not receptive to his message and turn to Christ, he lost patience and became hostile towards them. With the benefit of hindsight, we could say it was not yet time for the restoration of the Jews. Exasperated with them, he spoke in 1530 through a series of "Table Talk," in which he lampooned them as stiff-necked, haughty, and presumptuous. A few years later, he wrote an essay entitled "The Jews and Their Lies" (1543) in which he launched a vitriolic attack on them. An extract from the thesis:

> Whoever has a desire to lodge, nurse, and honor such poisonous serpents and young Devils, that is, the worst enemies of Christ our Lord and of us all; and permit himself to be abused, plundered, robbed, spit upon, cursed and suffer all evil, let the Jews be commended to him. If this be not sufficient, let him also be put into his mug or crawl and worship such a sanctuary, and afterward boast that he had been merciful, had strengthened the Devil and his young Devils to blaspheme our dear Lord and the precious blood with which He has bought us. In that way, he will be a perfect Christian, filled with deeds of mercy, for which Christ will reward him on Judgment Day with the Jews and eternal hell fire! [13]

A few months later, he produced a booklet, "Vom Schem Hamphoras" (Of the Unknowable Name), a Jewish fable, using language in its extreme borders on blasphemy.

The Russian Pogroms

The Russian Pogroms happened in the early years of the Late Modern Era (AD 1800-present). Pogrom is a Russian word meaning "to wreak havoc," an organized massacre of a particular ethnic group. In this case, the Russian Pogroms was directed mainly at the Jews in the Russian Empire.

Until the late 18th century, there were no Jews living in Russia. Then, Catherine the Great (AD 1729-1796), the renowned Russian female leader, annexed part of the Polish–Lithuanian Commonwealth. It came under the control of the Russian Empire. The annexed territory was subsequently called the Pale of Settlement, a vast ghetto (Jewish quarter) inhabited by mostly Jews. The area of the Pale is today Eastern Europe that encompasses Ukraine, Moldova, Poland, Belarus, and the Baltic states of Lithuania, Latvia and Estonia. By the end of the 19th century, that territory was home to the largest Jewish population in the world estimated at 5 million.[14] From the annexed territory, the Jews slowly began to migrate to the interior provinces of Russia, particularly to the capital cities of Moscow and St. Petersburg. Gradually, the number grew until it reached a few millions.

Between the years, 1821 to 1921, series of pogroms broke out within the Pale of Settlement and in Russia. The first pogrom occurred in 1821 in Odessa, in present day Ukraine. Over a dozen killed by the Greek over economic disputes. Then, following the assassination of Tsar Alexander II in 1881, pogroms broke out in the major cities of Kiev, Warsaw and Odessa. It lasted three years. After this, a much bloodier wave of pogroms broke out in several hundred towns and cities from 1903 to 1906, leaving an estimated 2,000 Jews dead and many more wounded.

The Bolsheviks Revolution from 1917-1920 that the Jews had a hand in, led to the Communist take-over and subsequent formation of the USSR. The after effect of the pogroms and the Revolution saw over 2 million Jews fled the region with most going to the United States.

There are differing views regarding the relationship between the Russian state and the Jews. One view sees Jews as the preeminent victims of the tsarist autocracy, whose treatment of the Jews was marked and defined by governmental anti-Semitism. Thus, the Russian state, jointly supported by the Orthodox Church, was to be blamed for the pogroms. Another view did not see anti-Semitism as the motivating force of the authority's treatment of Jews. They argue that pogroms against Jews were not orchestrated or even approved of by the state but were rather spontaneous and unplanned outbreaks of urban violence caused by social and economic forces. Irrespective of which view is correct, the Jews did suffer persecution during that period.

The Holocaust (Shoah)

Eastern Europe and Russia had the largest concentration of Jews in the world at the dawn of the 20th century. The First World War and the Bolshevik Revolution in Russia had forced many of them to immigrate to the United States and elsewhere. Roughly, 9.5 million chose to stay put, a number made up of about 60% of world Jewry of 15.3 million.[15]

Again with the benefit of hindsight, we now know the time for the restoration of the Jews had come. Their long, arduous journey began for them with the destruction of Jerusalem in AD 69. Their journey onwards was somewhat like a river whose course had been affected by an earthquake. The greater part of its water had descended into a chasm created by the quake. There it continued to flow, but, for the most part, its course was underground. Many people assumed that the river had ceased to flow altogether. Even those who knew that the river was still flowing were not aware of the exact course that it was following.[16]

Well, we finally know the course it would take when the river resurfaced from the underground, so to speak. It was the time God desired them to move on to Palestine, to have the nation of Israel reestablished, to give them back their homeland. But will they move? Are they willing to be uprooted from their familiar surrounding? How are they to be persuaded to migrate? No matter how you view it, it was a monumental task to move millions of them from Europe to the Middle East.

We believe God allowed the Second World War to loosen up the Jewish communities all over Europe—sort of like "the eagle stir her nest." It was an episode out of expediency to force them to immigrate.

In Germany, Hitler, and the German people had grown increasingly resentful of the Jews. The strong Jewish presence in German society had heightened animosity towards them. Several contributing factors which eventually compel him to take the course that led to the War. They include:

a. Hitler developed a hatred for the Jews from the teachings of the Church. The diatribe of Martin Luther and the Catholic Church had significantly molded his thinking.
b. A sense of humiliation that Germany lost the First World War and was forced to sign the Treaty of Versailles. The terms were highly disadvantaged to Germany. He felt the Jews were partly to be blamed.
c. He resented the fact that Jews who only constituted 1% of the population were dominating the economic sectors especially banking, the media; and the professional sectors such as lawyers, doctors, and teachers. Also, there were many Jews in significant government positions.
d. He believed Judaism handled the rise of Bolshevism in Russia since most of their leaders were Jews. After the First World War, Bolshevism overran Russia, which he viewed as a threat and an enemy of Germany.

The War began when Hitler set out to reclaim territories that were part of Czechoslovakia and the annexation of Austria, both with the large German population. His actions triggered the War which the United Nations estimated cost 60 million lives by the time it ended.

During the War, the Nazis had a particular target for the Jews. It was called the Final Solution. The Final Solution required the systematic removal of millions of Jews from German soil. To this end, countless labor camps and six concentration camps were set up. Below is the list of the concentration camp location with their corresponding number of deaths:

- Auschwitz-Birkenau (1,000,000)
- Chelmno (150,000)

- Treblinka (870,000)
- Sobibor (250,000)
- Maidenek (50,000)
- Belzec (600,000)[17]

The total deaths from the six camps numbered 2.9 million. Commonly, it is quoted that 6 million Jews died during the Holocaust (A Greek word meaning "whole" and "burnt"). This number is being disputed. In recent years, the figure has been revised downwards again and again. The Encyclopaedia Judaica in its second edition listed the updated figure at 3 million.[18] This number seems more realistic, taking into account those who died outside the camps. Anyhow, the number is still high relative to the overall Jewish population.

The Church's Regret

The return of the Jews to their homeland had corrected a misconception in many people's minds regarding their standing in the eyes of God. They previously thought the Jews were beyond the reach of God's mercy and forgiveness for their ancestor rejection of Christ.

On her part, the Roman Catholic Church had admitted her mistakes of nurturing hatred against the Jews based on this theological misinterpretation. On October 28, 1965, the Vatican Council II approved by an overwhelming majority a declaration on "The Relation of the Church to Non-Christian Religions." In that declaration, a statement on the Jews was made deploring all hatreds, persecutions, displays of anti-Semitism leveled at any time or from any source against the Jews.[19]

The document was promulgated by Pope Paul VI and became part of official Catholic doctrine, binding on every member of the Church throughout the world. The Catholic Church began to instruct their local parishes to deliver sermons expressing sincere regret for the anti-Semitic stance taken by the Church.

The returned of the Jews to their homeland also helps to dispel lingering doubts in the mind of some Christians whether the Jerusalem Temple will be rebuilt. The Third Temple will surely be rebuild and is necessary for the fulfillment of certain scriptures relating to the activities of the Antichrist. More shall be said about this later.

Refutation of Replacement Theology

Why are people subscribing to this view that the Christians have replaced the Jews? This belief is base on what ground? Is it fully back up by Scriptures? Let us examine the view and see whether or not there is any basis to it.

We have already cited about the Abrahamic Covenant containing the promise made to Abraham. And there are three aspects to that promise amplified to Abraham's descendants. For convenience, we shall restate them here:

I. Abraham's descendants would possess the land on which he set his foot on
   [This aspect of the promise has to do with the *land*. It is being called the Palestinian Covenant promise land]
II. God will make Abraham himself great, and his descendants will be a great nation
   [This aspect of the promise has to do with the *seed*. It is being called the Davidic Covenant promise seed]
III. "All the families of the earth," that is, the Gentiles will be blessed by Abraham's descendants
   [This aspect of the promise has to do with the *blessings*. It is being called the New Covenant promise blessings]

For our current purpose, we shall examine these three amplified covenants in reverse order.

First, let us look at the New Covenant. By this covenant, God's plan to bless "all the families of the earth" has been fulfilled through Christ. It was what the apostle Paul was attempting to explain in the Book of Galatians. Some of the notable verses are Galatians 3:8-9; 14, and 28-29. The fact that the New Covenant blessed us Gentiles Christians greatly does not mean the other two—Davidic Covenant and the Palestinian Covenant are no longer valid. The

New Covenant is just one of three (1 of 3). Although the three covenants are different from each other, they are inter-linked. We need to be reminded that all these three covenants are irrevocable.

What about the Scriptures that say the New Covenant had replaced the Old Covenant? The apostle Paul made statements to this effect in Hebrews 8:7, 8, and 13. If we read the whole Chapters 8 and 9, we would realize the Old Covenant he was referring to was the Mosaic Covenant. As explained before, this covenant is revocable (can be canceled). He was not referring to the Abrahamic Covenant as some have misunderstood, as the Abrahamic Covenant is irrevocable (cannot cancel). The three covenants; New Covenant, Davidic Covenant, and the Palestinian Covenant all have their roots in the Abrahamic Covenant (3 in 1). This being so, how could the New Covenant (1 of 3) replaced the main covenant?

Second, let us look at the Davidic Covenant in which God promised He will make Abraham's descendants a great nation. God partially and temporary fulfilled this promise in the life of King David. At the height of his reign, David was told his seed will proceed out from him to inherit his *kingdom,* his *house*, and his *throne* forever. Christ was that seed who inherited the promise (Luke 1:31-33).

(i) According to Replacement view, the kingdom of David that Christ inherited is now the Kingdom of God here on earth (Acts 19:8; Romans 14:17). They point to Matthew 21:43 where Jesus said the kingdom of God would be taken from the Jews and given to the Gentiles. It is true. But the decision is a temporary one. We know because the disciples brought up this matter to Jesus just before He was taken up to heaven. They asked Him when Israel will regain the kingdom. He could not say when as it is His Father's prerogative to reveal. Be that as it may, His statement did imply that the kingdom will be restored back to them (Acts 1:6-7).

(ii) According to Replacement view, the house of King David that Christ reign over is now the household of faith (the Church). One of the scriptures they made reference to is Ephesians 2:19-22. The Church is the household of faith with Gentile believers brought in and built upon the foundation of the apostles and prophets. It is true. In the Book of Romans, the apostle Paul described it in another way. Using the olive tree as an example, he said the original olive branches (Jews) were broken off. And wild olive branches

(Gentile Christians) are being grafted in their place (Romans 11:15-22). However, this trade-off is transitory. At the appropriate time in the future, the Jews will be grafted back (Romans 11:23)! To fend off Replacement view, we note that God has not cast away the Jews (Romans 11:1-5). They will experience mercy and restoration into fellowship with Him (Romans 11:28-31).

> There is only one olive tree and the root is Jewish

(iii) According to Replacement view, the throne of King David that Christ inherited is now the throne at the right hand of God the Father in heaven (Ephesians 1:20-23; Colossians 3:1). Adherents of this view refer to Acts chapter 2:25-36. In that passage of the Scriptures, the apostle Peter mentioned the prophecy of King David (Psalm 16:8-11). David foresaw Christ would one day rose from the dead, this same Christ who will proceed from his body. He understood that the resurrected Christ will inherit his throne. Peter announced to the Jewish crowd this transaction is being accomplished in their presence. The sign indicating this accomplishment is the outpouring of the Holy Spirit with the speaking in tongues. Again this is true, but the understanding is incomplete. The following will provide a complete understanding:

a) Since the kingdom of David will be restored back to Israel as discuss earlier in (i), the throne will also have to be restored.
b) Thus, Christ's throne in heaven includes the physical throne of King David in Jerusalem. While the right to David's throne is already His, the throne is still not available for Him to sit on. The dilemma Christ is facing right now is similar to what David encountered in his early years. We recall that Samuel the prophet had anointed David to be the next king to replace Saul (1 Samuel 16:13). David was just a teenager then. Did David immediately ascend to claim the throne? No. King Saul was not about to relinquish it. In fact, he set out to kill David. To escape his pursuer, David was forced to flee to the neighbor territory of the Philistine. After about 15 years of being a fugitive, relief came when Saul died. The people of Judah immediately acknowledged him as their king (2 Samuel 2:4). From Hebron, he ruled over the inhabitants of Judah for 7 years (2 Samuel 2:11). It was not complete because the rest of the population of Israel who was

more devoted to Saul, refused to acknowledge David as their king. This hung situation lasted for 7years until they finally surrendered to his kingship. David went on to rule the whole of Israel for another 33 years from Jerusalem. He was 30 years old by then. In all, he reigned over Israel for 40 years (2 Samuel 5:3-5). The lesson of this episode tells us that Christ will return bodily and physically to sit on the throne of David in Jerusalem, but only after Israel goes through a national repentance. They will surrender to His Lordship when they believe He is their Messiah.

Third, let us look at the Palestinian Covenant, which promise that Abraham's descendants will possess the land. According to Replacement view, there is no necessity for the fulfillment of this Covenant. They say we should not attach any more importance to the Jews returning to their ancestral homeland. To rebut this, we wish to make several statements:

a) The land promised to the children of Israel is not on a temporary basis but forever, or as an everlasting possession (Genesis 13:15; 17:8).
b) The Palestinian Covenant is irrevocable. Hence, the promise contained within cannot be declared null and void.
c) The Jews are long absent from the land for almost 1,800 years. It is true that there was a long break whereby there was no throne for kings to abide continuously. This temporary setback cannot be a sign that God had withdrawn the promise. As a matter of fact, God had forewarned them about this (Deuteronomy 30:1-10). If they sin, they will be driven out but will be allowed back to the land when they repent. They have already returned to the land, which attest to the validity of the Palestinian Covenant.
d) That they did not yet rebuilt the Temple in which Christ could return to sit on it should not be an issue. The fulfillment of the prophecy is still ongoing, and God's time is the best.

Before we leave this subject, we wish to respond to a few other scriptures used by Replacement Theology advocates to support their view.

(i) Romans 2:28-29
Since a real Jew is to be determined by the heart and not the skin, why is there a need to have physical Israel restored to their homeland?

Response: Paul is here addressing his fellow Jews, not Gentiles (Romans 2:17). The Jews like the Gentiles, need to be born again to have eternal life. The plan of God is to have all Jews born again. Those, not born-again are considered lost, from the time of the Apostles until now. Are there any born-again Jews during the long period of their dispersion? Yes, even during the Dark Ages. How could that be? God had said He will always have a remnant of the Jews to keep His plan alive, even in the days of Prophet Elijah (1 Kings 19:18; Romans 11:5). Are all Jews living in Israel today saved? No. Only those who believed in Jesus as their Messiah or the so-called Messianic Jews are saved. Why then are the Jews called God's covenant people, God peculiar people if only a remnant is saved? The answer to this is, many are called, but few are chosen (Matthew 20:16). We reiterate that God's plan is to have all Israel saved, to have every Jew born again at His second coming. When He finally reigned over the nation of Israel with Jews who are all born again, it will be the complete fulfillment of the covenant He made with Abraham.

(ii) Galatians 3:28-29
Through Christ, Gentile Christians are Abraham's seed and are heirs to the promises made to Abraham. Then, why is there a need for the Jews to return to the land? Why is there a need for Israel to be restored? Who needs the physical Jews now that there is neither Jew nor Greek?

Response: God's purpose or program for Israel and the world is yet to be completed. There will be neither Jew nor Gentile after God created the new heavens and the new earth (Revelation 21:1; 1 Corinthians 15:24-28). In the meantime, the distinction is still evident. What Paul said is a spiritual reality hindered from expression by the old world, old creation. Is it not true with male and female? Presently, it is still obvious but one day there will be neither male nor female. There will be no marriages and no procreation (Matthew 22:30).

So back to the question, "Have the Christians replaced the Jews?" or, "Has the Church replaced Israel?" Our conclusion points to the fact that they have not. As a strategic move, they have been temporary set aside so that God could reach out to the Gentiles. We are living in the days when God's dealing with the Gentiles are about to come to an end. When the full number of the Gentile believers has come in, God's attention will revert to His ancient people (Romans 11:25). We are witnessing the restoration of Israel to their land. The issue of whether to acknowledge Christ as their Messiah or not will be presented to them again. This time around they will be compelled to accept Him.

Chapter 6

JEWISH GLOBAL INFLUENCE

The Jews have come a long way in their struggle to survive. In the end, they not only survived against insuperable odds but succeeded comfortably; even thrive on the world stage. Looking at their current number, Jews made up only two-tenths of one percent of the global population but see what they have achieved. The scope of their success is neatly summed up by the confession of one of their own: "As a group, Jews are the most successful in terms of income and wealth. They have reached the echelons, the highest echelons of power in every field—in transportation, distribution, publication, movies, theatre, art, science, medicine, law, architecture, astronomy, archaeology, and anthropology. But all of this was developed through their mastery of trade and commerce. It is their success in trade that fueled all the other areas of Jewish life."

In centuries past, the Jews were discriminated and marginalized with the restriction imposed where only certain jobs were accessible to them. One of those few jobs or professions available was money-lending. The charging of usury (excessive interest) was deemed a sin or immoral in Christian Europe. The Bible discouraged the practice but is permissible in the Talmud. Jews are allowed to make loans with interest to non-Jews. With little choice, they took up this profession and since then, have become superb at it. Moneylending is the precursor of finance and banking that is at the heart of trade and commerce. The Jews are masters of it.

From the lofty position of power, the Jews are forcefully bringing their influence to bear on the world. The evidence is all there for the picking. The agenda of world Jewry has overtaken other agendas to the chagrin of the rest of the world. The list of their agenda is pretty long, which includes:

- Anti-Semitism
- New World Order
- Israel, the Palestinians, and Arab Neighbors
- Israel and the International Community
- Relations between Israel and North American Jewry
- Energy and Environment
- Women in the Work Force, Family, and Reproductive Rights
- Gay and Lesbian Rights
- Racism
- World Jewry and Threatened Jewish Communities
- Militarism and the Nuclear Arms Race

Having strong financial and political clout, they can defend their rights and interest as a minority. They acquired a particular quality of working togetherness, and a special conspiracy of the objective. The intense adhesiveness of their race put them in the admirable state in a period of severe trials. They have enemies aplenty, but a good number have been silenced or neutralized. But the perennial problem of anti-Semitism does not seem to go away. Unfortunately, at the time of this writing, the media is reporting a resurgence of anti-Semitism in a dozen of countries such as France, Germany, Poland, the Scandinavian countries, Argentina and South Africa.

The Jewish presences are noticeable where ever they live. Being fervid, they tend to flourish especially when their number is significant. Since the establishment of the nation of Israel, she is constantly on the news. To friends and foe alike, Israel is not about to go anywhere. She is here to stay, for the Jews have an appointment with destiny.

Today, the world's 14.2 million Jews are found mainly in two places: Israel and the United States. Israel has the largest Jewish population, slightly more than 6 million, excluding Arabs who are Israeli citizens. The United States has about 5.7 million. Europe, including Russia, has a Jewish population of roughly 1.4 million. There are about 1 million Jews scattered across the rest of the world, including significant communities in Argentina, Brazil, Mexico, South Africa, Australia, and Canada.[1]

Jewish Wealth

At the World Economic Forum, an international organization that meets annually in Davos, Switzerland, thousands of top business leaders, international political leaders, selected intellectuals, and journalists came together to discuss the most pressing issues facing the world. In its November 2013 Meeting, a summary was made of its annual report, and part of the perturbed report states that:

- Just one percent of the world population owned almost half of the world's wealth.
- The wealth of the one percent richest people in the world amounts to a USD10 trillion. That is 65 times the total wealth of the bottom half of the world's population.
- The bottom half of the world's population owns the same as the richest 85 people in the world.[2]

This report is shocking, but is it accurate? Is there more to what is being reported? There are financial institutions in the world which are privately owned. A good example would be the Jewish- owned Federal Reserve (the Fed) which has trillion of dollars in their book. Since no one could audit their account, not even the US Congress, it is not possible to come up with an accurate record. Furthermore, it is common knowledge the mega-rich use complex offshore structures, in offshore financial centers, to operate secret accounts, manage companies and hold assets. The financial institutions in this offshore haven are legal institutions but runs unregulated activities. Hedge funds, unlisted derivatives and credit default swaps are facilitated through these institutions across the global financial system without regulatory oversight—it is a form of shadow banking. Thus, wealth generated in this environment is certainly not included in the report roll out at the World Economic Forum.

What about the Jewish share of the world's wealth? Forbes, the media companies that tracks and publishes the list of the world's top rich individuals, announced in its 2013 global list that there were 1,426 billionaires living in the world. Its subsidiary, Forbes Israel, further declared that 11% of the 1,426 billionaires were Jews, and their collective wealth amounts to USD812 billion.[3]

As it is, 11% of the top richest people in the world are Jews seems very impressive, considering their tiny population. Regardless, their share should be much higher. Why? We need to reiterate, that there is wealth which are not accounted for, which Forbes could not possibly have tracked as they have no access to private-owned banks. In the case of wealth managed through shadow banking, not all belongs to the Jews of course, but assuredly a considerable percentage does belong to them.

Take the case of the Rothschild. The Rothschild family fortune is reputed to be the biggest in the world. A lot of their wealth is managed by their privately owned banks or by banks which they controlled. Back in the 18th century, the family already had the capability to provide finance to governments and the financing of the war effort in Europe. By the 19th century, they had crossed the Atlantic, owning and operating banks in major cities across Europe and in the United States. By the 20th century, their footprint could be seen distinctly in international finance. They played a major part in the ownership and operation of the Federal Reserve. They controlled the International Monetary Fund (IMF), the World Bank, Bank of International Settlement (BIS), and the European Central Bank; not to mention a number of very large banks such as JP Morgan, Goldman Sachs and Deutsche Bank. Through these financial institutions, their domination of the global wealth is well entrenched.

Let us take a look at the history of this remarkable family.

The Rothschild Banking Family

The Rothschild Banking Group is the largest and oldest family-controlled financial entity in the world. The following extract taken from the company website describes who they are:

"We are a global financial advisory group that is family-controlled and independent. We have been *at the center of the world's financial markets for more than*

200 years. From our historical roots in Europe, we have developed a unique global footprint. Today we have full-scale advisory businesses across the world including locally staffed offices in China, Brazil, India, the United States of America, the Middle East and Asia Pacific. Our Group includes four main arms—Global Financial Advisory, Wealth Management & Trust, Merchant Banking and Institutional Asset Management—as well as specialist financial businesses." [4] (Emphasis added)

It would be interesting to know how it started for them and how their path was and is being laid with gold. It all started with their founder, Mayer Amschel Bauer. Below is the historical timeline of the Rothschild family.

First a Few Points to Note:

(i) The name Rothschild is derived from two German words: "Rot" means red, and "Schild" means shield—a red shield sign he used to hang outside his shop.[5]

(ii) M.A.Bauer (Rothschild) also had five daughters. According to Jewish customs, Jewishness is based upon matrilineal descent, that is, the child of a Jewish mother is a Jew while the child of a Jewish father is not a Jew. However, in March 1983, the Central Conference of American Rabbis (Reform Movement) adopts a resolution accepting the principle of patrilineal identity. The resolution was opposed by the Orthodox and the Conservative sects. As of today, there is no consensus of opinion on this policy within Judaism.

(iii) To ensure the wealth remains in the family, inbreeding is common, that is, among first and second cousins.

(iv) Through intermarriages, the Rothschild Jewish bloodline had extended to family names such as Astor (German); Bundy (English); Collins (English); duPont (France); Freeman (English); Kennedy (Irish); Morgan (Welsh); Oppenheimer (German); Rockefeller (German); Sassoon (Iraq); Schiff (German); Taft (Scandinavian); and Van Duyn (Dutch).

(v) Apart from the above, some Rothschild members have their names changed, for security reasons.

1743: Mayer Amschel Bauer (Rothschild) was born in Frankfurt, Germany. He was a money lender and the proprietor of a counting house. M.A. Rothschild (1743-1812) had five sons. In the years following, they were sent to various cities in Europe to set up banking houses.

1) Amschel Mayer Rothschild was sent to Frankfurt
2) Salomon Mayer Rothschild to Vienna
3) Nathan Mayer Rothschild to London
4) Kalmann Mayer Rothschild to Naples
5) Jacob Mayer Rothschild to Paris

1760: Through business dealings, the Rothschild family became close associates with Prince William IX of Hesse-Hanau, one of the richest royal houses in Europe. Loaning money to sovereign and royalty is more profitable than loaning to individuals. This experience prompted them to seek more business opportunities with people in authorities and with royalties.

1790: In the midst of the French Revolution (1789-1793), laws were passed giving bankers control over the nation's finance. It led M. A. Rothschild to boldly state: "Permit me to issue and control the money of a nation, and I care not who makes its laws!"

1791: The Rothschild, acting through Alexander Hamilton (their agent in George Washington's cabinet) managed to set up a central bank in the U.S. called the First Bank of the United States.

1798: From Frankfurt, Nathan Mayer Rothschild went to England to set up a banking house in London. He was the third son and twenty-one years of age.

1803-1815: During Napoleonic Wars, the Rothschild family funded Napoleon's army (France) and the opposite side, Wellington's army (England). By the end of that war, the Rothschild had controlled over the British economy, and England was forced to relinquish control of the Bank of England to them. [Note: Although it is a state bank, as at today, over 95% of the bank money supply is privately controlled].

Through control of the Bank of England, they replaced the method of shipping gold from country to country to using the system of paper debits and credits practiced today. With celebrated success, Nathan Mayer Rothschild made this statement: "I care not what puppet is placed upon the throne of England to rule the Empire on which the sun never sets. The man who controls Britain's money supply controls the British Empire, and I control the British money supply."

1810: The second son, Salomon Mayer Rothschild went to Vienna, Austria and set up the bank, M. von Rothschild und Söhne.

1816: The American Congress passed a bill permitting the Rothschild to set up the Second Bank of the United States.

1821: The fourth son, Kalmann (Carl) Mayer Rothschild was sent to Naples, Italy. He would end up doing a lot of business with the Vatican, and Pope Gregory XVI subsequently conferred upon him the Order of St. George.

1835: The Almadén quicksilver mines in Spain was taken over by the Rothschild. At the time quicksilver was a vital component in the refining of gold or silver. It gave the Rothschild a monopoly control on this activity.

1836: Nathan Mayer Rothschild passed away, and the control of his bank, N. M. Rothschild & Sons, was handed over to his younger brother, James Mayer Rothschild.

1840: The Bank of England appointed the Rothschild to be its bullion brokers.

1844: Salomon Mayer Rothschild bought up the United Coal Mines of Vítkovice and Austro-Hungarian Blast Furnace Company. These companies eventually became one of the top ten global industrial companies.

1850: By this time, the Rothschilds had reaffirmed their position as Europe's pre-eminent lender to governments. Germany, Britain, France, Turkey, Austria, Prussia, Belgium and the Papacy had all issued bonds through one or more of the Rothschild houses.[6]

1852: N M Rothschild & Sons began refining gold & silver for Royal Mint and other international customers.

1863: With John D. Rockefeller, the Rothschilds started an oil business called Standard Oil which is the forerunner of today's Exxon Corporation.

1868: Jacob (James) Mayer Rothschild died, the last of Mayer Amschel Rothschild's sons to pass away.

1886: De Rothschild Frères, the French Rothschild bank, managed to secure substantial amounts of Russia's oil fields. The Caspian and Black Sea Petroleum Company was formed which quickly became the world's second-largest oil producer.

1887: The Rothschild took control of the Kimberley diamond mines in South Africa and the De Beers, precious stones mines in Africa and India.

1895: The youngest son of Jacob (James) Mayer Rothschild, Edmond James de Rothschild, visited Palestine. He founded the first Jewish colonies there. It was a first step of the Rothschild effort to assist the Zionist movement to bring about the creation of a Jewish homeland.

1896: Theodor Herzl, founder of the World Zionist Organization, said this in his book, "When we sink, we become a revolutionary proletariat, the subordinate officers of all revolutionary parties; and at the same time, when we rise, there also rises our terrible power of the purse." [7] He was partly referring to the purse of the Rothschild family.

1897: The Zionist Congress was co-founded by the Rothschild to promote the Zionist agenda. One of the agenda was to establish a homeland for the Jews. The first meeting held in Basle, Switzerland wth Theodor Herzl as the first president.

1913: The Rothschild, through their agent Paul Warburg, help set up the U.S. Federal Reserve Bank. It is the U.S. Central Bank and is 100% privately owned by the Jews.

1914-1918: During the First World War the Rothschild funded both sides of the conflict: the German on the one side, and the British and French on the other. Their power to sway opinion was further enhanced, by their control of the three European news agencies: Wolff in Germany, Reuters in England, and Havas in France. Not surprising that around this time, the Rothschild are rarely reported in the media.

1917: The Rothschild Zionist leaders managed to persuade the British to give the land of Palestine to them. On November 2, the offer letter was issued (Balfour Declaration) by British Foreign Secretary, Arthur Balfour to Lord Walter Rothschild. A few weeks later, General Allenby led the British army offensive against the Ottoman army and succeeded in retaking Palestine by December 30, 1917.

1926: N. M. Rothschild & Sons refinanced the Underground Electric Railways Company of London Ltd, which had a controlling interest in the entire London Underground transport system.

1930: The Bank for International Settlements (BIS) established in Basle, Switzerland. This mother of all central banks is Rothschild-controlled.

1944: The International Monetary Fund (IMF) and the World Bank were set up in Bretton Woods, New Hampshire at the end of world war two. Another two Rothschild-controlled world financial institutions.

1948: Due to conflict between the Jews and the Arabs living in Palestine, the British transferred its control of the area to the UN in 1947. The UN subsequently partitioned Palestine into two states. Thus, the nation of Israel was born on May 14, 1948. With a strong influence from the Rothschild, the U.S. under President Harry Truman became the first country to recognize Israel.

1953: N. M. Rothschild & Sons found the British Newfoundland Corporation Limited to develop 60,000 square miles of land in Newfoundland, Canada. The development included a power station to harness the power of the Hamilton

Falls, one of the largest construction projects ever to be undertaken by a private company up to that time.

1962: It is being stated, "Though they control scores of industrial, commercial, mining and tourist corporations, not one bears the name Rothschild. As a privately held partnerships, the family houses never need to, and never do, publish a single public balance sheet or any other report of their financial condition." [8]

As already stated, from about the second decade of the 20th century, the Rothschild family began to fade slowly from mainstream media attention. The reason cited was that their fortune had diminished. It was not the actual cause, however. They made that decision partly to hide their identity for security consideration, and partly because the family grouping had grown too large.

Jews in America

The first Jews to set foot on American soil were in 1654. Fast forward to the dawn of the 20th century there were approximately a million Jews in America. For the next four decades, roughly a million were added for each decade. By the onset of the Second World War in 1939, there were about 4.8 million Jews living in America.[9] By then, the nation had become home to the world's biggest concentration of Jewish people, thanks to American liberal immigration policies. They immigrated mostly from Central and Eastern Europe. The earlier batches were mostly poor, arrived on crowded boats, and employed in manual work. The later batches were slightly better off, and they scattered across the continent and set up businesses, from small stores and factories to running financial institutions like Lehman Brothers and Goldman Sachs.

Even in America, the Jews faced discrimination in the workplaces due to anti-Semitism. On the East coast, most of them lived in crowded and filthy slums in New York – Brooklyn and the Lower East Side. In a short span of time, they emerged from poverty and made faster progress than any other group of immigrants. In a study done, it showed that even before the outbreak of the Second World War, about 20% of the Jewish men had free professions, double the rate in the entire American population. Anti-Semitism weakened after the Second World War, and the restrictions on hiring Jews eased and later canceled as part of the 1964 Civil Rights Act. The struggle of the liberal activists, many of whom were Jews, finally bore fruit. This success was to be a foretaste of many more to come as the Jews, who were socialists in Europe, tend to be active in labor unions and workers' strikes and protests. The Jews established many trade unions.

In 1957, 75% of Jews were white-collar workers, compared to 35% of all white people in the US. In 1970, 87% of Jewish men worked in clerical jobs, compared to 42% of all white people, and the Jews earned 72% more than the general average. As they prospered, they seamlessly integrated themselves into society. They moved from the slums to the suburbs, abandoned Yiddish (Germanic dialect commonly spoken by Jews in Europe) and adopted the clothes, culture and slang, dating and shopping habits of the non-Jewish elite.[10]

In comparison with other groups of immigrants, the Jews succeeded more than everyone. Another area where they excelled in is education. Hillel International, the largest Jewish campus organization in the world, found that 9 to 33% of students in leading universities in the US are Jewish. In a survey carried out by Pew Research Center in 2013, it reveals most Jews are college graduates at 58%, including 28% who say they have earned a post-graduate degree. By comparison, 29% of U.S. adults say they graduated from college, including 10% who have a post-graduate degree.[11]

Because of better education, Jews have better opportunities to advance their careers. They have quick perception and know how to seize opportunities. A competitive environment gives Jews an advantage. New fields of science, engineering, research, law, and finance were emerging, and the Jews entered these areas with gusto.

The American Jewish community today is considered, on the whole, prosperous and well-established. David Brooks of the New York Times, on January 12, 2010, article, wrote: "Jews are a famously accomplished group. They make up two-tenths of 1 percent of the world population, but they are 54 percent of the World Chess Champions; 27 percent of the Nobel Physics Laureates; and 31 percent of the Medicine Laureates. Jews make up 2 percent of the United States population, but 21 percent of the Ivy League

Student Bodies; 26 percent of the Kennedy Center Honorees; 37 percent of the Academy Award-winning directors; 38 percent of those on the recent Business Week list of "Leading Philanthropists"; and 51 percent of the Pulitzer Prize winners for nonfiction."

Without a doubt, they have established themselves very well in United States.

Federal Reserve and the Mega Banks

Every nation has their central bank, controlled by their respective governments. In the US, the Federal Reserve (the Fed) is the nation's central bank but with a significant difference: it is not owned by the US administration, although there is a certain degree of supervision. The Fed is a private entity wholly owned and managed by several private Jewish banks. And just who owns the Federal Reserve Bank? The owners are the Rothschild of London and Berlin, Lazard Brothers of Paris, Israel Moses Seif of Italy, Kuhn Loeb and Warburg of Germany, Lehman Brothers and Goldman Sachs, and the Rothschild-controlled Rockefeller interests of New York.

The Federal Reserve System was set up in 1910 by a group of seven bankers and government officials including J. P. Morgan, William Rockefeller, Paul Warburg and their associates in a secret meeting in Jekyll Island off the coast of Georgia.[12] It was made an official institution when the US Congress passed the Federal Reserve Act bill in 1913. The Fed system has twelve regional reserve banks located in major cities across the US with its main branch in New York. These regional reserve banks only do business with the US Treasury and their member banks, not with the public at large. They do not lend money to individuals. Their main assets are U.S. government securities such as Treasury bonds. Each bank branch is presided over by a governor, and one of the governors will be appointed Chairman by the US President. Since its inception, there have been 15 Chairmen. Out of these, 11 were Jews including the current Chairwoman, Janet Yellen. She is the first woman to head the Institution.

Among others, there are two primary functions of the Fed.

First, it acts as a lender to banks that want to borrow money to meet their reserve requirements. The Fed does this mainly to keep the system stable and function as the "lender of last resort." Traditionally, banks are required to keep

10% of their funds in reserve while lending out 90%. It is called Fractional Reserve Banking. From the client or depositor point of view, the higher the reserve the bank has, the safer it would be. But from the bank's perspective, they could expand the money supply higher with a lower reserve.

In recent years, the Fed had loosened its regulations. Since 2007, for example, the required Reserve Ratio of 10% set by the Fed applies to deposits by individuals but no longer applies to deposits by companies or institutions.[13] It means huge swaths of loans given out from the deposits in the banks are subjected no longer to any reserve requirements. So, if a bank wishes to provide a loan of $900 the bank is not required to have a reserve of $100.

Prior to this, in 1999, the Fed pushed through the repeal of the Glass-Steagall Act in Congress. This act was passed in 1933, following the 1929 Wall Street stock market crash, to separate investment and commercial banking activities. While it is entirely appropriate for investment banks to get involved in the high-risk stock market investment, it is improper for commercial banks to do so as it posed a significant risk to depositors' money. With the repeal of Glass-Steagall Act, commercial bank deposits have been used to speculate in every type of investments, in increasingly risky and complicated securities, buying and selling mortgages, collateralized debt obligations, and other derivatives. Because of the financial instruments' complexity and the institutions' vulnerable positions, many banks faced stark losses during the 2008 financial crisis. Many went bankrupt and had to be acquired by larger banks or were bailed out by the Federal Reserve. The crisis hit both commercial and investment banks.

The Fed policies had caused banks to prefer capital market activities over commercial banking activities. This state of affair was compounded following the 2008 financial crisis. When bank borrow from the Fed, the Fed charges interests that are called the discount rate. The imposing of higher discount rate would have forced the banks to be more discipline in their activities. Instead, the Fed lowers its interest rate to almost zero percent. According to their rationale, it is to stabilize the U.S. economy and financial system. Taking advantage of this, the banks borrow at 0.25% or less, and then turn around and invest those funds say, in a 5-year US Treasury note at 2.50% gaining an almost risk-free profit of 2.25%. Or they use the cheap money to engage in unregulated speculation.

Through merger and acquisitions, there are now several megabanks such as JPMorgan Chase, Bank of America, Citigroup, Wells Fargo, Bank of New York, and Goldman Sachs. These banks are so big in terms of their market capitalization they have to be bailed out by the Fed when they fail because they have become too-big-to-fail (i.e. too big to be allowed to fail).

Second, the other function of the Fed is to control the money supply in the economy. Regrettably, the Fed is doing the opposite since the crisis in 2008. Through the Quantitative Easing (QE) programs, trillions of dollars are being issued out of thin air to buy the US sovereign debts. A few trillion are loans to those too-big-to-fail banks at near zero interest, who in turn loan to other banks and foreign governments at high interest. This financial malfeasance is flooding the world with debts. Just these few years, the Fed's balance sheet exploded from $800 billion to $4.5 trillion between 2008 and 2014. When the banks failed, the Fed bailed them out. When (not if but when) the Fed failed, who is going to bail out the Fed? All of these financial institutions are overleveraged. The situation has become untenable and redressing it is unavoidable.

While the Jews now controls the insane amount of wealth, in the form of fiat US dollars, they have to let it go. There is a need for a reset, a need to observe the Shemitah.

Jewish Lobby

To protect their needs and interests, the Jewish community set up various organizations. There are about three hundred such groups in United States catering to a broad spectrum of interests. This unwieldy group of organizations is known collectively as the Jewish Lobby. They aim to stick together. In their united stand, they wield enormous power and influence over the US bureaucracy. One of their primary interests is the security of Israel.

Below is a list of some of these groups:[14]

- The American Israel Public Affairs Committee (AIPAC): AIPAC is the most prominent governmental lobbying organization on behalf of Israel. It frequently writes legislation for members of Congress, which extraordinarily large majorities of both parties typically endorse. AIPAC's annual conventions are typically a who's who of high state office from both parties pledging their loyalty to Israel.

- Conference of Presidents of Major American Jewish Organizations (CoP):
  This group of 51 Zionist organizations also advocates on behalf of Israel, including a focus on Iran. All members of the CoP sit on AIPAC's executive committee. The Conference of Presidents focuses on lobbying the Executive branch while AIPAC concentrates on Congress.

- The Washington Institute for Near East Policy (WINEP): WINEP is an extremely influential think tank that pushes Israel-centric Middle East policies. It is frequently called upon by both the government and the media to provide expert analysis on Middle East issues.

- Anti-Defamation League (ADL):
  The ADL bills itself as a civil rights institution devoted to stamping out anti-Semitism. It is an architect of "hate crimes legislation" that effectively criminalizes criticism of Israeli policies. The ADL is a member of the CoP.

- International Fellowship of Christians and Jews:
  Founded in 1983 by Rabbi Yechiel Eckstein "to promote understanding between Jews and Christians and build broad support for Israel," it supports advocacy for Israel among mostly right-wing Christians.

- Christians United for Israel (CUFI):
  CUFI is a right-wing Evangelical Christian organization founded by John Hagee to advocate for American support for Israel based largely on Biblical prophecy. It has a nationwide membership of over one million advocates for Israel who can be called upon to flood their Congressmen with letters and phone calls at the slightest hint of legislation not approved by Israel. CUFI has high-level contacts

within the Israeli administration, including with the Prime Minister, who sometimes speaks at their events.

- America's Voices in Israel (AVI):
  A project of the Conference of Presidents, AVI works to "strengthen American understanding of and support for Israel by inviting U.S.-based radio talk show hosts to see Israel and broadcast their programs live from Jerusalem." It also brings celebrities and other opinion makers on guided tours of Israel.

- The Jewish Agency for Israel:
  The shorten form is The Jewish Agency. According to its website, founded in 1929, this links "Jews around the world with Israel as the focal point…" Major activities include Jewish Zionist education and building a global Jewish community.

- Zionist Organization of America (ZOA):
  The Zionist Organization of America was established in 1887, making it the oldest pro-Israel organization in the US. Their goal is to spread the Zionist message wherever in all aspects of American life. Their objectives include spreading Zionism on American campuses, work to advance the interests Israel and Jewish people within the American legal system.

The United States continues to support Israel fervently and defend its policies. She supports Israel financially, militarily and diplomatically. Financially and militarily, Israel has been the largest annual recipient of direct U.S. assistance since 1976, and the biggest total recipient since World War II. Israel receives about $3 billion in direct foreign aid each year, which is roughly one-fifth of America's foreign-aid annual budget. Israel is allowed to spend part of the military aid on its domestic arms industry while all other recipients of U.S. military aid have to use it to purchase U.S.-manufactured weapons. It enables Israel to consolidate its arms exporting sector. Another advantage Israel has over other recipients is that she has access to the most advanced weapons systems in the U.S. arsenal that she purchases with the U.S. aid. In per capita terms, the United States gives each Israeli a direct subsidy worth about $500 per year. This largesse is especially striking when one realizes that Israel is now a wealthy industrial state.

Control of the Media

The media is a mass communication channel through which news, entertainment, and educational messages are disseminated. Media includes every broadcasting and narrowcasting mediums such as newspapers, magazines, TV, radio, billboards, direct mail, telephone, and the internet. Decades ago there were thousands of independent companies providing such services. Increasingly, through merger and acquisition, the number of media companies has shrunk.

There is a report that presently, six mega-corporation controls 90% of media in America. They are Time Warner, Walt Disney, Viacom, News Corporation, CBS Corporation & NBC Universal. Together, the big six dominate news and entertainment in the United States. But even those areas of the media that the big six do not control are becoming increasingly concentrated. For example, Clear Channel now owns over 1000 radio stations across the United States. Companies like Google, Yahoo and Microsoft are increasingly dominating the Internet.[15]

Who owns the big six? Of the 12 senior executives of these media corporations, 9 are Jews or have Jewish spouses. Theoretically, it means they own 75% share. Contrast this with the fact that Jews only makes up approximately 2% of the U.S. population. Apparently, it can't be disputed Jews control the media in America.

Influence in the Judiciary

Another area where the Jews have a strong influence in the U.S. is in the Supreme Court. Of the current nine U.S. Supreme Court justices, three are Jews: Ruth Bader Ginsburg, Stephen G. Breyer, and Elena Kagan. The Supreme Court has undergone a dramatic transformation. For centuries, the justices were predominantly Protestants. It had its first Catholic justice member in 1836 and the first Jew in 1916. For the first time in its history, the current bench since 2010 comprises the three Jews and the remaining six who are Catholics. It has no Protestant representatives.

The current justices have taken an active stance on the separation of Church and State. It is one of the causes of the erosion of Evangelical influence in the nation's public life. Needless to say, Jewish thinking and preferences will sway the decisions and verdicts of the Supreme Court.

US Congress

The US Congress and the White House are dominated by Jews either directly or indirectly via the various Jewish lobby groups. For the 113th Congress (2013-2015), there is a Jew from the Republican Party and 21 from the Democratic Party out of 435 members of the House of Representatives. In the Senate, Jews are represented by 11 Democrats out of 100 members.

Kevin MacDonald, a psychology professor at the University of California, Long Beach, noted: "there are approximately 300 national Jewish organizations in the United States with a combined budget estimated in the range of $6 billion—a sum greater than the gross national product of half the members of the United Nations." Strong financial standing of the Jewish Lobby coupled with evangelical Christians supports produces a positive influence on Congressional votes on issues relating to Israel. Supporting Israel is popular among Congressmen.

Diplomatically, America's support for Israel is best observed at the United Nations. The United States has cast its veto a total of 39 times to shield Israel from Security Council draft resolutions that condemned, deplored, denounced, demanded, affirmed, endorsed, called on and urged Israel to obey the world body. The first time it took place was on September 10, 1972—condemned Israel's attacks against Southern Lebanon and Syria. The U.S. vetoed the resolution. The latest was on October. 5, 2004 in which the U.S. vetoed the draft resolution condemning Israel's military incursion into Gaza that caused many civilian deaths and extensive damage to property. [16]

Chapter 7

THE SHEMITAH

The Shemitah is a Hebrew word meaning "to release," "to remit" or "to let go." God told Moses to instruct the children of Israel to observe the Shemitah while they were in the wilderness of Sinai. They were to adhere to it when they enter the Promised Land, land that will soon be their inheritance. They were required to be responsible towards the property. The responsibility necessitates they do not exploit the land. The Shemitah principle is to guide them to be scrupulous in the use of it. According to set time and season the Shemitah is to be practiced or observed on these occasions:

a. To observe it on the Sabbath Day (Leviticus.23:3).
   In a week cycle, the seventh day is the Sabbath Day, a day of rest. They are allowed to work for six days, but God command them not to do any work on the seventh day. Therefore, the Sabbath Day is the Day of the Shemitah.

b. To observe it on the Sabbatical Year (Leviticus 25:3-7).
   In a seven-year cycle, the seventh year is a Sabbatical Year, a year of rest for the land. For six years the people could sow the field, prune the vineyard and harvest the produce, but should refrain from these activities for the seventh year. What is produced from the land in the seventh year they should leave it to others (such as friends, servants or strangers) to harvest. They should not claim the produce as their own. Hence, the Sabbatical Year is the Year of the Shemitah.

c. To observe it on the Jubilee Year (Leviticus 25:8-17).
   Multiplying the seven-year cycle by 7 times equals forty-nine years. The following year that is the fiftieth year is the Jubilee Year, a year of complete rest for the land, and the people. All fields and houses sold during the past forty-nine years were to revert to their original owners. Slaves are to be released. Throughout the year, there should be no cultivation of the land and no claim to the produce of the land as one's own. It is a year to proclaim a liberty for all. Accordingly, the Jubilee Year is also the Year of the Shemitah.

Notice that there is a *Day* of the Shemitah and the *Year* of the Shemitah. The Shemitah is a call to take a breather instead of holding on to the possession or blessing without a break. And the call is packaged as a command of God. The question that immediately arose from this command is how they would survive without an income for a whole year and have the resource to plant (or invest) for the eighth year? To this, God promises He would make up the shortfall by increasing His blessing via a greater abundance of the produce in the sixth year:

> **Leviticus 25:20-22**
> **20** And if you say, "What shall we eat in the seventh year since we shall not sow nor gather in our produce?" **21** Then I will command My blessing on you in the sixth year, and it will bring forth produce enough for three years. **22** And you shall sow in the eighth year, and eat old produce until the ninth year; until its produce comes in, you shall eat of the old harvest.

It is without question the Shemitah is a biblical command. Since delivered through Moses, is it considered part of the Mosaic Covenant? Bear in mind that the Mosaic Covenant is already being canceled and replaced by the New Covenant (See Chapter 4). God required the children of Israel to observe the Shemitah when they dwell in the Promised Land (Leviticus 23:10). Moses presented to them the land title deed with its conditions just before they entered the land to possess it (Deuteronomy 30:1-10). The requirements state their need to obey God's voice and to comply with all His commandments for them to enjoy the inheritance. The relationship of the people to the property is link inseparably to their relationship with God. The Shemitah ties them to the land, and the land comes under the Palestinian Covenant. As this covenant is irrevocable, it implies that the command of the Shemitah is still relevant for the Jews to observe today.

It is obligatory to keep the Shemitah as long as the Jews are back in their land. Indeed, since 1948 they have returned to their homeland. In ancient time, Israel was an agrarian society but has since progress into an industrial society similar to most nations in this modern era. Utilization of land is no longer restricted solely to agriculture use but has been allocated for commercial and industrial purposes (excluding residential purpose). For a whole year, the Shemitah requires cessation of all work, land to return to its original owners, slaves (servants or workers) released and the cancelation of all debts. Observing the Shemitah in an agrarian society would be much simpler and straight forward compare to the modern setting. In the contemporary environment, the ramifications of these requirements are so vast and complex it caused the Rabbis to come up with ways to get around the Shemitah requirements.

One of the ways relates to the idea that the Shemitah applied only to Jewish-owned land. So, in the Year of the Shemitah, Jewish farmers would sell their lands to non-Jews and continue to work. The sale of the property is under an agreement in which the land would revert to the Jewish farmer at the end of the Shemitah year. Another way was devised to avoid the cancelation of debts. The Rabbinical sage Hillel the Elder of the first century BC developed a system called the *pruzbul*, where the creditor can transfer his debts to a religious court. Since a tribunal is not an individual, the obligation would survive the Year of the Shemitah. In one form or another, the Shemitah is being observed but not in an altruistic manner.[1] This inexorable practice would continue until the Messiah returns to put an end to it.

God attach great importance to His people observing the Shemitah. The Shemitah bears witness that the land belongs to Him: "The land shall not be sold permanently, for the land is Mine...." (Leviticus 25:23). Naturally, He only entrusted it to His people on a stewardship basis. God wants to be first in the hearts and lives of His people. He does not want material or physical things to take His place. The people should lessen their focus on material pursuits, and concentrate more on their spiritual lives in their relationship with Him and their fellow men. He wants His people to have a genuine appreciation for Him, and to continue looking to Him in faith for their needs.

Now, what happens when the Jews fail to observe the Shemitah? Failure to carry out the Shemitah would mean they disobeyed the command of God. It would be as though they had committed idolatry. There will be judgment, as God had explicitly warned:

Leviticus 26:31-35
31 I will lay your cities waste and bring your sanctuaries to desolation, and I will not smell the fragrance of your sweet aromas. **32** I will bring the land to desolation, and your enemies who dwell in it shall be astonished at it. **33** I will scatter you among the nations and draw out a sword after you; your land shall be desolate, and your cities waste. **34** Then the land shall enjoy its Sabbaths as long as it lies desolate, and you are in your enemies' land; then the land shall rest and enjoy its Sabbaths. **35** As long as it lies desolate it shall rest-- for the time it did not rest on your Sabbaths when you dwelt in it.

The land, together with the cities, will be forced into desolation. The people will be driven out and scattered among the nations. Notice that while the land was left desolate, the land enjoyed its Sabbaths. In reviewing Israel past, there were several occasions of this occurring. A good example was during their exile to Babylon in the days of Prophet Jeremiah. Jeremiah had prophesied of the impending judgment on Jerusalem if the people do not repent of their sins. God had revealed to him that the inhabitants of Judah would be taken captives to Babylon for seventy years:

Jeremiah 25:8-11
8 "Therefore thus says the Lord of hosts: 'Because you have not heard My words, **9** behold, I will send and take all the families of the north,' says the Lord, 'and Nebuchadnezzar the king of Babylon, My servant, and will bring them against this land, against its inhabitants, and against these nations

all around, and will utterly destroy them, and make them an astonishment, a hissing, and perpetual desolations.
10 Moreover, I will take from them the voice of mirth and the voice of gladness, the voice of the bridegroom and the voice of the bride, the sound of the millstones and the light of the lamp. **11** And this whole land shall be a desolation and an astonishment, and these nations shall serve the king of Babylon seventy years."

Why were they exiled to Babylon for seventy years? Was there any significance to the seventy years? In 2 Chronicles 36:20-22, we were made to understand, the seventy years was because they fail to keep the Sabbaths:

2 Chronicles 36:20-22
20 And those who escaped from the sword he carried away to Babylon, where they became servants to him and his sons until the rule of the kingdom of Persia, **21** to fulfill the word of the Lord by the mouth of Jeremiah, until the land had enjoyed her Sabbaths. As long as she lay desolate she kept Sabbath, to fulfill seventy years. **22** Now in the first year of Cyrus king of Persia, that the word of the Lord by the mouth of Jeremiah might be fulfilled, the Lord stirred up the spirit of Cyrus king of Persia, so that he made a proclamation throughout all his kingdom, and also put it in writing, saying .....

The Babylonians began besieging Jerusalem in 606 BC. By 587 BC, the city fell and was totally overran. In a span of nineteen years, the Jews were taken exile to Babylon in three batches. They were there until the Persian Empire conquered the Babylonian. In the first year of the reign of the Persian king, King Cyrus issued a decree allowing the Jews to return to Jerusalem. That year was 536 BC. Thus, they were in exile for seventy years (606 – 536 BC) in fulfillment of Jeremiah's prophecy.

The Babylonian captivity came to an end once the land kept its Sabbaths. The Shemitah effect had ceased. But what brought an end to the Babylonian power? It was another world power, the Persian Empire. And the rise of the

Persian Empire coincided with the end of the Shemitah. Apparently, world powers were drawn into the affairs of the Shemitah effect on Israel. On that account, the impact of the Shemitah was not just an isolated matter for Israel to contend. The world was not immune from it. There were grave consequences for the world when Israel was forced to observe the Shemitah.

Israel of the New World

The Shemitah is a Jewish matter. A command God gave them to observe in the land of Israel where six million of them are currently living. Or in America, with a Jewish population of almost an equal number. Here, it is not an assumption that the Shemitah is pertinent to America just because it has a large Jewish population. This reason alone is not sufficient to warrant it. There is more.

It is a fact well known that America was founded as a Christian nation. Christopher Columbus was the first European Christian to set foot in the Americas in 1492. He had discovered the New World, the old world being Africa, Europe, and Asia. More than 100 years later, the first English settlement was established in Jamestown, Virginia in 1607. The knowledge that there is an existing colony of the British Empire gave the Pilgrims the added courage to immigrate to America. The Pilgrims (a.k.a. Separatists) were facing persecution back home from the Church of England. With grave concerns of the problems impeding the godly development of their children, coupled with the burning desire to promulgate the gospel, they made the historic decision to immigrate.

The Mayflower, the ship with 102 Pilgrims, left Plymouth, England and arrived at Cape Cod, Provincetown Harbor in what is today Massachusetts in 1620. While still on board the ship, the surviving members of the group created a charter for self-government signed by all the men, which they named it— the Mayflower Compact. This classic document became the cornerstone of the United States Constitution which was drawn up much later in 1787.

The Pilgrims began their new life in America in an area they named the Plymouth Colony, Massachusetts. In the ensuing years, the Puritans arrived to set up many other British colonies on the east coast. By 1775, the American Revolutionary War broke out between the colonies and Great Britain over the objection by the Americans to taxes imposed by the British parliament, taxes that they claimed were unconstitutional. On July 4 the following year, a confederation of thirteen colonies declared independence from Britain. Fifty-six men, representing a combined population of about three million people, signed the Declaration of Independence. Fifty out of the fifty-six men were Trinitarian Christians i.e. they held to the doctrine of the Trinity. About half of the signers had seminary degrees.[2] No doubt the Declaration was a religious as well as a secular act for these people. Thus, the American nation was founded on Biblical principles with a Judeo-Christian root.

Another factor that strengthens the case as to why the Shemitah is pertinent to America is the role of the Jews—they play a central role in the life of the nation. The relatively tiny Jewish population is concentrated mainly in New York, currently at 2.1 million. From there, they hold sway over the country's finance through controlling the Wall Street, the Federal Reserve, and five to six of the megabanks. From Washington, they dominate the US Congress and the Judiciary. The Jews regulate American public opinion through the mass media that are mostly owned by them. Apart from these, they influence American culture through controlling Hollywood and some of the prestigious universities. Given this development, in which Jews play such a dominant role, America can indeed be called the Israel of the New World.

The Sabbatical Year

America is the proverbial promised land to the Jews therefore America has to observe the Shemitah. The Shemitah takes effect in both the Sabbatical year and the Jubilee year. First, let us determine the Sabbatical year. Is the current year (2015) a Sabbatical Year? Based on the Hebrew calendar, the current year is 5775. The Hebrew calendar is not synchronous with the Gregorian calendar. In comparison, the Hebrew civil year commence on 1 Tishri around September-October. It ends on 29 Elul, that is, 1 Tishri being the Jewish New Year Day and 29 Elul being the Jewish New Year Eve. The Jews called the New Year Day Rosh Hashanah. Now, let us match the two different calendars for the current year:

1 Tishri 5775 — 29 Elul 5775
25 September 2014 — 13 September 2015

For the following year:

1 Tishri 5776 — 29 Elul 5776
14 September 2015 — 2 October 2016

According to Jewish Rabbis, the current year 5775 is a Sabbatical year. They ascertain it this way. From the time of creation to the destruction of the Second Temple in Jerusalem is the year 3829. That year corresponds to AD 68-69 of the Gregorian calendar. They also endorsed it as a Sabbatical Year, interpreting the Temple destruction as the result of the Shemitah effect. The number of years from the destruction of the Second Temple to the present is 1,946 years, that is, 5775 – 3829 = 1,946 years. The Sabbatical Year is a cycle of seven. Hence, 1946 years divided by the 7-year cycle equals 278 cycles (1946/7=278). As 278 is a round number, this confirms that the current year is a Sabbatical Year.

Shemitah Effect on Wall Street

Being a Sabbatical Year, this year 5775, i.e. 25 September 2014-13 September 2015 is the Year of the Shemitah. The Shemitah calls for the release of the land, stoppage of work, and cancelation of debts. The people, especially American Jews, will not observe it voluntarily. Therefore by force, the command will apply to America. In what way is it going to be forced on America?

In today society, for America and many other nations as well, the principal source of wealth is through financial activities. It is the largest and quickest way to generate wealth. It stays ahead of other economic activities such as manufacturing, agriculture, transportation, education, tourism, and others. America is the world leader in offering financial services. Located in Wall Street in New York is the world largest stock exchange, the New York Stock Exchange (NYSE). The Exchange operates the Dow Jones Industrial Average (DJIA) indices. It offers equities-based trading. Plying their trade there includes the world biggest investment banks, commercial banks, hedge funds, mutual funds, asset management firms, insurance companies, broker-dealers, currency and commodity traders, and financial institutions. These companies together control trillions of dollars in financial assets, and the exchange daily trading volumes exceed $5 trillion. Therefore, whatever happens to the Dow Jones, when the point movement rises or fall, will substantially impact the world's financial markets. As the US dollar is the medium of exchange, coupled with its role as the world reserve currency, any adverse effect on the dollar will impact the Dow Jones and the global financial market as well.

The Dow Jones (Wall Street) will have the Shemitah applied to it. How certain is that? Looking at the history of the Dow Jones, the Shemitah effect is explicitly noted. Consider what happened on Monday 17 September 2001 (29 Elul, 5761). Six days earlier on 11 September, the world witnessed the destruction of the New York World Trade Centre Twin Towers. Due to the chaos, the NYSE was closed. When Wall Street opened for business on Monday 17 September, the Dow Jones Industrial Average fell 684.81 points, which was the worst ever one-day drop to date. The decline wiped out 7.1% of stock value, setting a record for the biggest loss in the exchange history for one trading day.

Thus, the trigger for this event was the collapsed of the Twin Towers.

Seven years forward, the world witnessed another Shemitah effect on Wall Street on Monday 29 September 2008 (29 Elul, 5768). Beginning in August 2007, a liquidity crisis broke out in the banking and insurance industry related to subprime mortgage-backed securities and other collateralized debt obligations. It grew worse by early 2008 when Bear Stearns, one of the most prominent global investment firms, collapsed. It was taken over by JP Morgan Chase with a loan from the Fed. Then, by the middle of September 2008, AIG, the world largest insurer was bailed out by the Fed, as the company was too-big-to-fail (i.e. too big to be allowed to fail). Around this time, Lehman Brothers, the fourth-largest investment bank in America, went under but was not bailed out.[3] The debacle around Lehman Brothers precipitated the Dow Jones Industrial Average to plunge 777.7 points, the greatest one-day drop in the history of the stock market. The lost points translated into approximately $1.2 trillion in market value.[4]

This episode happened on Monday 29 September 2008 (29 Elul, 5768). The trigger for this event was the failure in time of the US Congress to pass the Emergency Economic Stabilization Act (passed on Oct. 3, 2008). If the Bill were to pass on time, it would provide $700 billion in Troubled Asset Relief Program (TARP) to finance the bailout of Lehman Brothers.

Again, fast forward seven years, we shall arrive on Sunday 13 September 2015 (29 Elul, 5775) — in the current year. Will the world witness yet again the collapse of Dow Jones Industrial Average due to the Shemitah? Two earlier consecutive Sabbatical Years have shown the Shemitah did not spare America. Will it let-off America this time? If not, how severe will the Shemitah effect be? As the date is still in the future at the time of writing, we shall wait and see. If United States is not let-off, we can expect the Shemitah effect to be worst, much worst, then compare to the previous episodes. The 2008 collapse will be like a dress rehearsal compared to what the United States and the world are going to face in the next one.

It is of interest to note that the Shemitah effect erupted on 29 Elul, the last day of the Year of the Shemitah. Throughout the year, distress in the economic landscape had been building up but the authorities were powerless to defuse it. Similarly, for the current Year of the Shemitah, there is clear evidence the economic and financial distress is growing steadily worst. This time, it involves the US dollar itself—it is being abused by the Fed. Through Quantitative Easing (QE) into infinity, the Fed had rendered the US dollar worthless. Since December 2008, the Fed's policy to maintain a near-zero interest rate, provides cheap money to the banks, who borrow it to speculate at the Dow Jones. While the US economy continues a downward trajectory, the Dow Jones keeps rising. It is one sure sign something is amiss. What is going to happen this coming 29 Elul (13 September 2015)? [5] What would be the trigger to collapse the Dow Jones? Will it be the global abandonment of the US dollar that will bring on the total or near-total crash of the Dow Jones?

The Jubilee Year

The Jubilee Year is also the Year of the Shemitah. The Jewish people today do not observe the Jubilee Year, neither in America nor Israel. Among other reasons, they state they could not keep the Jubilee Year until the Third Temple is built. Opinion is that only the High Priest could officially announce the beginning of the Jubilee Year. As instructed in Leviticus, the announcement by the High Priest is by way of sounding the trumpet on the Day of Atonement

(Yom Kippur). Jubilee in Hebrew is *yobel* which means "trumpet blast." [6] The next Yom Kippur will be 10 Tishri, 5776 (23 September 2015).

Furthermore, there are differences of opinion among the Rabbis in determining the Jubilee Year. Some say it is every forty-ninth year. Others say it should be the fiftieth year as stated in the Bible (Leviticus 25:8-12).

The Shemitah Effect on the Temple Mount

Notwithstanding the controversy over the timing as to when to observe the Jubilee Year, some Rabbis recognized the year 5678 (17 September 1917 - 6 September 1918) as a Jubilee Year. Why? In that year, a paramount event transpired: the British wrest control of Palestine from the Muslim Turks. Let us relate that memorable event.

Foreign powers continuously overrun the Holy City and the Land of Israel from the time the Romans destroyed Jerusalem in AD 69. The foreign powers included the Romans, other European powers, and lastly by the Muslim Ottoman Empire or the Turkish Empire. Since 1516, the Turks held the land for nearly 400 years. For most of the time, the land was left desolated and in ruin.

Towards the end of the First World War, in early 1917, the Jewish Zionist leaders persuaded the British to give them Palestine. In granting the request, the then British Foreign Secretary, Authur James Balfour, issued the Balfour Declaration (dated 2 November 1917) expressing that intention to the Zionist leaders. A few weeks later, General Allenby led the British army offensive against the Muslim Ottoman army and succeeded to retake Palestine on 30 December. Although the British did not immediately transfer the land to the Jews, it was nevertheless, an occasion to celebrate. The Balfour Declaration provided the assurance the land will eventually be theirs.

The date 30 December 1917 falls within the Jewish year 5678 (17 September 1917 - 6 September 1918). In retrospect, the Jewish Rabbis reckon that the year would be a pivotal year. For so long they have been kept from returning to their homeland. We are aware they do not believe Jesus Christ is the Messiah. They could not accept the fact their Messiah was crucified. It is a stumbling block to them (1 Corinthians 1:22-23). We know they do not accept the fact, that their rejection of Christ was the main reason they cannot return to their homeland. We understand they refuse to acknowledge, that they could not return to reclaim the land until the Shemitah effect finished its course. The Shemitah effect seems to sustain for so long. And it lasts so long because it must commensurate with the seriousness of rejecting Christ. But then suddenly, the land appears to beckon them to come home.

"Somewhere over the rainbow, skies are blue. And the dreams that you dare to dream really do come true," as the song goes. The lyric of this song, "Over the Rainbow" was written by Edgar Yipsel Harburg and put to music by Harold Arlen, who were both Jewish, was felicitous at that juncture in their history. The song, written in 1939 saw the fulfillment of the "dream" in 1948.

The transfer of the land from the Turks to the British was an indication the Shemitah effect had ended. The British wanting to obtain international legitimacy for what they were doing sought the United Nations mandate. Under the UN auspices, part of Palestine was handed over to the Jews. With that, the nation of Israel became a sovereign state on 14 May 1948. It was wonderful except the old City of Jerusalem and the area known as the West Bank remained under Jordanian control.

The next Jubilee Year from the release of the land in 5678 (17 September 1917 - 6 September 1918) is derived by adding another forty-nine years. It brings us to 5727 (15 September 1966 – 4 October 1967). Amazingly, further release of the land took place that year. This time it was the release of the old City of Jerusalem. In what was known as the Six Day War (5-10 June 1967), the Israeli army fought and won against a combined Arab army. On 7 June, the Israeli army wrestled the old City of Jerusalem from the Jordanian. Apparently, 7 June 1967 falls within the year 5727.

When the Israeli captured the old City, it included the Temple Mount. It was known formerly as Mount Moriah, the little hill where Abraham offered his son Isaac to God. It is the site where Solomon Temple and the Second Temple once stood. Presently, erected on the site are the Muslim Dome of the Rock and the Al-Aqsa Mosque. After the Israeli army captured the site, the then Defense Minister, Moshe Dayan, decided to forgo taking possession of it. It was regrettably handed back to the Jordanian to manage it. To this day, the Israeli are not allowed access to the site freely except with permission from the authorities. Daily, Israeli security personnel keeps the peace, preventing clashes between the Israeli and the Arabs.

Again, fast forward to the next Jubilee Year by adding another forty-nine years, we arrived at the year 5776 (14 September 2015 – 2 October 2016). It is the current and the next year in the Gregorian calendar. What is the significance of this Jubilee Year? What do the Jewish people expect? Back in 1917, the land of Palestine was finally released, and subsequently handed over to the Jews, although not in its totality. Then, in 1967 they came into possession of the old City of Jerusalem, but minus the Temple Mount. The Temple Mount is the heart of the city of Jerusalem, and by extension, the nation of Israel. Axiomatically, the Jewish people yearn to take ownership of it. Could this Jubilee Year be the year the Arabs have to release the Temple Mount to them? If so, the world can expect another regional war to break out because the Arabs will not surrender it willingly.

Chapter 8

THE BLOOD MOON

In 2008, Mark Biltz, the founder of El Shaddai Ministries began talking about the blood moon phenomenon.[1] The appearance of blood moon is not something unusual that people should be unduly concern. However, Mark discovered their presence in concurrence with the Jewish annual feast days as something rare that deserve scrutiny. Furthermore, he believes the phenomenon might be conveying an important message to the world.

Before we delve into what Mark discovered, we want first to determine what a blood moon is. We know the moon orbits around the earth, and the earth in turn orbits around the sun. Of these three, only the sun gives out the light; the earth and the moon merely reflect. When the earth comes between the sun and the moon, the shadow of the earth is projected onto the moon. From the earth, the moon appears reddish; hence, the term "blood moon" or "the moon became as blood." The obscuring of the sunlight is called an eclipse, and, in this case, Total Lunar Eclipse occurs when the Earth completely blocks the sunlight from reaching the moon.

The rotation of the earth and moon around the sun creates another situation: Total Solar Eclipse. It occurs when the moon passes between the sun and the earth. View from a particular angle, when it covers the entire disk of the Sun the Moon appears black "like sackcloth of hair" as it completely blocks out the sunray.

How frequently do blood moon appears? Blood moon appeared during partial and total lunar eclipses. Partial lunar eclipses are very common. In comparison, total lunar eclipses are less frequent. Now it would even be less frequent when there is tetrad, that is, four successive total lunar eclipses occur, each separated by six months. In other words, two total lunar eclipses occur in the first year followed by another two total lunar eclipses in the next year. In the last 500 years, tetrad appeared only eight times. Of these eight times, three times the tetrad coincided with Jewish feast days of Pesach (Passover) and Sukkot (Feast of Tabernacle). The current tetrad showing the matched Jewish feast days is as follows:

- 2014
  Total lunar eclipse: 15 April (Pesach/Passover)
  Total lunar eclipse: 8 October (Sukkot/Feast of Tabernacle)
- 2015
  Total lunar eclipse: 4 April (Pesach/Passover)
  Total lunar eclipse: 28 September (Sukkot/Feast of Tabernacle)[2]

Natural vs. Supernatural Phenomenon

Is the blood moon phenomenon alluded in the Bible a natural phenomenon or is something supernatural? There are three passages of scriptures specifically mentioned the blood moon, and we shall quote them here:

> **Joel 2:30-31**
> **30** "And I will show wonders in the heavens and in the earth: Blood and fire and pillars of smoke. **31** The sun shall be turned into darkness, And the moon into blood, Before the coming of the great and awesome day of the Lord."
>
> **Acts 2:20**
> **20** The sun shall be turned into darkness, And the moon into blood, Before the coming of the great and awesome day of the Lord.
>
> **Revelation 6:12 & 17**
> **12** I looked when He opened the sixth seal and behold; there was a great earthquake, and the sun became black as sackcloth of hair, and the moon became like blood.

> **17** For the great day of His wrath has come, and who is able to stand?"

It is interesting to note that when the Scriptures mention the moon turned into blood it also states the "sun turned into darkness." The expression the "sun turned into darkness" could mean either the sun will not give out light (stop shining) or is a reference to a total solar eclipse. Now, these two celestial bodies cannot display the phenomena at the same time. Based on the natural phenomenon, total lunar eclipse, and total solar eclipse should be at least one to six months apart of each other. Furthermore, if the phenomena are to occur simultaneously, and the sun stop giving out its light, this will rule out the possibility of there being a total lunar eclipse (blood moon). Why? The explanation is, without the presence of sunlight there can be no eclipse. If they both were to occur simultaneously then, these phenomena must be of a supernatural origin. In any case, it is a supernatural phenomenon for the sun to stop shining!

In the Olivet Discourse, Jesus Himself made reference to the phenomenon while speaking to His disciples about His second coming. The text is found in the Matthew and Mark gospel. We shall quote just the Matthew account here:

> **Matthew 24:29-31**
> **29** "Immediately after the tribulation of those days the sun will be darkened, and the moon will not give its light; the stars will fall from heaven, and the powers of the heavens will be shaken. **30** Then the sign of the Son of Man will appear in heaven, and then all the tribes of the earth will mourn, and they will see the Son of Man coming on the clouds of heaven with power and great glory. **31** And He will send His angels with a great sound of a trumpet, and they will gather together His elect from the four winds, from one end of heaven to the other."

Jesus did not say the "moon turned into blood" but use the phrase the "moon will not give its light." We know the moon does not shine on its own. Jesus must have meant the moon will not reflect sunlight. Could it be that at the time of these phenomena, the sun first stop shining, followed by the moon not reflecting light, but instead turned into blood-like appearance? We are inclined to believe that the blood moon stated in the Bible will not be of a natural phenomenon but rather of a supernatural kind. God can cause the moon to become like blood without the aid of an eclipse.

Finally, all the scriptures quoted above make mention of the appearance of the blood moon with their relation to the coming of the Lord. We are indeed living in the end times, very close to the Lord's coming. These natural blood moon tetrad in 2014 and 2015 will come and go. Soon, in few years from now, the supernatural blood moon will be seen in the sky just before the appearance of the Lord in the heaven. We are confident, the world will not have to witness the next natural blood moon tetrad scheduled to take place in 2032–2033, as the Lord presumably will return before that date.

If the blood moon of the Bible is not the same as the blood moon the world is witnessing in 2014 and 2015, what then is the significance of the natural blood moon tetrad? John Hagee, pastor of Cornerstone Church, in his book "Four Blood Moons," popularizes what was initially discovered by Mark Biltz. In it he explains the relations the tetrad had with the Jewish people and the nation of Israel. They learned that during past occurrences of the tetrad, some very significant events befell the Jewish people. Apparently, the tetrad is a sign to the world of what God is doing with His ancient people.

Significance of the Tetrad

There are three previous tetrads that coincided with the Jewish feasts in the last 500 years. Those three times were as follows:

- Tetrad of 1493-1494
- Tetrad of 1949-1950
- Tetrad of 1967-1968

Significant events affecting the Jewish people had occurred around the time of those tetrads. Observe that the events in question either occurred a year before or in the midst of the tetrad. There is no reason to rule out the possibility the event could transpire a year after the tetrad.

Expulsion from Spain in 1492

The tetrad of 1493-1494 which coincided with the Jewish feast days:

- 1493
  Total lunar eclipse: 2 April (Pesach/Passover)
  Total lunar eclipse: 25 September (Sukkot/Feast of Tabernacle)
- 1494
  Total lunar eclipse: 22 March (Pesach/Passover)
  Total lunar eclipse: 15 September (Sukkot/Feast of Tabernacle)

During the period of the Spanish Inquisition, Jews were expelled from Spain. It happened on 30 March 1492 when the Majesties of Spain, King Ferdinand, and Queen Isabella, issued the edict that all Jews should leave the kingdom. They could stay if they converted to Catholicism. Four months later, on 30 July, nearly the entire Jewish community of some 200,000 people were expelled. In the same month the edict was issued, the Majesties gave orders to Christopher Columbus to make an expedition of discovery to the Indies. With help from some Jewish friends, Columbus (an Italian explorer born in the Republic of Genoa, Italy) made the journey on 3 August 1492. It was his first of 4 voyages to the Americas. Columbus was believed to be the first European Christian to set foot in the New World. Many years later, America was founded. Eventually, the nation became the secondary homeland for the Jews—Israel of the New World.

Rebirth of the Nation of Israel in 1948

The tetrad of 1949-1950 which coincided with the Jewish feast days:

- 1949
  Total lunar eclipse: 13 April (Pesach/Passover)
  Total lunar eclipse: 7 October (Sukkot/Feast of Tabernacle)
- 1950
  Total lunar eclipse: 2 April (Pesach/Passover)
  Total lunar eclipse: 26 September (Sukkot/Feast of Tabernacle)

Fourteen May 1948 saw the establishment of the State of Israel. In 1949, Israel had its first legislative election. The Israeli parliament (Knesset) convened for the first time, and it voted to transfer the seat of power from Tel Aviv to Jerusalem. The first Knesset meeting then held in Jerusalem. Israel's first Prime Minister, Ben-Gurion, proclaimed Jerusalem as Israel's capital, but without the old City.

Israel Reclaimed the Old City of Jerusalem in 1967

The tetrad of 1967-1968 which coincided with the Jewish feast days:

- 1967
  Total lunar eclipse: 24 April (Pesach/Passover)
  Total lunar eclipse: 18 October (Sukkot/Feast of Tabernacle)
- 1968
  Total lunar eclipse: 13 April (Pesach/Passover)
  Total lunar eclipse: 6 October (Sukkot/Feast of Tabernacle)

During the Six Day War from 5-10 June 1967, the Israeli army captured the old City of Jerusalem on 7 June, thus, reunited Jerusalem as the capital of Israel. Also, Israeli forces had taken control of the Gaza Strip and the Sinai Peninsula from Egypt; the West Bank, including East Jerusalem, from Jordan; and the Golan Heights from Syria.

Current Tetrad & What Significant Event Might Occur With the Jewish People

According to John Hagee,[3] he believes either one of these two events could happen with regards to the current tetrad:

a. Israel might go to war with Iran. Israel is against the Iranian developing nuclear weapons and is eager to launch a pre-emptive strike to destroy the various nuclear facilities in the country. A nuclear-capable Iran is an existential threat to Israel.

b. Russia, together with a confederation of nations, could launch an invasion (Invasion of Gog) of Israel in fulfillment of the prophecy in Ezekiel Chapters 38 & 39.

Considering other factors explained in later chapters in this book, the above first suggestion is more likely. We believe there are two other possible events that could transpire:

a. The mass migration of Jews from America to Israel. The coming severe financial and economic troubles in America will cause the Americans to revolt against their government (See Chapter 7 The Shemitah). In the midst of social upheaval, anti-Semitism (blaming the Jews and persecution against them) will arise in earnest, resulting in Jews fleeing the country in large numbers. There are presently about 5.7 million Jews residing in America. God wants them to move (make aliyah) to Israel.

b. Arab nations attack Israel in fulfillment of Psalm 83. Some people believe this Psalm refers to a war yet to see fulfillment. The confederacy of nations, stated in verses 5-8, seeks to destroy Israel. They attempt to "cut off Israel from being a nation" verse 4. Could this war result in Israel taking complete control of the Temple Mount? (See Chapter 7 The Shemitah).

The events listed above could occur in the current year 2015 or 2016, and it could be just one of the events or a combination of events.

Chapter 9

AMERICA

El-Elyon— the Most High God has blessed America like no other nations on earth. She has come to occupy center stage in modern world history as the greatest economic, financial, military, political and cultural power in the world. All these wonderful blessings were bestowed to enable her to perform three crucial tasks. The first task is a spiritual one, that is, for her to carry out the mission of world evangelization. She is to bring the gospel message of the saving knowledge of Christ to the ends of the earth. The second task is the political and economic aspect of supporting the principles of democracy, free markets, and civil liberty around the world. The third task is that she could extend unwavering support and the defense of Israel against international antipathy. It would allow Israel space to grow and to establish itself in her homeland.

Let us look briefly at each of these tasks, and reflect on how America attains her greatness through these undertakings.

America's Role in World Evangelism

What prepare America beforehand to embark on the mission to bring evangelical Christianity to the world were several movements of spiritual revival that began in the early part of the eighteen century. During the period from the 1730s to 1743, known as the First Great Awakening, God used men like Jonathan Edward and George Whitefield to revive His people.

Jonathan Edward, who became pastor of the church in Northampton, Massachusetts, began holding prayer meetings among the youth in the church.

Revival broke out which soon spread to other towns, and his reputation as a preacher of extraordinary power grew. Influenced by Martin Luther's theology, he preached on justification by faith alone. Also, his sermons focused on man's relationship to God in such a way that they can experience the supernatural grace of God beyond merely depending on intellectual and cultural experiences. This spiritual state was the norm for Christians in seventeenth-century England. Most who migrated from England to America brought with them this spiritual vapidity. As a theologian with a keen mind, he wrote several books. His most celebrated work is "The Freedom of the Will" (1754). His writings together with his fiery preaching, including his most famous sermon entitled, "Sinners in the Hands of an Angry God," help genuine conversion of souls.[1]

Complementing the effort of Jonathan Edward was an Evangelist from England, George Whitefield. In 1740, Whitefield returned to America (his second of seven trips), where he preached in a series of revivals. He traveled throughout the American colonies and drew great crowds with his messages. He was an excellent orator, strong in voice and adept at spontaneity. In one of his open air meetings, there was a crowd of over thirty thousand people. Whitefield's sermons were widely reputed to capture his audience's enthusiasm. Many of them as well as his letters and journals, were published during his lifetime. In "Thankfulness for Mercies Received, a Necessary Duty" and "The Heinous Sin of Drunkenness" two of his well-known sermons, he addressed his belief in predestination and regeneration through the new birth.[2]

Jonathan Edward was a friend of John Wesley. The latter visited America for a short stint. Contemporaneously, these revivals brought about the rise of the Baptists and Methodists from obscurity to their traditional position as America's two largest Protestant denominations.

The Second Great Awakening arose in 1800. These revivals were looked upon as social movements to reshape the American society through such reforms as temperance, women's rights, various benevolent and betterment societies, and the abolition of slavery movement. One of the prominent revivalists during this period was Charles G. Finney.[3] He was a lawyer, and he was a masterful pulpit orator who devoted his energies to preaching revivals in New York, Philadelphia, Providence, and Boston. By the 1820s, Evangelical Protestantism became the dominant expression of Christianity in the United

States. As a result of the 19th-century evangelization of America, the nation became home to the largest number of Christians in any country and is also the most evangelized society on earth.

Foreign Missions

The Christians sensed the burden to spread the gospel to foreign lands. From the second decade of the 19th century, a small number of Americans began to venture forth to India, Burma, and Hawaii. By 1900, more mission field destinations were added including the Middle East, Africa, China, Japan, and Korea. By then, American missionary numbers increased substantially to about 5,000. All the major denominations had formed their missionary societies. Many began to build up a large resource base to funnel significant funds to carry out building programs for churches, schools, hospitals and clinics, orphanages, and publishing houses in the mission fields. American businessmen contributed generously through organizations such as the Laymen's Missionary Movement. The number of Americans swelled on the world's mission fields. Soon after 1900 Americans outstripped their forerunners the British in numbers, and by the late 1920s Americans constituted about 40% of the more than 30,000 Christian missionaries worldwide.[4]

The United States has been the chief vehicle for bringing Christianity to the world in the twentieth century. That said missionaries activity decline by the mid-20th century, partly because of shrinking in the number of new converts and partly because it had largely succeeded in establishing permanent parishes overseas.

According to a report published by the Pew Research Center in May 2015, Christian share of the U.S. population is slacking off. Conversely, the number of U.S. adults who do not identify with any organized religion is growing. The drop in the Christian share of the population has been driven mainly by declines among mainline Protestants and Catholics. It reported the percentage of adults (ages 18 and older) who describe themselves as Christians had dropped by nearly eight percentage points in just seven years, from 78.4% in 2007 to 70.6% in 2014.[5]

America's Role in Democracy Promotion

America desires to promote democratic values in the economic and political life of developing countries. She got involved in democracy promotion from the late 19th century. America felt it a call of duty she must not neglect. As President Woodrow Wilson in his public address in Boston in February 1919 said, "We set this Nation up to make men free, and we did not confine our conception and purpose to America." He was saying America has a mission to fulfill.

There had been waves of democratic moves in the past. According to Samuel Huntington, he identified the current movement that began in the mid-1970s to the present as the third wave of democracy. In this current wave, America has adopted democracy promotion as the guiding principle of her foreign policy. It is a priority, at least for Washington.

What is a democracy? There are many attempts to define what democracy is. The Oxford Dictionary defines it as "A system of government by the whole population or all the eligible members of a state, typically through elected representatives." Another person defines it as "a system of governance in which rulers are held accountable for their actions in the public realm by citizens acting indirectly through the competition and cooperation of their elected representatives."

Take note that there is a difference between the democracy of ancient Greece and contemporary democracy. Classical Athenian democracy was based on the ideals of full political participation of all citizens, a strong sense of community, the sovereignty of the people, and equality of all citizens under the law. On the other hand, modern democracy relies on elected representatives and tends to draw a distinction between the public and private spheres. It tends to erode the bonds of community and foster individualism. [6]

Whatever the variation may be, most contemporary definitions of democracy have several common elements. First, democracy is a country in which there are institutional mechanisms, usually elections that allow the people to choose their leaders. Second, prospective leaders must compete for public support. Third, the power of the government is restrained by its accountability to the people. These are the essential characteristics of political democracy.[7]

Benefits of Democracy

People living under a democratic form of rule tend to have a better quality of lives. Compared to inhabitants of nondemocracies (authoritarian regimes), citizens of democracies enjoy greater individual liberty, political stability, freedom from governmental violence, and a much lower risk of suffering a famine.

Respect for the liberty of individuals is an inherent feature of democratic politics. Leadership that is accountable to the public is less likely to deprive its citizens of human rights. The spread of democracy is likely to bring greater individual liberty to more and more people. It is an observation that even in countries with imperfect democracies tend to offer more liberty to its citizens than autocracies, and liberal democracies are very likely to promote liberty.

Democratic political systems—especially those of liberal democracies constrain the power of governments, hence, reducing their ability to commit mass murders of their populations. Democratic politics allow the opposition to express openly and have regular processes for the peaceful transfer of power. If all participants in the political process remain committed to democratic principles, critics of the leadership need not stage violent revolutions and governments will not use violence to repress opponents.

Democracy is not necessarily synonymous with prosperity. Nevertheless, there is a strong relationship between the two. A country that is democratic is more likely to have a market economy, and market economy tend to produce economic growth over the long run. Most of the world's leading economies implement market economies, such as the European Union nations, Japan, the economies of Southeast Asia, and, of course, the United States. Another point is that a democratic state is more likely to have the political legitimacy necessary to embark on difficult and painful economic reforms. Some of the former communist countries have to grapple with this matter, and they manage to succeed like in Vietnam and some Eastern European countries.

There is yet another benefit of democracy. As someone keenly observe, the citizens of democracies do not suffer from famines. There are two reasons for this. First, in a democratic country the government is accountable to its population and its leaders have electoral incentives to prevent mass starvation. As they want reelection, politicians are motivated to ensure that their people do not starve. Second, the existence of a free press and the free flow of information in a democratic country prevent famine. It works by serving as an early warning system on the effects of natural catastrophes such as floods and droughts that may cause food scarcities.

Examples of non-democratic countries lacking press freedom that suffered famine include China, Sudan, and Ethiopia. During the 1958-61 famine in China that killed 20-30 million people, the Chinese authorities overestimated the country's grain reserves by 100 million metric tons. The disaster could be avoided if there were transparency in the government management. Contrast this with situations faced by India, Botswana, and Zimbabwe, who managed to avoid famines, even when they have suffered large crop shortfalls. Botswana's food production fell by 17% and Zimbabwe's by 38% between 1979-81 and 1983-84, respectively. Still, they could prevent famine.[8]

Spreading Democracy

America is not the only country spreading democracy. But as the world leading economic power, she has the resources to do more than others. The effort at spreading democracy include providing assistance to countries holding elections, both election observing, and technical aid for election administration. Another area of support is strengthening political parties, and providing assistance to non-governmental organizations or civil societies.

What are some of the successes of American effort at spreading democracy to other nations? Japan is a good example. Prior to the Second World War, Japan was governed by an imperial Emperor Hirohito, whose word was law and who ruled with an iron hand. His subjects consider him as a god. Following Japan surrender, he was forced to reject the traditional claim explicitly that he is divine. General Douglas MacArthur, Chief of Staff of the United States Army, brought this to bear on him offering not to prosecute him for war crimes in return. Today, Japan is a constitutional monarchy but with a parliamentary democracy headed by a Prime Minister.

Another country is Germany. Germany was a democracy before the Second World War but became a dictatorship under Hitler. After the war, it was split into East and West Germany. West Germany returned to a democratic form of rule guided by the Western Allies. On the other hand, East Germany, which was controlled by the Soviet Union, became communist. With the fall of the U.S.S.R in 1991, East Germany was reunited with West Germany. The country is now wholly democratic.

The collapse of the former Soviet Union was a windfall for the West, particularly to those promoting democracy. Practically all the old states of the Soviet empire have become democracies albeit in varying degrees.

America's Role in Defense of Israel

This role is the third crucial task God has entrusted America to do. As describe earlier in chapter 6, God bless the Jews in America so that they could influence the U.S. government to extend support to Israel. We noted that America helped Israel in three areas: financially, militarily and diplomatically. We will not repeat what we already said. What we wish to highlight here, is the further diplomatic support Israel is receiving from America.

First, America defends Israel's right to possess nuclear weapons.

Israel is the only country in the middle-east alleged to have nuclear weapons. Alleged because Israel refuses to declare openly, she has those weapons. She maintains a policy of "nuclear ambiguity." Other countries adopting this policy include India, Pakistan, and North Korea. Regardless, it is an open secret Israel develop nuclear weapons in the Dimona facilities located in the Negev Desert. It was the French who provided the initial assistance to help build a nuclear reactor there in 1956. Israel refused to sign the Nuclear Non-Proliferation Treaty and did not allow the International Atomic Energy Agency (IAEA) team of experts to inspect Dimona. Without verification, it is a rough guess that Israel has 75-400 nuclear warheads.[9]

The Arab regimes in the middle-east are nervous about Israel alleged possession of nuclear weapons. They contemplate developing their own, especially the Saudi. But the American diplomatic handle on the situation has prevented this issue from becoming contentious. The Saudi is an ally of the American and has a growing peaceful relationship with Israel. With over a dozen military bases in the region, the American can keep the peace.

However, the Iranian is not in favor of the status quo. They are planning to develop their nuclear weapons. It is a worrisome development for the Israeli who has explicitly state they will attack Iran to destroy those nuclear sites. In the meantime, the American administration is using the diplomatic channel to resolve this issue.

Second, America looks away in the face of Israeli housing ministry expansion of new settlements in the occupied territories.

In June 1967 Six-Day War, the Israeli army defeated the combined Egyptian, Jordanian, and Syrian armies. It concluded with Israel gaining control of the Gaza Strip and the Sinai Peninsula from Egypt, the West Bank, and East Jerusalem from Jordan, and the Golan Heights from Syria. Within months, the UN Security Council adopts Resolution 242 to create a framework for a formal peace treaty based on an exchange of "land for peace." The Resolution states in part:

"(1) Withdrawal of Israel armed forces from territories occupied in the recent conflict" and "(2) termination of all claims or states of belligerency and respect for and acknowledgment of the sovereignty, territorial integrity and political independence of every State in the area and their right to live in peace within secure and recognized boundaries free from threats or acts of force." [10]

This resolution remains the mainstay of all future negotiations between the interested parties. With regards to (1) above, Israel completed the return of the Sinai Peninsula to Egypt in 1982. It was in accordance to the Camp David Accords, an agreement between Egyptian President Anwar Sadat and Israeli Prime Minister Menachem Begin signed in the presence of President Jimmy Carter in September 1978. Some 7,000 Israeli settlers withdrew from northern Sinai.

Another withdrawal was from the Gaza Strip. The area was handed back to the Palestinian control when about 9,000 settlers permanently left the place in August 2005. It happened under Israeli Prime Minister Ariel Sharon's watch. This move was first agreed in 1994 between the Israeli Prime Minister Yitzhak Rabin and Palestinian leader Yasser Arafat in an agreement signed as a follow-up to the 1993 Oslo Accord. It was temporary put on hold because Rabin was assassinated a few months after inking the deal.

While Israel did disengage and dismantle settlements in the Sinai Peninsula and Gaza Strip, she expanded new settlements in the West Banks and Golan Heights. From 1967 until the current year, approximately 780,000 Israelis now live in those territories. In January 2015, Israel's Interior Ministry gave the figures of 389,250 Israelis living in the West Bank, and 375,000 Israelis living in East Jerusalem.[11] A further 20,000 are known to be living in the Golan Heights.

America is the chief middle-east mediator, getting involved in the contentious issues right from the start. She is working with the international community through the United Nations and sometimes launches her direct effort. There were several initiatives launched such as the Camp David Accords in 1978, the Reagan Plan in 1982, the Madrid Conference in 1991, the Oslo Accords in 1993, and the Quartet in 2002. The Quartet comprises the United States, the United Nations, the European Union, and Russia.

Plainly, for all the effort spent through the many agreements and accords these 47 years, there appears to be no long-term solution in sight in meeting the requirements of U.N. Resolution 242. Instead, Israel has blithely pursued the enlargement of civilian settlements in the occupied territories. Not only is she the chief mediator, America is also Israel's chief protector. To be fair, America did not support Israel's actions and had raised objections again and again. But God has so ordained that America should just close one eye. Let Israel shrug off international pressure and continue to build more housing for the many diaspora Jews who are making aliya to Israel.

Third, America supports but did not force the "two-state solution" proposal on Israel.

Before Israel became a State in 1948, the British royal commission of inquiry issued the Peel Commission in 1937 that first proposed splitting Palestine into two areas— one for the Jews and the other for the Arabs. Later in 1948, the United Nations proposed a similar Partition Plan to establish the boundary of the new State of Israel. A year into her statehood, Israel's border enlarged a little bit as the Israeli took control over the land left behind by the Arabs who fled due to the War of Independence. The state boundary widened even more after the Six Day War in 1967. It continues to enlarge to the present day through the construction of more and more new settlements in the occupied territories. The situation on the ground now looks impossible for Israel to return to the pre-1967 borders. It is no longer feasible for them to comply with the U.N. Resolution 242.

For the Palestinians, they feel their cause is getting very difficult but not entirely lost. They still hope to achieve a "two-state solution" with Israel.

This proposal calls for the setting up of its own Palestinian State made up of the West Bank, including East Jerusalem, and the Gaza Strip. As to the status of Jerusalem, they want it to be their state capital, but the matter could be decided on a later date. From the beginning, the Palestinians were against this proposal but have shown serious interest in it since the mid-1970s, and its mainstream leadership has embraced the concept since the 1982 Arab Summit in Fez, Morocco. In 2002, the Arab League drafted the Arab Peace Initiative, formally backing the two-state solution.

Over the years, more and more countries are sympathetic to the Palestinian cause. The latest U.N. resolution passed in November 2013 with 165 countries in favor of the two-state solution. Six states voted against it. They are the United States, Canada, Israel, Federated States of Micronesia, Marshall Islands, and Palau. Another six countries abstained.

The Americans and the Israelis supported this proposal all along. It has been Washington official policy. However, the Israeli government under Benjamin Netanyahu is appearing to show tepid interest in it. There was a report that the U.S. Undersecretary of State had warned Jewish leaders. If the Israeli authority does not demonstrate its commitment to the two-state solution, the U.S. will have a difficult time continuing to assist its efforts to halt international initiatives on the Palestinian issue at the United Nations.[12]

Chapter 10

MORAL DECLINE & CHANGING OF GOD'S LAW

Moral decline is the underlying cause of the weakening of America's role in the world. Decline implies losing height, a downslide from a higher to a lower level of standard. America once had a high moral standard. The standard is a reference point for morality to be upheld and for degeneration to be adequately measured. There are many religious groups and philosophies in the world advocating their standard, or they may have no standard at all. For some their standard is subjective, that is, they set it up without a belief in God. But America's standard is the moral code laid down in the Bible adopted at the time of her founding as a nation. The moral code referred to in the Bible is God's law.

God Himself is governed by law. His essential attributes are determined by His law like love, holiness, mercy, anger and so on. God is the Lawmaker, and also the Lawgiver. When He created the universe, He established laws to govern it. Without law, the universe would degenerate into chaos. The law provides the order.[1]

When God created the angelic beings, they have been established as free-willed beings guided by God's law. The same applies to human beings. Adam and Eve, our first parent, were created with free will. They were to serve and worship the Lord God by the law of loving obedience. As long as they submitted their free wills to God's good, perfect, and acceptable will, there was order, peace and harmony in their lives, and in the Garden of Eden.[2]

As our Creator, He knows what the right way is, and what not the proper way to live is. His law is likened to the manufacturer's "Instruction Manual." If one follows the instructions found in the Manual, things will go well and fine.

Otherwise, there will be mishap, injury, malfunction or destruction. Precisely, this was what happened to Adam and Eve. When they did not obey God's instructions, they sinned and fell from God's moral standard. The Bible used the phrase, "....they fall short of the glory of God" (Romans 3:23). Following that fall, they began their journey on the road to death and destruction.

Note that there are different types of God's laws in the Bible. There is the Moral Law, the Civil Law, Food Law, Health and Hygiene Laws, and the Ceremonial Law. Some of these laws have been done away with following Christ's redemptive act on the cross of Calvary. But the Moral Law is very much relevant and significant for a person to observe even in this modern age and time because it transcends time.[3]

Evidence of Moral Decline

The following are some facts taken from a compilation carried out by Michael Snyder in April 2014 entitled "100 Facts About The Moral Collapse Of America That Are Almost Too Crazy To Believe." [4]

- Approximately one-third of the entire population of the United States (110 million people) currently has sexually transmitted diseases, according to the Centers for Disease Control and Prevention. Every single year, there are 20 million new STD cases. At this point, one out of every four teen girls in the U.S. has at least one sexually transmitted disease. America has the highest STD infection rate in the entire industrialized world.

- The United States has the highest teen pregnancy rate in the entire industrialized world. For women under the age of 30, more than half of all babies are being born out of wedlock.

- Law enforcement officials estimate that about 600,000 Americans are trading dirty child pictures online. It is estimated that 89 percent of all pornography is being produced in the United States.

- In the United States today, more than half of all couples "move in together" before they get married. America has the highest divorce rate in the world by a good margin.

- In a massacre that is almost unspeakable, more than 56 million American babies have been slaughtered in the country since Roe v. Wade decision in 1973. About one-third of all American women will have had an abortion by the age of 45. Planned Parenthood Founder Margaret Sanger once said: "The most merciful thing that a family does to one of its infant members is to kill it." And she is praised in the halls of the United States Congress.

- America has the highest incarceration rate and the largest total prison population in the entire world by a wide margin.

- In the United States today, prescription painkillers kill more Americans than heroin and cocaine combined. America has the highest rate of illegal drug use on the entire planet.

- For the first time, Protestants do not make up a majority of the U.S. population. In 2007, Protestants made up 53 percent of the U.S. population, but now they only make up 48 percent of the U.S. population. Way back in 1972, Protestants made up 62 percent of the U.S. population. Sixty-six percent of all U.S. adults believe that religion is "losing its influence on American life".

- An all-time high of 59 percent of all Americans believe that the traditional definition of marriage needs to be changed. They are calling for the legalization of gay marriage.

Ultimate Evidence of Moral Decline

Generally speaking, there are two kinds of laws in the world: man's law and God's law. The government could change man's law even those that are enshrined in the Constitution to suit the times and circumstances but should never do the same to God's law. The United States Supreme Court very recently did just what is prohibited—they changed God's law to allow gay marriage in America.

God had reproved through the Bible the abomination of this sin. He repeatedly warned through His servants the Prophets and Ministers of the Gospel in this generation. Because the people kept pushing for their "rights," God gave them what they desired. They were given a President, who supported it, and a Supreme Court to legalize it.

Changing God's Law

God revealed the President of the United States would alter the nation's Constitution, and enact a final abomination in the nation. This revelation was given to Pastor T D Hale, a pastor of Calvary Christian Center in Gallipolis, Ohio. In a span of twelve months, he had four dreams in which God made known to him what would soon come to America. He shared his dreams with radio host, Rick Wiles of TruNews.com. Below are transcripts of his first and second dreams, followed by a short remark.[5]

Pastor TD Hale
First Dream

With the situation that we see going on in America, with the president and the administration certainly there are warning signs coming up. On December 28, 2011, I had been seeking the Lord for a word to give to our assembly. I went to bed that night just like any other night. The Lord just really dealt with me in the middle of the night concerning things that were coming.

I certainly was shocked when I saw what I saw. In the dream, I began to see myself going across America. I was floating, suspended in the air going across America. I had no fear of what I was seeing. Then all of a sudden I began to see bombs had landed everywhere. The land was totally destroyed. It looked like things were totally just wiped off, grass, trees, everything. Everything was gone, burned. There was nothing left. There was nothing on the trees. There was just a total disaster. I don't know if it was everywhere, but it was everywhere that I could see, from the point I was at.

When I saw this, I saw people standing around their homes and things that were left, holding onto each other. I saw people that laid dead, and I heard the cries of the people saying, "This should never have happened, this should never have happened." It was like they just kept saying it over and over again, "This should never have happened, oh Lord, this should never have happened."

You could tell that life had changed. There was no food. There was no water. I could see babies crying, grownups, men all crying, holding onto their families. They were begging God for mercy. As I moved along, I saw people running; looking for their loved ones who were missing and they were complete, completely out of their minds. Insanity had taken over. I could see people slinging themselves off of bridges, committing suicide. It was just so vivid what I could see.

Then I came to a big city that looked like Columbus, Ohio. That is when all of a sudden I saw mass hysteria, riots and all kinds of things breaking out in the streets of the city. There were windows being busted. There were people just grabbing things left and right. But when I saw it, I did not see them grabbing things like TVs and electronics. They were grabbing food. They were grabbing chips. They were grabbing water. They were grabbing anything they could get their hands on to sustain their lives. It was all about survival. I could tell that this was different from riots that we have seen in the past. They had come into the stores by the thousands, as many as could come in. I saw them pushing shelves over and pushing electronics aside. They were trying to grab the food, the bread, and cases of water. They were seeking everything they could get for survival. The rioters were fighting among themselves. I saw one man grab a gun out of his pocket and shoot another man right in the head.

The next part of the dream was the most startling for me. As I left that place, I was going like at the speed of light. I found myself standing on the back side of the White House. As I stood there, I looked up. I heard a voice say, "Look up to the Truman balcony." I knew what a balcony was, but I did not know the balcony had a name. I did not know that there was a Truman balcony until I later shared this with a friend who told me there is a balcony by that name at the White House. In my mind, I believe the Lord identified that to let me know that my dream was from the Lord.

I saw the president of United States, President Obama, standing on the balcony and I saw in his hands a shotgun. All of a sudden, to my left-hand side I heard a loud scream, real loud. When I turned my head to see where the scream was coming from I saw flying high in the air was a majestic eagle flying in the air around Washington DC. I knew that scream. I knew it was an eagle. All of a sudden I saw the president of United States point that shotgun and shot that Eagle dead and it fell to the ground. When it did, I looked back up at him, and he just had a smile on his face like a smirk. And these were the words I heard in the dream, "I've done it, and I won't have to deal with this in my administration."

Then there was dead silence. Then I heard a voice say "Tell the people that this is my will, that this is my hand, this is the hand of the Almighty both upon the generation of the righteous and the cursed. The righteous will find their way and will know what to do. The cursed will wander around with no compass because the cup is full."

There will be people running around saying we don't understand why these things are happening, but people need to understand that God has everything under control. The Lord let me know that this is His will. It is His hand upon the righteous and the cursed, and we have to accept that. It amazes me how people have their heads buried in the sand when God is sending so many warnings to people through all kinds of His servants, and yet they still will not believe. It is just like in the Bible (with ancient Israel). God sent the prophets and warned them there is going to come destruction, there's going to come trouble, the nations are going to come in and take over. But the people said, "No that is not going to happen, God is not going to let that happen. God won't do something like that." But then it did happen. Then the people went back to God and apologized to him and said we are sorry, but it was too late. It is like people have fallen asleep. They don't have a prayer life. They constantly just go on as if nothing is going to happen. They act like life is going to continue as it is, like America is going to continue as it is, and there is no urgency. They have their heads buried in the sand, but God is saying "it is time to wake up. Things are getting ready to happen. It is going to move at a fast rate. It is time to get a prayer life back."

At that point in the dream I knew we were coming to a showdown between good versus evil. I saw people gathering in their homes, and there were prayer meetings. People were praying in the spirit. Then I heard the Lord say, "Tell my servants and my handmaidens a special anointing will reside on you in the last days. Hold not back your voices but speak your hearts for out of them comes the issues of life. Pick up the mantle of prayer and cover yourselves in a secret place of prayer. Your eyes will be anointed with a special anointing. There will be others who will be blinded to my word. All things will be revealed in their due course. There will be a supernatural wave of the spirit that will come over this generation very soon."

The final voices are in the land to speak one last time. Through the ministries of tapes and DVDs and books that people would have in their possession that God will give them that spiritual food to sustain them during these times that are coming upon us. The Lord said, "There are harsh days coming."

All of a sudden, things changed in the dream, and I began to hear a voice, the voice of God. I saw in front of me an ancient antique table. I knew there had been documents signed on this table, special documents. I am hesitant to say this, but I saw a voting ballot lying there on the table. As I looked at the ballot, I saw two names on it. I saw the President's name, and I saw Mitt Romney's name on it. Then all of a sudden I looked and I saw the president of United States name check marked. I knew then what that meant. I looked at the ballot, and I saw written on the ballot, "This is the will of the Lord." Then I woke up. America's days are numbered. The handwriting is on the wall. I am telling my church to be prepared and to get their houses in order. I am telling them that whatever they need to do for their families do it quickly.

Second Dream

The very next night (December 29, 2011) I had a second dream in which I saw the American people going into slavery. In this dream, I came upon a wooded area where I saw some people that were camping. They were not camping like we usually think. They were hiding. They were all standing by their tents. There were two tents. The people looked tattered. They looked like they had not taken a bath in ages. There were gallon jugs of water, and they were trying to light a fire, but they didn't want to bring attention to themselves. But they had already been found out. I saw some federal officials coming up around, and they took these families. They handcuffed the adults and took them to the cars, and they took their children with them. I also saw two elderly people and they took them and put them in the car. I saw the federal agents and they said "We are from the United States government, and you are under arrest."

I knew that these people had been running to get away from being arrested. They took these people to some processing place. I was standing in front of this building where I watched them being taken in and processed. To me, it was like I was looking at the days of Hitler again. The building looked like it had been modernized and updated and painted, but it looked tattered and things were very run down. I knew they were old military bases that had been shut down. I saw them take the people inside where they were being processed. I even saw them being fingerprinted. I saw rail cars that came up beside this place. I did not go into the rail cars, so I did not see inside them. That frightened me. It disturbed me. I knew America was in trouble when I saw that. I knew we were headed down a path that was not going to be turned around. I felt like I had entered into a death camp. What I saw sickened me. I knew that America was about to change.

End of the dreams

Remarks

(i) In the first dream, Pastor Hale saw President Obama and Mitt Romney's names on the ballot in the 2012 election. It was about six months before Mitt Romney even secured the Republican nomination; even before the Presidential Primaries officially began. Moreover, he saw Obama won the re-election that came to pass on November 6, 2012 election result.

(ii) The first dream has four parts:
Scene One — Total destruction by bombs
Scene Two — Mass riots in a large city in America
Scene Three — President Obama shooting the American Eagle
Scene Four — Election ballots with Obama winning re-election

It appears God showed him the scenes in reverse chronological order in its fulfillment. Let us place them in reverse chronological order:

Scene Four — This was fulfilled in November 2012.
Scene Three — The eagle symbolizes American constitutional form of government and the freedoms enshrined within it. It looks like Obama is slowly but surely changing the constitution to strengthen his dictatorial rule.
Scene Two — The riot ultimately will lead to a martial law in many parts of America, with most of the violence and suffering concentrated in large urban areas. It would be a good idea to stock up on canned foods, rice, beans, water, batteries, cash, and things like that. It sounds like a massive disruption is coming to the food and water supplies.
Scene One — Pastor Hale did not say what part of the country was hit or if all of it was hit. It is clear that this is a warning to all who have ears to hear in America. God is calling His people to repent and turn to Him.

(iii) Pastor Hale's second dream was also very disturbing. Others have shared similar words about American citizens being forced into concentration camps or FEMA camps (Federal Emergency Management Authority). They sounded similar to the horrible camps now used in North Korea and the Nazi camps of World War Two.

Pastor TD Hale also was shown the third and the fourth dream. Below are the transcripts of the dreams followed by a short remark.[6]

Third Dream

I received this third dream in the summer of 2012. In the dream, I found myself standing in front of the Kirtland Temple in Ohio, a building I previously knew nothing about other than what was shown to me in the dream. I went inside and found Mitt Romney and two staircases on either side of the stage. I then saw an Egyptian-like, falcon-like creature (or hybrid) that continually blocked Governor Romney from ascending the stairs to the stage.

Remarks

Kirtland Temple is a Mormon Temple (The Church of Jesus Christ of Latter-day Saints), and Mitt Romney is a Mormon. The interpretation of the dream is that Governor Romney is being blocked from ascending to the Presidency of the United States. Clearly that dream was fulfilled already.

Fourth Dream

This dream was given to me on November 24, 2012. In this dream, I was immediately taken into the Oval Office. I was standing in the oval office looking at the President of United States. It was so real that I felt like I could reach my hand out and touch the man. He was standing behind the desk. When I stood in front of him all of a sudden, I heard a voice, and I knew it was the voice of God. I heard the voice say, "Weep and howl for the misery that shall come shortly."

Then all of a sudden I turned and when I turned I saw there on the floor of the oval office was that eagle that I saw him shoot back in the dream I had in December 2011. I saw the president walk behind the desk with that same smirk, that same arrogant smirk on his face that he had on the Truman balcony in my other dream. He came out from behind the desk, and he walked over to the eagle and he put his foot on the neck of the eagle. Then at this point he bent down, and he took it by its head, and then he twisted it three times until the head of the eagle came off of its body. Then at that point I heard a voice say, "The spirit of Rehoboam."

As I began to look at him again, he was dressed in all black. He had a black suit on, a black tie, a black shirt, black pants everything was total black that I saw him wearing. Then as I was looking directly at him all of a sudden his chest cavity around his heart began to open up. His heart was exposed. As I was looking at his heart, this thick black, dark mist was swirling around his heart, and I knew that God was letting me see the evil that is really in that man.

Now at this point he walked over to the desk, and he picked up a gavel in his hand. The gavel was part wood and part stone. The handle was wood, and the head of the gavel was stone. On the desk of the president of United States, there is a document with these words written on it, "The final abomination." He then hit the document on his desk with the gavel and when he hit this document on the desk then all of a sudden I felt a shaking. Honestly, I felt like my bed was shaking. Literally, it was shaking, and I could feel it. When he hit this document, I shot up into the air, and I was standing up above the White House.

Then an earthquake hit Washington DC. Then I saw the earth open up, and it went towards the Washington monument then towards the Jefferson Memorial. At that point, I began to see an odd colored rain falling. It was the color of fire or something. It started slowly coming down then it intensified little by little. It was coming down faster and faster until the waters began rising. As the waters started rising, I went up higher into the atmosphere, and I saw the map of the United States. I could see the outline. The waters left Washington and began to flood across the whole United States. I saw them hit Maryland, West Virginia, Ohio, Michigan, Kentucky, Indiana, South Carolina until it completely went all across the United States. People began to scream across the nation, and all I could hear was a mournful sound. It was as if something had happened, a great loss, like if you went to a funeral home and somebody had passed away, and you were very close to them. It was that kind of mournful sound. Even in my dream I thought about the days of Noah and what it must have felt like for the people who were outside of the ark when the flood came, but they could not get in. They had not listened to the voice of Noah or the voice of God when he had spoken to them. This is the thing. God is speaking to them one last time. He is speaking through TruNews.com, he is speaking through you, he is speaking through me, and some other ministers that I know. God is speaking.

As I was in the air, I saw America in this state of being covered with these flood waters. Then all of a sudden as I was suspended in the air, I could see these beams of light quickly coming up out of the flood waters. Like at the speed of light, they were quickly going up into the air. There were millions it seems. Then at that moment I was taken higher above the earth, and I could see the round earth and all over the earth I started seeing those lights shooting up all over the world. Then I came back down to the earth as if I was back at the beginning of this dream. Then I heard a voice say, "The shifting has begun."

At this point I was looking over the top; I was going across the top of several churches in America. These were mega-churches. I saw them as I was going across them from the top of one to the other. I saw the names of the churches and the names of their leaders. I heard a voice say, "A breeding ground for sin for the people know not Me, but they play around their golden calf."

I knew that we had entered into the time of the end. It will not be these large churches, but it will be home prayer meetings where the saints will be gathering in secret and praying. It is going to get to the point where we are going to have to meet in secret. The days of persecution had come upon this generation. The Lord let me know a long time ago that there would be a remnant that would be called out. There would be a little here and a little there. Some of these mega-churches are not going to be around anymore. They are going to be shut down. God is going to have some people here and there who are going to be praying in secret. So speak in the last days because of the persecution that will come upon this generation.

At this point, I was looking again at the homes. I knew that these people loved and served God with all of their heart. I saw the homes of men and women that were gathered together in deep intercessory prayer across the nation. And then I heard a voice says, "The season is upon this nation because you have set abomination before my eyes, I will set judgment before yours." Then I asked the Lord, "When will it happen?" I heard the voice answer, "After he is sworn in." Then I woke up.

End of the dreams

Remarks

(i) The Spirit of Rehoboam

Rehoboam succeeded King Solomon after his father's death. In an incident recorded in 1 Kings Chapter 12, the people gathered together at Shechem and demanded that he reduce their taxes. Rehoboam consulted with the younger generation and instead of reducing their taxes he increased them. The interesting thing is that the Scripture says he consulted with the younger generation that he had grown up with. He would not listen to the advice of the elders. He answered the people haughtily. He told them his father whipped them with whips, but now they would be whipped with scorpions. His administration was going to put more pressure and more trouble on them. His young advisers gave him unwise advice.

This same spirit of Rehoboam is on Barack Obama. Look at all the young people that rallied around Obama and put him in office. Like Rehoboam, Obama is listening to the voice of younger people, people he grew up with, people who have no experience because they have not yet experienced life. It is like a young person saying you should do this and this with your child but yet he has never been a parent before. Just like Rehoboam, Obama refuses to listen to the voice of the elders.

(ii) The Final Abomination

On September 21, 1996, President Clinton signed the Defense of Marriage Act (DOMA) of 1996 into law. This Act is a federal law that denies federal recognition of same-sex marriages and authorizes states to refuse to recognize same-sex marriages licensed in other states. DOMA was passed out of fear that a lawsuit in Hawaii would force that state to recognize same-sex marriages. Obama refused to defend this Act. On June 26, 2013, the United States Supreme Court ruled the Act is unconstitutional. By striking down Section 3 of DOMA, the Supreme Court has affirmed that all married same-sex couples deserve equal legal respect and treatment. Then, on June 26, 2015, the Supreme Court ruled that gay marriage is legal nationwide. When he took office in 2008 gay marriage was legal in only two states. Just before this final court verdict, 37 states allowed it. Now, it is legal in all the 50 states in America.

(iii) The Falling Rain of Fire

The falling rain that looked like fire represents judgment. I think the judgment is going to start falling on America this year, next year, and the year after. I do not believe it is going to be happy times. I think more people are going to go mentally insane as things begin to grow progressively worse. When people are hungry, they do crazy things. When people do not have money, they do stupid things. They do so when they do not have money to pay their rent and pay their bills. This generation is totally different from the generation that lived during the great depression of the 1930's. During the depression, people tried to help one another. Today I do not see that happening. All I can say is something is going to transpire. And it has been. We have been seeing month after month things beginning to change in Washington DC.

(iv) The Shifting Has Begun

When something shifts, it moves back and forth. So we are getting ready to move from what is happening now to something in this dream. The mega-churches are going to shift deeper into apostasy. It is going to get to the point in America where these churches will just accept anything. When the new laws come into effect, we are going to see that pastors will be required to marry homosexual couples.

(v) A Breeding Ground for Sin

We have several pastors of these mega-churches going on television saying things like, "Well, I'm not sure if homosexuality is wrong. Gays might get to go to heaven." They say things like, "I don't know if Jesus is the only way. There are different ways to get to God and Christ is not the only way." We are seeing these ministers beginning to deny the Scriptures. They are compromising. So that is why God said "A breeding ground for sin because the people know not Me but they are playing with their golden calf."

The Supreme Court Verdict

June 26, 2015, was a very dark day in the U.S. history, and indeed, for the whole world because a Supreme Court decision on this day is bound to have widespread moral ramifications. It is remembered as the day men attempted to change God's divine law. God created human beings, male and female, for a purpose that they may procreate and raise a family. Two men cannot procreate, neither can two women. For this reason, He created Adam and Eve. He did not create Adam and Steve, nor Helen and Eve.

Who are these Supreme Court justices, particularly the ones who favor the verdict? Are they not learned people? It seems too much learning has not brought them the truth as the Bible describes them saying, "they are always learning and never able to come to the knowledge of the truth" (2 Timothy 3:7).

The U.S. Supreme Court justices had always had a majority of Protestant members. For the first time in its history, there is neither Protestant nor Evangelical members in the current one that is made up of six Catholics and three Jews. It means it does not represent a cross-section of the American population. It therefore does not represent the Evangelicals.

The verdict on this case was 5:4. The 5 who favored the verdict include two Catholics and all of the three Jews.

The four justices who disagreed with the majority opinion include the Chief Justice John Roberts. Each wrote their dissenting opinion laying out just why they believed the majority to be wrong. Let us hear what they have to say (extract).[7]

Chief Justice John Roberts

He said, "Five lawyers have closed the debate and enacted their own vision of marriage as a matter of constitutional law."

"Understand well what this dissent is about: It is not about whether, in my judgment, the institution of marriage should be changed to include same-sex couples. It is instead about whether, in our democratic republic, that decision should rest with the people acting through their elected representatives, or with five lawyers who happen to hold commissions authorizing them to resolve legal disputes according to law," he wrote.

"Supporters of same-sex marriage have achieved considerable success persuading their fellow citizens—through the democratic process—to adopt their view. That ends today," Roberts wrote.

"Stealing this issue from the people will for many cast a cloud over same-sex marriage, making a dramatic social change that much more difficult to accept."

"If not having the opportunity to marry 'serves to disrespect and subordinate' gay and lesbian couples, why wouldn't the same 'imposition of this disability,' ... serve to disrespect and subordinate people who find fulfillment in polygamous relationships?" he writes. "I do not mean to equate marriage between same-sex couples with plural marriages in all respects. There may well be relevant differences that compel different legal analysis. But if there are, petitioners have not pointed to any."

Justice Antonin Scalia

"Until the courts put a stop to it, public debate over same-sex marriage displayed American democracy at its best," Scalia wrote. "But the Court ends this debate, in an opinion lacking even a thin veneer of law."

Scalia attacked his colleagues' opinion with his signature flourish. "The opinion is couched in a style that is as pretentious as its content is egotistic," he wrote.

"When the Fourteenth Amendment was ratified in 1868, every State limited marriage to one man and one woman, and no one doubted the constitutionality of doing so," he wrote.

"They [the majority] have discovered in the Fourteenth Amendment a 'fundamental right' overlooked by every person alive at the time of ratification, and almost everyone else in the time since."

Scalia called out the majority for acting like activists, not judges. "States are free to adopt whatever laws they like, even those that offend the esteemed Justices' 'reasoned judgment'," he wrote.

The majority began its opinion with the line: "The Constitution promises liberty to all within its reach, a liberty that includes certain specific rights that allow persons, within a lawful realm, to define and express their identity." Scalia wrote that if he ever were to join an opinion that began with that sentence he "would hide my head in a bag," saying such language was more like the "mystical aphorisms of the fortune cookie" than, say, legendary Chief Justice John Marshall.

Elsewhere, the majority wrote, "The nature of marriage is that, through its enduring bond, two persons together can find other freedoms, such as expression, intimacy, and spirituality." Scalia scoffed at this assertion, saying, "Really? Who ever thought that intimacy and spirituality [whatever that means] were freedoms? And if intimacy is, one would think Freedom of Intimacy is abridged rather than expanded by marriage. Ask the nearest hippie."

Justice Clarence Thomas

Echoing a grievance expressed by many conservative politicians, he lamented that the Supreme Court's decision was enshrining a definition of marriage into the Constitution in a way that put it "beyond the reach of the normal democratic process for the entire nation."

Thomas additionally warned that the Court's "inversion of the original meaning of liberty will likely cause collateral damage to other aspects of our constitutional order that protect liberty." Further, he argued that the decision would threaten religious liberty by creating an unavoidable collision between the interests of same-sex couples and some religious organizations. "In our society, marriage is not simply a governmental institution; it is a religious institution as well," Thomas wrote. "Today's decision might change the former, but it cannot change the latter. It appears all but inevitable that the two will come into conflict, particularly as individuals and churches are confronted with demands to participate in and endorse civil marriages between same-sex couples."

Justice Samuel Alito

"For today's majority, it does not matter that the right to same-sex marriage lacks deep roots or even that it is contrary to long-established tradition. The Justices in the majority claim the authority to confer constitutional protection upon that right simply because they believe that it is fundamental," Alito wrote.

"At present, no one—including social scientists, philosophers, and historians—can predict with any certainty what the long-term ramifications of widespread acceptance of same-sex marriage will be. And judges are certainly not equipped to make such an assessment," Alito wrote.

Alito's belief is also that traditional marriage has existed between a man and woman for one key reason: children. His argument was: "For millennia, marriage was inextricably linked to the one thing that only an opposite-sex couple can do: procreate. Adherents to different schools of philosophy use different terms to explain why society should formalize marriage and attach special benefits and obligations to persons who marry. Their basic argument is that States formalize and promote marriage, unlike other fulfilling human relationships, in order to encourage potentially procreative conduct to take place within a lasting unit that has long been thought to provide the best atmosphere for raising children."

"By imposing its own views on the entire country, the majority facilitates the marginalization of the many Americans who have traditional ideas. Recalling the harsh treatment of gays and lesbians in the past, some may think that turnabout is fair play. But if that sentiment prevails, the Nation will experience bitter and lasting wounds," he wrote.

Statements from Evangelical Leaders

The son of Billy Graham, Franklin Graham made this statement: "With all due respect to the court, it did not define marriage, and, therefore, is not entitled to re-define it. Long before our government came into existence, marriage was created by the One who created man and woman —Almighty God—and His decisions are not subject to review or revision by any manmade court. God is clear about the definition of marriage in His Holy Word: 'Therefore a man shall leave his father and his mother and hold fast to his wife, and they shall become one flesh' (Genesis 2:24). I pray God will spare America from this judgment, though, by our actions as a nation, we give Him less and less reason to do so." [8]

Founder of the Christian Broadcasting Network (CBN) Dr. Pat Robertson expressed disappointment with the court's decision. Robertson said, "Marriage from time immemorial has been a sacrament of the church. I think the Supreme Court erred in extending the Due Process Clause of the Fourteenth Amendment to force homosexual marriage on states that have clearly rejected the concept." "I agree with Chief Justice Roberts that the Supreme Court is not a supra legislature, but this is what it has become while ignoring the explicit tenets of constitutional law," he added.[9]

Chapter 11

ECONOMIC DECLINE & COLLAPSE OF THE USD

We stated in the preceding chapter that moral decline is the underlying cause of the weakening of America. The economic malaise is a significant indication of that weakening.

Evidence of Economic Decline

America is in the throes of a horrifying economic decline that is the result of decades of wrong decisions. Thirty years ago, the U.S. national debt was about one trillion dollars. Today, it is around 18 trillion dollars. Forty years ago, the total amount of public and private debt, comprising sovereign, business, and consumer debt, in the United States was about 2 trillion dollars. Today, it is more than 57 trillion dollars. As the debts are climbing, the nation economic infrastructure is breaking down. Since 2001, the United States has lost more than 56,000 manufacturing facilities, and millions of good jobs moved overseas, especially to China. The U.S. share of global GDP declined from 31.8 percent in 2001 to 21.6 percent in 2011. The percentage of Americans that are self-employed is at a record low, and the percentage of Americans that are dependent on the government is at a record high.

The following are some statistics on the fall of the U.S. economy.[1]

- During President Obama's first term, the federal government accumulated more debt than it did under the first 42 U.S. presidents combined. The U.S. national debt is now more than 23 times larger than it was under the administration of President Jimmy Carter.

- The United States has fallen in the global economic competitiveness rankings compiled by the World Economic Forum for four years in a row.

- Overall, the United States has run a trade deficit of more than 8 trillion dollars with the rest of the world since 1975.

- Back in 1985, the U.S. trade deficit with China was approximately 6 million dollars for the entire year. In 2012, the deficit grew to 315 billion dollars. It was the largest trade deficit ever recorded between nations in world history. According to the Economic Policy Institute, the United States is losing half a million jobs to China every single year.

- There are fewer Americans working in manufacturing today than there was in 1950 even though the population of the country has more than doubled since then.

- Small business sector is rapidly dying in America. At this point, only about 7 percent of all non-farm workers in the United States are self-employed. That is at a record low.

- According to the U.S. Census Bureau, 49 percent of all Americans live in a home that receives direct monetary benefits from the federal government. Back in 1983, it was less than a third of all Americans. Overall, the federal government runs nearly 80 different welfare programs, and at this point more than 100 million Americans are on the enrollment in at least one of them.

- Back in 1965, only one out of every 50 Americans was on Medicaid. Today, it is one out of every 6. It is being projected that Obamacare will add 16 million more Americans to the Medicaid rolls.

- It is being projected that the number of Americans on Medicare will grow from 50.7 million in 2012 to 73.2 million in 2025. At this point, Medicare is facing unfunded liabilities of more than 38 trillion dollars over the next 75 years. That comes to approximately $328,404 for every single household in the United States.

- Forty-five percent of all children in Miami are living in poverty, more than 50 percent in Cleveland, and about 60 percent in Detroit.

- Today, more than a million public school students in the United States are homeless. It is the first time it has ever happened with this number.

The Future of America

Only God knows the future. He knows what will become of America. He had warned this nation to repent of her wicked ways, but she has not taken heed of His warning. He is about to judge her for her sins. The judgment will fall in a series of severe catastrophe. They will come in very quick succession, almost back to back. The final catastrophe will be a thermonuclear destruction. We will cover this last desolation in the next chapter.

In the middle of 2012, God revealed the future of America to Pastor Shane Warren. He is the Senior Pastor of First Assembly of God in West Monroe, Louisiana. Pastor Warren was interviewed by Sid Roth on the television program "It's Supernatural!" [2] Below is a transcript of the interview.

Collapse of the American Dollar & An Earthquake Splitting America Into Two

One evening around the middle of 2012, I was sitting on my couch. I thought I had fallen asleep when in reality, I was in an open vision. I had a large TV screen in my living room, and as I sat watching, there was a weather broadcast. There was a news anchor who said, "The most surprising thing is going on right now. It is tragic, it is tragic." He said, typically the hurricane hit on the coastline, but there is a hurricane that seems to be spreading down on the heartland of America.

At that point, he showed a satellite image of America. I was horrified as I watched a storm covering the Northern border to the Southern boundary, from East to West. It is this massive storm with the eye right over the middle of America, coming across the center of America.

Immediately, it came back to the anchor. This anchor said, "We have somebody on the ground in the eye of the storm. We are going to him now."

The scene switched. The news reporter was reporting as the wind is blowing violently, and toss to and fro. He said, "This is the most amazing thing, and I don't understand it. It is not a natural storm. Look what it is raining?"

He reached down to the ground, and he picked up a fist of one dollar bills. He said it is raining dollar bills, and it looks like it is worthless.

About that time it came back to the anchor. He said, "Ladies and gentlemen, another tragedy has hit America. Right in the heartland of America on the New Madrid Faultline, a major earthquake has just hit."

Immediately, pictures of devastation all over America popped up. The earthquake caused entire cities to crumple. While I was sitting there, I heard a booming voice behind my ear that said,"They have divided My land. Now, I will divide their land." I knew immediately in this vision that He is speaking about Israel, and specifically Jerusalem. With all that is taking place there now, it feels like this vision is about to unfold.

I saw incredible changes in the price of currencies. I saw silver, not gold, but silver drastically increased in value. I saw riots break out in major cities all over America. People are carrying placards, "Give us our entitlement! Give us our entitlement!" It was a civil war within our borders. It is over the issue of devaluation of money.

Then, immediately I was caught up, and I was sitting in a room with world leaders— China, Iran, Russia— Putin was there. In this meeting, the world leaders were talking about how to devalue the American dollar by buying oil with another currency. It will drive down the value of the dollar.

I woke up and realized I was not in a dream. I was sitting on the couch and watching the TV and realized this was an open vision. God was showing me the storm that is about to come to America. We are in troubling days.

However, there is hope. I saw churches become places of refuge. All of a sudden, the body of Christ stood up like a mighty sleeping giant in the earth.

People began to come to them for ministry. I saw signs and wonders being poured out all over America. People couldn't go to the government anymore, they have to get back to the Church for help. I saw cities of refuge — there was light, glory, peace and the presence of God there. The revival was taking place.

On one hand, there is judgment but, on the other hand, the glory of God was poured out. When judgment comes there always is unto mercy. I believe we are running out of time.

End of the vision.

Remarks

(i) Collapse of the US Dollar Like a Hurricane

Typically, hurricane moves in towards the land from the Atlantic Ocean. But Pastor Warren saw the storm hit the center of America suddenly. It means there is no time to "evacuate" for a lot of people. There is a saying that when "it rains, it pours." This storm that symbolizes the collapse of the U.S. dollar is pouring down the valueless dollars. Since the dollar is the world's reserve currency, it will drag down the currencies of the rest of the world. Understand that the global derivatives market value estimated at 1.2 quadrillion dollars is like a humongous bubble ready to burst.

What triggers the collapse seems to be the result of a decision by a group of world leaders. Pastor Warren saw them gathered in a meeting room somewhere in a middle-eastern city. The leaders are from Russia, China, and Iran. In another interview he gave elsewhere, he also mentioned the presence of Egypt, Syria, Turkey and Saudi Arabia. The relationship between Russia and Saudi Arabia has not been close these many years. Recently, they have a sharp disagreement over several geopolitical issues such as stopping Iran's nuclear program, and supporting the Assad regime in Syria. The situation is slowly changing. The son of the present Saudi ruler recently visited Russia. An invitation is extended to the Saudi king to visit Russia, and the Russian leader is invited to visit Saudi Arabia.

This group of world leaders will make a decision to abandon the dollar together. It is not an understatement to say that the U.S. dollar is the most abused currency in the world. The dollar appears to be in demand due to its reserve currency status, being so established at the Bretton Woods Conference in 1944. It was pegged initially to the gold standard, that is, back up by the amount of gold Uncle Sam possessed.

After over issuing the currency due to over spending, President Richard Nixon in 1971 decoupled the dollar from gold. From that point, the dollar became a fiat currency similar to other currencies of the world. To prop up the value of the dollar, Nixon in 1973 went to Saudi Arabia to negotiate a deal with the Saudi. The U.S. commits to buying crude oil from the Saudi, who in turn will use the dollar to invest back in the U.S. by purchasing some of America's debt. The arrangement sets the dollar up as the "petrodollar." Other countries are required to buy or sell crude oil in U.S. dollars. For this reason, the dollar is in demand.

There are some countries that are already reducing their use of the dollar in their international transactions. They do it through bilateral trade arrangements using their respective currencies. This is so among Member countries of BRICS: Brazil, Russia, India, China and South Africa. It is true, also, between the BRICS and other nations. There is a growing lack of confidence in the U.S. dollar these days. The last straw to break the camel's back will be when the Saudi decouple crude oil from the dollar. This action carries weight as Saudi Arabia is the world largest crude oil exporter and the leading member of OPEC (Organization of Petroleum Exporting Countries).

(ii) Nationwide Riot

Pastor Warren saw masses of people rioting on the streets. Carrying placards, they demand their entitlements—their retirement benefits such as the 401(k) (In other countries it is the EPF or CPF). The collapse of the dollar has created a severe lack; no jobs, no food, and no government welfare aid.

People everywhere will wake-up to the realization that a fiat currency has no intrinsic value. There is a saying, "If it is written on a piece of paper, then it is worth the paper it is written on." What is the value of a small piece of paper? Suddenly, the price of silver (gold and other precious metals) will drastically increase in value. What is found in the ground is real value, for God put them there.

(iii) Earthquake Hit the New Madrid Seismic Zone

The New Madrid Seismic Zone, also called the New Madrid Fault Line, is an earthquake prone area. The center of the zone, located in the town of New Madrid, Missouri, lies along the Mississippi River. The Fault Line is about 150 miles (240 km) long. History records three main shocks that hit the site: in December 1811, in January 1812, and in February 1812. The past quake was recorded to have affected 5 million square km area. Due to low population density in those regions in those days, casualties were low. The Federal Emergency Management Agency (FEMA) warned that the next quake could result in the "highest economic loss due to a natural disaster in the history of the US." Damage will be felt across the states of Alabama, Arkansas, Illinois, Indiana, Kentucky, Mississippi, Missouri, and Tennessee.

Pastor Warren heard the voice of the Lord said, "They have divided My land. Now, I will divide their land." (Leviticus 25:23 and Joel 3:1-2). The earthquake will be so powerful that it will split America into half along the Mississippi River, from the Great Lakes in the North to the Gulf of Mexico in the South.

The severe judgment will come, after the U.S. pressured Israel to accept the "two-state solution" with the Palestinian (See Chapter 9).

(iv) Cities of Refuge

There appears to be hope in the midst of this terrible judgment. It is a two-edged sword. God intend to wake up His people. They will seek Him in earnest, discarding their sins and worldliness. The churches will be full again. Many who did not acknowledge Christ as their Saviour will respond to Him then. The churches will be a refuge as they will not be able to get help from the government. God will work wonderfully among His people, pouring out His grace, mercy, and anointing. Great miracles will occur, of cleansing, healing, and provisions.

PART TWO

Some Major Events Leading To The Second Coming Of Christ

Chapter 12

COMING JUDGMENT OF AMERICA

> Surely the Lord God does nothing unless He reveals His secret to His servants the prophets.
>
> [Amos 3:7]

Abraham was in Mamre near Hebron for a brief period, pitching his tent by the terebinth trees (Genesis 18). One hot afternoon he was sitting at the door of his dwelling tent. In the land of extreme heat, it was customary to take a break at the hottest point of the day. Looking up he saw he had some visitors, three men were walking towards his tent. Being hospitable, he rose quickly and ran to greet them. Would they mind staying a while to refresh before continuing their journey, he asked. The three visitors were happy to oblige. Rushing to inform his wife Sarah to prepare some cakes, and to his servant to cook a meal with a tender calf, he was delighted to present the afternoon meal to his guests when it was ready.

The three guests were theophany or at least one of them, who was none other than the Lord Jesus Christ while the other two were angels. As they were enjoying the good meal, the leader among the guests, the Lord, blessed Abraham and his wife with a promise that the latter will give birth to a long awaited child. After that sumptuous lunch, it was time for them to leave, to continue their journey to the twin cities of Sodom and Gomorrah. Abraham accompanied his guests for a short distance but the Lord suddenly stopped and thought aloud, "Shall I hide from Abraham what I am doing?"

What was the Lord planning to do in Sodom and Gomorrah? These twin cities, located approximately 40 kilometers to the south of the Dead Sea in present-day Jordan, were infamous for their wickedness, mainly homosexual sins. It appeared the time of judgment had finally arrived. The Lord was planning to wipe the cities off the face of the earth. The judgment was a serious matter. Should He do this without His friend Abraham being informed beforehand? Informing Abraham would be a nice gesture of their friendship, but what could he do about it?

Abraham was a righteous man and a prophet. When told of the Lord's intention, he immediately braced himself to intercede for the inhabitants of those cities. "If there were fifty righteous people alive in those cities would You destroy them along with the rest," he gently asked. "No, for the sake of those fifty righteous I will spare the place for their sake," the Lord replied. Abraham asked, "What if there were only forty-five righteous?" The Lord said, "For the sake of the forty-five I will not destroy it." He further supplicated, "What if there were only forty?" "I will not do it," the Lord replied. He implored, "What if there were only thirty?" The Lord again said, "I will not do it." "What if there were only twenty?" he entreated. "I will not do it," said the Lord. By now, Abraham felt embarrassed, almost afraid with his questioning. He pleaded the Lord to bear with him while he asked one last time, "Will You destroys the cities if there were only ten righteous people there?" Surprisingly, the answer was, "No, for the sake of the ten righteous I will not destroy it."

As the story goes, the two angels went down to those cities and hurriedly got Lot (Abraham's nephew), his wife, and his two daughters out of the place. Only four persons in the two cities were found to be righteous. Immediately after they left, the Lord rained down brimstone and fire that totally obliterated the twin cities.

Sodom and Gomorrah may be ancient cities with an old abominable sin of homosexuality. Through the ages, this particular sin has not disappeared from the earth, instead has become prevalent in our society today. While God loves the sinner and desires to see homosexual repent from it, He hates the sin. For that matter, He hates all types of sins. Unless mankind repents, judgment is unavoidable. God has set a time in which He will judge the world by His Son Jesus Christ, the Righteous One.

America is on the edge of a precipice. The world superpower is also the foremost world advocate of the homosexual lifestyle. To our knowledge, there has not been a leader (together with his vice-president) of a nation, out-rightly condoning and promoting homosexuality as the leaders of America is currently doing. Some assumed that time had mellowed God in His standard. It cannot be true because Jesus had irrevocably said that His word, His truth will not pass away even though heaven and earth may pass away (Matthew 24:35).

The judgment of America will not be a surprising act from God. Just as He had pre-informed His friend and prophet Abraham in days gone by, He has also revealed to His present day prophets what He is about to do to America. In the past eight to nine decades, God had shown in stunning details what will befall America soon. God had said He will use America's enemies to judge her. The judgment will be swift and devastating. By swift, it is implied that America will not have the time to put up a credible defense. All her early warning and missile defense systems will not be up to speed. The judgment will be so devastating it will reduce America's status from being a first-world to a third-world nation overnight, effectively removing her from playing the leadership role in the world.

There are at least a dozen, if not more, of God's modern-day prophets or servants who were shown details of the coming judgment that will befall America.[1] One of them was a Romanian minister of the gospel, Dumitru Duduman. Before we look into the details shown to him through a number of visions he received, we need to first find out who he is.

Who is Dumitru Duduman?

Dumitru Duduman was a prophet from Romania whose father was a pastor of a Pentecostal Church.[2] As a young man he joined the army when at that time Romania was still a communist country. Christians were facing severe persecution, and possession of Bibles was banned.

One day he was called to check for Bibles in a ship docking at the port of Constanta, Black Sea. The ship belonged to Open Doors. It was one of a few ministries smuggling Bibles into the country at that time. They found the Bibles. Although a Christian, in anger he seized those consignments with the intent to arrest the ship captain. However, he heard an audible voice speaking to him, "Don't confiscate the Bibles or I will punish you." Trembling with fear, he left the ship without taking the Bibles.

His father believed his son should be in the ministry rather than serving in the army. Due to the prayers of the church, soon he was discharged from the military. After his marriage, he began to distribute Bibles to Christians in places all over Romania, and later even into Russia. The Romanian authorities came to know about his activities. Several times he was called up by them for questioning. Each time without any pieces of evidence, they let him go. The Lord sent His angel, even angel Gabriel, to assist him.

One day he was caught, imprisoned and interrogated for five and a half months. They tortured him horribly. Among other torture methods, he was placed in an electrocution chair, twice. Angel Gabriel, who appeared to him many times throughout his life, instructed him to plead the blood of Jesus. When power was turned on, the electrocution knocked him unconscious with blood oozing out of his mouth, ears and nose. Because it was not his time to die, he survived.

Just before he was to be released, angel Gabriel told him to persevere one last time— he will be released but the chief persecutor will die. During the interrogation, five men in heavy military boots began to beat him up and to jump on him. As a result, nine of his ribs were broken. Faithful to the angel's word, he was released when the chief persecutor vomited blood and died.

Before his release, angel Gabriel told him in advance, that he will have four more years to distribute Bibles. That year was 1980. After that he will be arrested again and exiled to America. Gabriel also told him he will be banished from the country at 10.00 am on July 24.

After his release, it took him three months to fully recover. Eventually, he resumed distributing the Bibles to believers who were in need of them. He was arrested again in 1984. The authorities put him, his wife, daughter and grandson on a plane for America. While waiting for the flight to take off, he looked at his watch—it was 10.00 am on July 24, exactly as the angel Gabriel had informed him four years ago.

He and his family arrived in America and were provided accommodation in an apartment through some friends. One night he could not sleep ….. (he was shown the vision of the coming judgment of America).

Visions of Dumitru Duduman

From the time he was exiled to America until his death in 1997, Dumitru Duduman received a series of visions and dreams, majority of them had to do with the coming judgment of America. Reproductions below are three of those visions.

An Angel Revealed:
America is the Mystery Babylon

Vision received on September 1984

Late one night, I could not sleep. The children were sleeping on the luggage. My wife and daughter were crying; I went outside and walked around. I didn't want them to see me cry. I walked around the building, crying and saying, "God! Why did You punish me? Why did You bring me into this country? I can't understand anybody. If I try to ask anybody anything, all I hear is, "I don't know."

I stopped in front of the apartment and sat on a large rock. Suddenly, a bright light came towards me. I jumped to my feet because it looked as if a car was coming directly at me, attempting to run me down! I thought the Romanian Secret Police had tracked me to America, and now they were trying to kill me. But it was not a car at all. As the light approached, it surrounded me. From the light, I heard the same voice that I had heard so many times in prison.

He said, "Dumitru, why are you so despaired?" I said, "Why did you punish me? Why did you bring me to this country? I have nowhere to lay my head down. I can't understand anybody." He said, "Dumitru, didn't I tell you I am here with you, also? I brought you to this country because this country will burn." I said, "Then why did you bring me here to burn? Why didn't you let me die in my own country?

You should have let me die in jail in Romania! He said, "Dumitru, have patience so I can tell you. Get on this." I got on something next to him. I don't know what it was. I also know that I was not asleep. It was not a dream. It was not a vision. I was awake just as I am now.

He showed me all of California and said, "This is Sodom and Gomorrah! All of this, in one day it will burn! Its sin has reached the Holy One." Then he took me to Las Vegas. "This is Sodom and Gomorrah. In one day, it will burn." Then he showed me the state of New York. "Do you know what this is?" he asked. I said, "No." He said, "This is New York. This is Sodom and Gomorrah! In one day, it will burn." Then he showed me all of Florida, "This is Florida," he said. "This is Sodom and Gomorrah! In one day, it will burn."

Then he took me back home to the rock where we had begun. He said, "IN ONE DAY IT WILL BURN! All of this I have shown you." I said, "How will it burn?" He said, "Remember what I am telling you because you will go on television, on the radio and in churches. You must yell with a loud voice. Do not be afraid because I will be with you." I said, "How will I be able to go? Who knows me here in America? I don't know anybody here." He said, "Don't worry yourself. I will go before you. I will do a lot of healings in the American churches, and I will open the doors for you. But do not say anything else besides what I tell you. This country will burn!"

I said, "What will you do with the church?" He said, "I want to save the church, but the churches have forsaken me." I said, "How did they forsake you?" He said, "The people praise themselves. The honor that the people are supposed to give Jesus Christ, they take upon themselves. In the churches, there are divorces. There is adultery in the churches. There are homosexuals in the churches. There is abortion in the churches and all other sins that are possible. Because of all the sins, I have left some of the churches. You must yell in a loud voice that they must put an end to their sinning. They must turn toward the Lord.

The Lord never gets tired of forgiving. They must draw close to the Lord, and live a clean life. If they have sinned until now, they must put an end to it, and start a new life as the Bible tells them to live."

I said, "How will America burn?" America is the most powerful country in this world. Why did you bring us here to burn? Why didn't you at least let us die where all the Dudumans have died?" He said, "Remember this, Dumitru. The Russian spies have discovered where the nuclear warehouses are in America. When the Americans think that it is peace and safety—from the middle of the country, some of the people will start fighting against the government. The government will be busy with internal problems. Then from the ocean, from Cuba, Nicaragua, Mexico,...." (He told me two other countries, but I didn't remember what they were.) "…..they will bomb the nuclear warehouses. When they explode, America will burn!"

"What will you do with the Church of the Lord? How will you save the ones that will turn toward you?" I asked. He said, "Tell them this: how I saved the three young ones from the furnace of fire, and how I saved Daniel in the lions' den, is the same way I will save them."

The angel of the Lord also told me, "I have blessed this country because of the Jewish people who are in this country. I have seven million Jews in this country, but they do not want to recognize the Lord. They didn't want to thank God for the blessing they received in this country. Israel doesn't want to recognize Jesus Christ. They put their faith in the Jewish people in America. But, when America burns, the Lord will raise China, Japan, and other nations to go against the Russians. They will beat the Russians and push them all the way to the gates of Paris. Over there they will make a treaty, and appoint the Russians as their leaders. They will then unite against Israel. When Israel realizes she does not have the strength of America behind her, she will be frightened. That is when she will turn to the Messiah for deliverance. That is when the Messiah will come. Then, the church will meet Jesus in the air, and he will bring them back with Him to the Mount of Olives. At that time, the battle of Armageddon will be fought."

When I heard all of this I said, "If you are truly the angel of the Lord, and everything you have told me is true, then all you have said must be written in the Bible." He said, "Tell everyone to read from Jeremiah 51:6-15, Revelation chapter 18, and Zechariah chapter 14, where Christ fights against those who possess the earth." "After His victory," the angel said, "there will be one flock and one Shepherd. There will be no need for light. The Lamb of God will be the Light. There will be no sickness, no tears, and no deaths. There will only be eternal joy and God will be the ruler. There will be only one language, only one song, and no need for a translator!"

"....And Dumitru," he continued, "a word of warning. If you keep anything from the American people that you are told, I will punish you severely." I asked, "How will I know that this is for real —that it will really happen?" "As a sign that I have spoken to you, tomorrow before you wake, I will send someone to bring you a bed, and at noon I will send you a car and a bucket of honey. After which I will send someone to pay your rent."

The next day someone brought Dumitru a bed, and at noon a car arrived with the bucket of honey. His rent also was paid, as God had promised him. Then the angel left.[3]

China and Russia Strikes

Vision received on April 22, 1996

I prayed then went to bed. I was still awake when suddenly, I heard a trumpet sound. A voice cried out to me, "Stand!" In my vision, I was in America [Note: at the time he was in Romania for a short visit]. I walked out of my home and began to look for the one who had spoken to me. As I looked, I saw three men dressed alike. Two of the men carried weapons. One of the armed men came to me. "I woke you to show you what is to come." He said. "Come with me."

I didn't know where I was being taken, but when we reached a certain place he said, "Stop here!" A pair of binoculars was handed to me, and I was told to look through them. "Stand there, don't move, and look," he continued. "You will see what they are saying, and what they are preparing for America."

As I was looking, I saw a great light. A dark cloud appeared over it. I saw the president of Russia; a short, chubby man, who said he was the president of China and two others. The last two also said where they were from, but I did not understand. However, I gathered they were part of Russian controlled territory. The men stepped out of the cloud. The Russian president began to speak to the Chinese one. "I will give you the land with all the people, but you must free Taiwan of the Americans. Do not fear, we will attack them from behind."

A voice said to me, "Watch where the Russians penetrate America." I saw these words being written: Alaska, Minnesota, and Florida." Then, the man spoke again, "When America goes to war with China, the Russians will strike without warning." The other two presidents spoke, "We too will fight for you." Each had a place already planned as a point of attack. All of them shook hands and hugged. Then they all signed a contract. One of them said, "We're sure that Korea and Cuba will be on our side too. Without a doubt, together we can destroy America."

The president of Russia began to speak insistently, "Why let ourselves be led by the Americans? Why not rule the world ourselves? They have to be kicked out of Europe too! Then I could do as I please with Europe!"

The man standing beside me asked, "This is what you saw: they act as friends and say they respect the treaties made together. But everything I've shown you is how it will really happen. You must tell them what is being planned against American. Then, when it comes to pass, the people will remember the words the Lord has spoken."

"Who are you?" I asked. "I am the protector of America. America's sins have reached God. He will allow this destruction for He can no longer stand such wickedness. God, however, still has people that worship Him with a clean heart as they do His work. He has prepared a heavenly army to save these people."

As I looked, a great army, well armed and dressed in white, appeared before me. "Do you see that?" the man asked. "This army will go to battle to save My chosen ones. Then, the difference between the Godly and the ungodly will be evident." +

The Bear Awakes

The following is the last vision given to Dumitru Duduman in April 1997 just before he passed away.

I knelt to pray beside my bed, as I do every night before I go to sleep. After finishing my prayer, I opened my eyes but I was no longer in my room. Instead, I found myself in a forest. I looked around and to my right I saw a man, dressed in white, who pointed his finger and said, "See and remember." It took me a while to find out what he was pointing at. It was a small bear who seemed half dead lying on the ground. As I continued to watch this bear, it began to breathe deeper. With every passing minute, it seemed to revive itself, and as I watched, it also became angrier. It then started to grow. Soon it was larger than the forest floor and as it grew larger it continued to become angrier. It then began to paw the ground, so that when its paw would hit the ground, the earth would shudder. The bear continued to devastate all that stood in its path until it came upon some men with sticks trying to fend it off. By this time, the bear had grown so large that it simply crushed the men underfoot and continued to rampage.

I was stunned by what I saw and asked the man standing beside me, "What does this mean?" "At first, they thought the great bear was dead," the man said. "As it will begin to stir once again, they will consider it harmless. Suddenly, it will grow strong once more with purpose and violence. God will blind the eyes of those that continue to trample on the sacrifice of Christ's blood until the day the bear will strike swiftly. This day will catch them unprepared, and it will be just as you saw." The man then said, "Tell my people the days are numbered, and the sentence has been passed. If they will seek My face and walk in righteousness before Me, I will open their eyes that they may see the danger approach. If they only look to the approaching danger, they too will be caught up and trampled underfoot. Only in righteousness will they find safety." Suddenly, I was once again by myself in my room, on my knees, with sweat covering my face. [5]

End of the three visions.

Comments on the Visions

Mystery Babylon: For many years, students and teachers of eschatology have been asking how America would be engaged in the end times. As the world superpower, there surely must be a starring role for America. Since Russia, Egypt, Iran (Persia), Libya and even Ethiopia are cited in the Bible; they tried very hard to identify America in the Scriptures. Some link America to obscure names of either Sheba or Dedan, the merchants of Tarshish (Ezekiel 38:13). Others just plainly state, they do not believe the Bible mention America. This uncertainty and confusion were put to rest when an angel revealed to Dumitru; America is the Mystery Babylon referred to in Jeremiah 51:6-15, and Revelation chapter 18. We shall very briefly explain a point or two on these two Scripture references.

In the passage in Jeremiah quoted by the angel, verse 7 states, "The nations drunk her wine; therefore the nations are deranged." Truly, the nations are drunk with the 'wine' supplied by America. America has been exporting to the world her liberty in the form of wealth (petrodollars), filth, and lawlessness that the world is now getting drunk with it. In verse 13 it states, "O you who dwell by many waters, abundant in treasures," appropriately refers to America that border on the Atlantic Ocean, Pacific Ocean and the Gulf of Mexico.

In the Book of Revelation, both chapters 17 and 18 allude to the Mystery Babylon. However, about America the angel attribute it to chapter 18 only. Mystery Babylon characterizes a number of things. First, it describes a political system represented by the Babylonian Empire, which was active with their first king, King Nebuchadnezzar. Its ancient base was located in the present day Iraq. Second, it characterizes the religious system of the world represented by Roman Catholicism as described in Revelation chapter 17. Rome was the base for this religious system. Third, it refers to the commercial system of the world as represented by America which has its base headquartered in New York City.

Revelation 18 verse 3 says, "For all the nations have drunk of the wine of the wrath of her fornication, the kings of the earth have committed fornication with her, and the merchants of the earth have become rich through the abundance of her luxury." This description describes America's role in relation to the rest of the world.

Verse 7 says, ".... She glorified herself and lived luxuriously; .....and says in her heart, "I sit as queen, and am no widow, and will not see sorrow." It brings to mind America's female Statue of Liberty.

And Verses 17-19 says, "For in one hour such great riches came to nothing. Every shipmaster, all who travel by ship, sailors, and as many as trade on the sea, stood at a distance and cried out when they saw the smoke of her burning, saying, "What is like this great city?" They threw dust on their heads and cried out, weeping and wailing, and saying, "Alas, alas, that great city, in which all who had ships on the sea became rich by her wealth! For in one hour, she is made desolate." Notice shipmasters are watching the destruction of the great city (New York) from a distance, wailing and inconsolable.

How the Judgment is being prepared: Since the collapse of the Soviet Union in 1991 and the end of the Cold War, America has let her guard down. There was a series of military exchanges between the Americans and the Russians. In 2009, a treaty was signed to provide a new strategic framework for military-to-military engagement between the two nations. The U.S. allowed Russian troops into the country to take part in military drills in 2012. We understand that joint training on land, at sea and in the air will not compromise one's national security. But Russian military officers, were invited to visit the U.S. Northern Command Center located at Peterson Air Force Base in Colorado Springs, Colorado. The command center incorporates the North American Aerospace Defense Command (NORAD) housed in the nearby Cheyenne Mountain. The place is the nerve center that coordinates the Air Force Space Command, the Defense Intelligence Agency, the National Security Agency, and the Missile Defense Agency. What this boils down to is that the Americans had allowed the Russians to enter their inner sanctum. It was never allowed before. From this visit, had the Russians obtained critical information that will help them to breach the American defense system when the time comes? Whatever the answer to this question may be, Dumitru already knew that the Russian will penetrate America's defense. If not, how else could the Russian nuclear missiles be successful to strike multiple American cities? Another point revealed to Dumitru is that Russian spies have located where the American nuclear warehouses are. These are places where sea and air-launch ballistic missiles are kept, including the land base Inter-Continental Ballistic Missile (ICBM) lodge in underground silos. Those nuclear weapons held in the warehouses will be sabotaged at the time of the attack.

Russia's strength weakened gravely, and her national security thrown into disarray following the breakup of the Soviet Union. The world, especially the Western world, felt relieved to see Russia (the primary state within the Soviet Union) is no longer a threat to them, even though Russia still possesses thousands of nuclear warheads. If Western leaders and planners, particularly the Americans, have a clear vision, they would have been able to see that Russia will eventually regain her strength. But as Dumitru was told, God had blinded their eyes because of their continuous rebellion against Him, which is in effect a trampling on the sacrifice of Christ's blood. Their blurred vision causes them to have a wrong perception of Russia's strength and determination today.

The bear is awakened. The bear is Russia's national symbol. In the last twenty years, Russia has settled much of her national debt and carried out massive modernization of her military assets, notably her nuclear-powered submarines and very advanced ICBM. Russia was and remains to be the only nation that could effectively challenge America. With her nuclear triad capability, she could launch nuclear strikes via their long-range nuclear bombers, by way of the land base mobile ICBM, and through the much feared Submarine Launch Ballistic Missiles (SLBM). Russia's nuclear triad capability was not something new. If, during the long period of the Cold War, the two sides could successfully restrain themselves from waging war with each other, why cannot this continue? Moreover, the relationship between them started to thaw since 1991. The situation back then was cold and threatening.

During the Cold War period, both sides had a high degree of respect for each other, despite being enemies. One would think twice of attacking the other knowing it would be suicidal to do so. The one who is being attacked could counterattack, and in a thermonuclear exchange, both sides will be annihilated. This mutually assured destruction (MAD) military doctrine had kept both parties at a safe distance from each other. Thus, world peace was preserved.

Today we are slowly creeping back to the cold war situation, to a new Cold War 2.0, although world leaders do not want to admit this publicly yet. Harsh rhetoric and provocative military drills from both sides are heightening the tension between America and Russia not seen since the old Cold War. How did this tension develop?

The Soviet Union had fifteen Soviet republics, covering Eastern Europe and Central Asia. Moreover, the Soviet Union had a military pact with eight other nations called the Warsaw Pact Countries, all located in Eastern Europe. The dissolution of the Soviet Union meant all these nations are free to enter into a new alliance with whom they choose. There is the North Atlantic Treaty Organization (NATO) ever willing to receive them into its fold. However, a year before the dissolution, there were several discussions between Soviet and American & NATO leaders on the need to treat this matter carefully. Although there was no written agreement, NATO had verbally stated it will not expand eastward, that is, not accept these former Soviet republics as members. Whatever verbal agreement or real intention that may exist, it has been thrown to the wind, as one after another of these nations have become NATO members. As of today, two remaining countries in Eastern Europe have not joined either Russia or NATO: Moldova and Ukraine. It is important to note, Russia has no military alliance with any of the former Soviet nations of Eastern Europe. There is only an economic partnership with Belarus under the Eurasian Economic Union. However, Russia has established a military alliance with China and some Central Asian nations who were former Soviet states. They named that alliance, Shanghai Cooperation Organization (SCO).[6]

Let us focus on Ukraine. Ukraine is a strategic nation to Russia and wants her to be under her sphere of influence. She shares a common border with Russia and acts as a buffer between Russia and NATO. Needless to say, Russia does not want her to become a NATO member, although most Ukrainians are in favor of joining. NATO, already with 28 members, should take into account Russia's security need and not accede to Ukraine's request. Instead of heeding Russia's objection, NATO will take in Ukraine in five years' time. There is an on-going NATO plan to install the Aegis Ashore in Romania and Poland. Aegis Ashore is a land-based component of the sea-based Aegis Ballistic Missile Defense System (BMDS).[7] The United States is ready to supply 44 units of the anti-ballistic missiles to be placed in Romania by end of 2015, and other units in Poland by 2018.[8] The BMD systems were previously limited under the Anti-Ballistic Missile (ABM) Treaty between the US and Russia to avoid a strategic imbalance. The United States backed out of that treaty in 2001. When Ukraine becomes a NATO member, NATO's defense system will essentially be at Russia's doorstep. A crisis will erupt that will become the 1962 Cuban Missile Crisis in reverse.[9] Indubitably, this system will be a serious threat to Russia, as it will render Russian ballistic missiles useless. Why is NATO so persistent?

The angel told Dumitru, God had blinded the leaders of the West that they could not see the danger of Russia. Understand that the driving force behind NATO is America, as she contributes the largest share in terms of finance and military assets within the alliance. The push by NATO up-close to the border with Russia is a *nyet-nyet.* The world is witnessing the anger of Russia as she tries to put the message across to the West, especially America. The Russian bear is pounding the ground with her paws. Sadly, the Americans are nonchalant to the apprehension of the Russians and continued steadfastly with their hegemonic goal for global dominance to fulfill their New World Order agenda.

Chronology of the Attack: As shown to Dumitru, the Presidents of Russia, China, and two other nations are discussing their plan of attack against

America. Very likely, they are members of the SCO, which also include the Central Asian states of Kazakhstan, Kyrgyzstan, Tajikistan and Uzbekistan. First, the Chinese will invade Taiwan, an attempt to reclaim back the island lost to the Kuomintang in 1949. China currently has 1,600 ballistic missiles aimed across the Taiwan Strait. [10] This invasion is the canary in the coal mine—a signal that Third World War has begun. America will come to the defense of Taiwan, which will set off a Sino-American war. With the conflict underway in the Central Pacific Theater, the Russian submarines off the coasts of Alaska, in the Gulf of Mexico, and possibly off the eastern coast of Florida will launch surprise nuclear strikes on America. American defense shield will be penetrated. Contrary to American military commanders' and planners' expectation, America will not be able to unleash a retaliatory strike against Russia. Visions God gave to other prophets not included in this book support this scenario. America's Strategic Command will fail to activate their strategic nuclear force to launch a retaliatory strike. Why do they fail at that crucial moment? One possible reason could be the effect of EMP (Electromagnetic Pulse). EMP could be caused by a solar storm or Coronal-Mass Ejections (CME).[11] Alternatively, it could be the Russian use of EMP weapons causing interference, permanently damaging all microchips used in electronic equipment and systems on the U.S. continent.[12]

Before China makes the move against Taiwan, which will signal for Russia to make the move against America, watch out for the internal revolution to break out in the middle of America. Americans will rise in rebellion against their government. They are commencing to do this on a smaller scale like the incidents in August 2014 in Ferguson, Missouri and April 2015 in Baltimore, Maryland. The one to look out for is a very major one, likely due to the collapse of the US dollar. The American administration is holding an important military drill like the Jade Helm 15 exercises in preparation for such eventuality. The leadership will be busy quelling the internal unrest, and will be unprepared for the coming judgment.

God's People will be Protected: Dumitru asked the angel how God will save and protect His people during the time of chaos and destruction. The angel told Dumitru that His people will be delivered just like the deliverance of Daniel from the lions' den. God will supernaturally seize them and transport them out of harm's way, something similar to what happened to Philip when the Spirit of God caught him up and relocated him elsewhere (Acts 8:39-40).

Because of this revelation, we know the judgment of America will precede the Rapture.

Why Single Out America? Because of the Jewish people living in America, the nation is blessed. In turn, America is a blessing to Israel. Why will God judge America if this is so? There are several reasons for this. First, God wants to wane America from Israel. Israel has become too dependent on her 'big brother.' The time is fast approaching when Israel need to make amends to the Messiah who loved her, but whom she has been ignoring for so long. Israel will pass through a great trial when America is not able to help her. In the furnace of affliction, she will repent and acknowledge her Messiah.

Second, we need to take the cue from what befell Judah and Jerusalem in the days of prophet Jeremiah. Because Judah and Jerusalem failed to repent and turn away from their wicked ways, God sent the Babylonian armies against her—the holy city was utterly destroyed. If it happened to Judah and Jerusalem with the Holy Temple, it could happen to America and New York.

Third, America will be removed to pave the way for Russia to rise as the next global superpower. Russia is destined to fulfill the Scripture. The book of Ezekiel chapters 38 & 39 is a set program drawn up for her to fulfill. She will launch an invasion of Israel, believing no other superpower will be there to stop her.

Chapter 13

COMING RUSSIAN INVASION OF ISRAEL

Russia will be the next superpower, albeit for a short time, after defeating America in the coming global war. Some nations will be forced to realign, forming new alliances. There will be changes in the NATO leadership structure as America's role will diminish. In a worst case scenario, the Alliance will disband. Whatever the outcome may be, Russia will step up to helm the leadership role in Europe. There will be new alliance established between them. As God had shown to Dumitru, an agreement will be inked between Russia and the European in Paris. Since Paris is the venue, we assume France will lead the Europeans in extending hand-shake with Russia.

The European acquiescence of Russia as their new leader will be a sweet dream coming true for the Russians. Russia has a vast landmass covering two continents with the western side more developed and populated than the east. She is happy in her friendship with China, her big, rich and strong eastern neighbor, particularly when both need to stand up to American hegemony. Notwithstanding, she has a greater desire to covet the respect and honor of her western neighbor, the Europeans. Having achieved this position in Europe, she is under pressure to lead the world as expected of a superpower.

The Israeli-Palestinian conflict that has been simmering for decades will be a strong draw for Russia, and the European will egg her on, to resolve this issue once and for all. For Russia and her partners, they will opt for a military solution of invading Israel.

Confederation of Nations Headed by Russia

The Russian invasion of Israel also called the Invasion of Gog mentioned in Ezekiel chapters 38 & 39 is an event prophesied more than 2,500 years ago. The fulfillment of this event is still in the future. Before we proceed to identify which nations are in the confederation, we should keep in mind the following factors:

a. Some of the nations alluded to by Ezekiel already existed in his days, namely: Persia, Ethiopia, Tarshish, and Dedan. Prophet Jeremiah (Jeremiah 25:23), who was a contemporary of Ezekiel, mentioned Dedan as well.
b. Gog, the land of Magog and the chief prince of Meshech & Tubal are located to the *far north* of Israel (Ezekiel 38:6, 15; 39:2). As they were situated at a considerable distance to the north, they could not be referred to Lebanon and Syria, who are Israel immediate northern neighbors.
c. Israel's immediate Arab neighbors are not listed in the Confederation that comprises Egypt, Lebanon, Syria, Jordan, and Saudi Arabia. Why? Very likely, these nations are in no position to fight having already gone to war with Israel earlier. The regional war could be a fulfillment of Palms 83 in which they lost the war and had to return the Temple Mount to Israel (See Chapters 7 & 8 on Shemitah and the Blood Moon).
d. Chemical, and perhaps biological, weapons will be used by the invaders as is indicated in Ezekiel 39:14-15. Incidentally, Russia possesses the largest stockpile of chemical and biological arms in the world.

We restate here the confederation of nations listed in Ezekiel:

Ezekiel 38:2-3, 5-6

2 "Son of man, set your face against Gog, of the land of
Magog, the prince of Rosh, Meshech, and Tubal, and prophesy
against him, **3** and say, "Thus says the Lord God: Behold, I am
against you, O Gog, the prince of Rosh, Meshech, and Tubal.

5 Persia, Ethiopia, and Libya are with them, all of them with shield and helmet; **6** Gomer and all its troops; the house of Togarmah from the *far north* and all its troops--many people are with you." (Emphasis added)

Below are the probable identities of these nations:

- Gog – The word means leader similar to a President, Chairman or Tzar of the Confederacy.
- Land of Magog – The land located in Russia, the Caucasus and Steppes, to the far north of Israel.
- Prince of Rosh – The word "Rosh" has two possible meanings. First, it means Chief. Hence, Prince of Rosh would be Chief Prince. Second, it could refer to Russia. If so, Prince of Rosh would be Prince of Russia.
- Meshech & Tubal – These two could be nations currently aligned with Russia in the Eurasian Economic Community: Belarus & Kazakhstan.
- Persia – Should be Iran.
- Ethiopia or Cush – Should be present day Ethiopia.
- Libya or Put – Present day Libya.
- Gomer – Could be the European nations (France included).
- Togarmah – Could be the nation of Turkey.

At the time of the Russian invasion, some nearby countries will voice their objection but nothing more:

Ezekiel 38:13
13 Sheba, Dedan, the merchants of Tarshish, and all their young lions will say to you "Have you come to take plunder? Have you gathered your army to take booty, to carry away silver and gold, to take away livestock and goods, to take great plunder?"

These nations could be:

- Sheba (Sabean) – Possibly refers to Yemen.
- Dedan – Could be the Kingdom of Saudi Arabia.

- The merchants of Tarshish – Tarshish is possibly one of the Southern European port or city hence, these are Western traders. Prophet Jonah tried to flee to Tarshish from Joppa (Jonah 1:3).

Occasion for the Invasion and the Outcome

America has been Israel staunchest supporter from the time of her establishment as a sovereign nation. However, the situation is changing. It will be a new phase, a new normal going forward. Israel will sense a great lost without America's long-standing support. One thing has not changed; the Arabs, who harbor varying degrees of hostility towards her, continue to be her immediate neighbors. Who will extend a hand to her should another conflict erupt in the region? A sense of being alone will grip her national consciousness.

Israel has gone to war many times with her neighbors. On some occasions, it was war with a coalition of Arab armies. In those wars, she was outnumbered in personnel and equipment, yet came out victorious. She could defend herself valiantly, and God was on her side. In the process, she has gained much valuable experience. Through the years, she beefed up her military strength, even equipped itself with nuclear capability. Service wise, Israel is ranked sixth most powerful in the world today.[1] Although a tiny state, she is a formidable force to be reckoned with. Despite these positive factors in her favor, she will soon find herself come face to face with a gargantuan challenge never encountered thus far. She will have to defend herself against, not just another coalition of armies but a coalition headed by Russia, a superpower.

A Peaceful People

Ezekiel 38:10-11
10 "Thus says the Lord God: "On that day it shall come to pass that thoughts will arise in your mind, and you will make an evil plan: **11** You will say, "I will go up against a land of unwalled villages; I will go to a peaceful people, who dwell safely, all of them dwelling without walls and having neither bars nor gates"

Russia and her allies will be jealous of the peaceful situation in Israel. In the past, she had protection from America and could feel secure but the situation is beginning to change. Although Israel does possess nuclear warheads, for some reason, the invaders think she will not use them. The atmosphere of the time is very tempting to invade.

To Take Plunder

> **Ezekiel 38:12-13**
> **12** to take plunder and to take booty, to stretch out your hand against the waste places that are again inhabited, and against a people gathered from the nations, who have acquired livestock and goods, who dwell in the midst of the land. **13** ......Have you gathered your army to take booty, to carry away silver and gold, to take away livestock and goods, to take great plunder?

The Israeli economy is base sharply on a technologically advanced market economy. Of human capital, she has a very highly developed labor force. Her major industrial sectors include high-technology products, electronic and biomedical equipment, agricultural products, metal products, processed foods, chemicals, pharmaceuticals, and transport equipment. Furthermore, she is actively pursuing development in software, semiconductors, and telecommunication.[2] These industrial knowledge, discoveries and skilled workers are highly sought after in this modern era. All this will be a great booty for the Russian and her allies, especially European allies.

Israel does not declare how much national silver and gold reserve she has, a practice common to most nations. The Israeli are planning to build the Third Temple, and these precious metals are essential for the production of the Temple paraphernalia. It will be surprising if they do not have a large stockpile of these valuable metals. The invaders must be very much aware of this and will want to lay their hands on them.

Invaders will be Judge

> **Ezekiel 38:21-22**
> **21** I will call for a sword against Gog throughout all My
> mountains," says the Lord God. "Every man's sword will be
> against his brother. **22** And I will bring him to judgment with
> pestilence and bloodshed; I will rain down on him, on his
> troops, and on the many peoples who are with him, flooding
> rain, great hailstones, fire, and brimstone."

This battle belongs to God. He will fight for Israel. God will cause confusion in the enemy camp, and they will start killing each other. A mighty earthquake will hit the ground underneath their feet (38:19).

> **Ezekiel 39:4-6**
> **4** You shall fall upon the mountains of Israel, you and all
> your troops and the peoples who are with you; I will give you
> to birds of prey of every sort and to the beasts of the field
> to be devoured. **5** You shall fall on the open field for I have
> spoken," says the Lord God. **6** And I will send fire on Magog
> and on those who live in security in the coastlands. Then they
> shall know that I am the Lord.

There will be the massive burial of the dead invaders in the battle field. Not only that, but judgment will fall on Russia itself and her allies. God will hit Russia and her allies with fire. What will the fire send on Magog be? Could it be nuclear missiles?

Implements of War Used as Fuel for Seven Years

> **Ezekiel 39: 9-10**
> **9** "Then those who dwell in the cities of Israel will go out
> and set on fire and burn the weapons, both the shields and
> bucklers, the bows and arrows, the javelins and spears; and
> they will make fires with them for seven years. **10** They will

> not take wood from the field nor cut down any from the forests, because they will make fires with the weapons;

The Israeli will use the implements of war left behind as fuel for the duration of seven years. There will be huge volume of military fossil fuel abandoned in the battle field. Parts from military equipment and vehicles could be dismantled and use for fuel. This period of seven years will more or less coincide with the time of the Antichrist reign.

Seven Months to Bury the Dead

> **Ezekiel 39:12-15**
> **12** For seven months, the house of Israel will be burying
> them, in order to cleanse the land. **13** Indeed all the people
> of the land will be burying, and they will gain renown for it
> on the day that I am glorified," says the Lord God. **14** They
> will set apart men regularly employed, with the help of a
> search party, to pass through the land and bury those bodies
> remaining on the ground, in order to cleanse it. At the end of
> seven months, they will make a search. **15** The search party
> will pass through the land, and when anyone sees a man's
> bone, he shall set up a marker by it, till the buriers have buried
> it in the Valley of Hamon Gog.

The manner in which the Israeli handle the dead bodies indicates deadly contamination by chemical and or biological weapons. The invaders will come with these weapons, but they will be like returning boomerangs—be killed by their arms. It will take seven months for the Israeli to bury the corpses properly, and cleanse the land. For this reason, we believe there will be no nuclear weapons use as induced radiation will cause the ground to be radioactive, and it will remain so for an extremely long time.

Invasion of Gog is not the Battle of Armageddon or the Battle of Gog & Magog

The Invasion of Gog is not to be confused with two other wars stated to break out at the time of the end. In the sequence of events, what follows the Invasion of Gog is the event of the Rapture. Dumitru was shown this clearly. After the Rapture, the seven-year reign of the Antichrist will commence.

The Battle of Armageddon is a great war to take place at the end of the seven-year reign of the Antichrist, and just before Jesus returns bodily to the earth in His second coming. All nations of the earth will be mobilized to gather to fight against our Lord in Israel. He will return physically to defeat the horde of the wicked, and set up His Millennial (meaning 1000 years) reign here on earth.

The Battle of Gog & Magog is the last war recorded in the Bible. During His Millennial reign, Satan and all his demons will be bound and cast into the bottomless pit where they will remain for a thousand years. At the end of the thousand years, they will be released. Satan will then marshal the rebellious people in the earth to wage a final war with the Lord and His saints.

The table below shows the differences between the three wars.

Invasion of Gog	**Battle of Armageddon**	**Battle of Gog & Magog**
Definite allies are mentioned (Ezekiel 38:2, 5, 6)	All nations are engaged (Revelation 16:14-16)	All nations are engaged (Revelation 20:8)
Since the Israeli used the implements of war as fuel for 7 years (Ezekiel 39:9-10), this indicates the second coming of Christ is still a few years in the future	This battle will end with the second coming of Christ, His feet touching down at Mount of Olives (Zechariah 14:1-7)	This battle occurs after the second coming and at the end of the one thousand years reign of Christ (Revelation 20:7-9)

The invasion is against the land of Israel only (Ezekiel 38:14-16)	The battle is against the land of Israel only (Zechariah 14:2; Revelation 16:16)	This satanically led battle is not only against Jerusalem & Israel but also against the camp of the saints (Revelation 20:9)

Chapter 14

RAPTURE

The world is in a state of war, the Third World War. Russia had teamed up with China to fight America. It was not to be a protracted war like the previous two world conventional wars. This time it was a thermonuclear one. It takes a much shorter time to determine the victor. After a brief break, perhaps a few months to a year, Israel will be dragged into the war as well when the Russian with her allies invaded her tiny state. Thus, in a short span of a few years, the world will have witness a global conflict fought in at least three regions of the globe: in the Pacific, the Atlantic, and the Mediterranean.

What has become of God's people in this tempestuous period? It is the time of the great tribulation His people have to pass through. It is the period of the fifth and sixth seals (See Chapter 3). Some are asking why God could allow the church to go through the Third World War. It is going to be a horrible time. Yes, it is going to be awful, so were the years during the First and Second World War. The church made it through, though, for God was with His people. We, the people of this generation, had only experienced peace, omitting the localized conflicts here and there. However, this test and the trial is needed to prepare His people, millions of them all over the world for the grand exit—to be raptured from the earth.

The Blessed Hope

Hope is the anchor for our souls. Our God is a God of hope, a very present help in times of trouble. He will make a way when there seems to be no way. He will rescue His people in the nick of time that we may praise His name for evermore. He redeems the soul of His righteous ones, and none who put their trust in Him will be disappointed. As King David of old had once said, "I have been young, and now am old, yet I have not seen the righteous forsaken…." (Psalm 37:25).

Revelation of the Rapture

Not forsaken, the rapture will be a blessing to the righteous. This English word "rapture" is derived from the Latin verb "rapere" found in the fourth century Latin Vulgate version of the Bible translated by St. Jerome. This Latin word was translated from the original Greek word "harpazo" meaning "snatch up" or "catch up" used in the Greek New Testament (1 Thessalonian 4:16-17). The New Testament was written originally in Greek, Koine (common Greek), and the language was widely spoken by the populace in the region at the time. It was written not in Hebrew as some mistaken it to be.

One day, in His conversation with His disciples, Jesus told them that He will be going away to a place where they cannot follow Him for now. Ill at ease at this announcement, Peter asked Jesus where He plans to go. The fervid Peter was prepared to die with Him if he is expected to. To calm their anxiety, Jesus explained His need to return to His Father in heaven so that He could prepare their heavenly mansions for them. After it is done, He will return to take them there (John 14:1-3). On some other occasions, Jesus did remind them of this matter. The last instance was at the Mount of Olives after His resurrection. As they gazed up at Him, Jesus was lifted up into the heavens. Two angels discreetly stood nearby said to them that the Lord will come back just the way they witnessed Him go up (Acts 1:9-11).

The disciples were very well aware of Jesus return from heaven—His second coming. From their vantage point, the time of His second coming will be far into the future, like a high mountain on the distant horizon. At first the solitary mountain was all there was to it, that is, Jesus coming will be in one act, one installment, so they thought. Soon they began to realize, as the Holy Spirit revealed to them, Jesus coming will be in two installments. It started to dawn on them that behind the mountain that they could plainly see was another mountain—the one in front blocking the one behind. Just veering off a bit to the side they could view two high mountains instead of one distinctly.

A careful examination of the more than three hundred Scripture references on the second coming of Christ attests to the fact that there are two phases to His return. Consider the hint that many scriptures are inconsistent with each other even though they refer to the same subject. We know there are no contradictions in the Word of God. Therefore, we conclude there must be one coming in two stages. First, He will come abruptly in the air to rapture His church, and lead them in a triumphant procession to heaven. There the saints, the Bride, will participate in the marriage supper of the Lamb. Second, about seven years later, He will return to the earth with His saints to set up His Millennium reign.[1]

The Rapture Event

The rapture event involves several parties. First of course is the Lord our Redeemer. Then, there are the redeemed saints who are already in heaven, the angels and last but not least, the faithful ones who are eagerly looking for the Lord's return. There are many Scripture verses alluding to this event. From these verses, a chronological order can be constructed, and it gets underway with the Lord descending from heaven ….

a. The Lord Himself will descend from heaven where He has prepared a place for us, to receive us to Himself (John14:1-3).
b. He will descend, accompanied by the voice of an archangel and the trumpet of God (1 Thessalonians 4:16).
c. When He comes, He will bring along with Him the redeemed who are now in heaven that they may resurrect first (1 Thessalonians 4:14-16).
d. Then, we who are alive and remain will join them, we will also be gathered in the cloud with the Lord (1 Thessalonians 4:17).
e. To join those in the cloud, we must go through translation. Our bodies that are corruptible will be made incorruptible, and that are mortal will be made immortal (1 Corinthians 15:51-54). The transformation will occur in a moment, in the twinkling of an eye.

f. From the gathering place in the cloud, the Lord will bring us with Him to heaven (John 14:3).
g. The redeemed, the saints, the Bride of Christ will attend the Marriage Supper of the Lamb (Revelation 19:7-9).

Blessed are those *invited* to the Marriage Supper of the Lamb!

When will be the Rapture?

Jesus personally asserted that no one knows the day or the hour in which He will return not even the angels nor Himself, but His Father only (Mark13.32). When He said that, He was still on earth. Now He is in heaven and ready to return; He could have known it by now. His declaration precludes anyone from attempting to set a date for His return. It will be an exercise in futility to do so. Even so, as we cannot know the day, can we know the season?

Some teachers of eschatology believe in the imminence of the rapture. The word "imminence" means "likely to happen soon." By that, they understand the rapture could take place anytime, without prior signs or scheduled events. It implies it could happen in the period of the early church or during the middle-ages or in our day. They draw our attention to certain Scripture references such as Matthew 24:42-44, Mark 13:35-37, Luke 21:34-36, 1 Thessalonians 5:1-6 and Revelation 3:3. These are some of the Scripture verses warning believers to be ready at all times. Yes, believers throughout the ages and everywhere should be prepared at all times. Even if the Lord delays His coming, one should be ready lest one suddenly passed away. A believer should passed away (Paul calls it "sleeps" 1 Thessalonians 4:13-14) in readiness, that is, in holiness not in sin. Otherwise, his salvation is in jeopardy.

Although the admonition to be ready at all times is a good take, there are factors to support the belief that the rapture will only occur after certain scheduled events have come to pass. For example, consider the cases of the return of the Jews to their homeland and the task of world evangelization currently in its tail-end. It is obvious Jesus did not come prior to these two developments. To press the point, He could not come, say, during the middle-ages, could He? Without a doubt, He could not. If He were to come then, there would be no Christian support for Israel in her effort to reclaim her homeland. Also, the task of world evangelization could not be accomplished.

Another event is the great falling away pointed out by the Apostle Paul (2 Thessalonians 2:1-12). Paul said the great falling away or the backsliding of the Church will occur prior to the Rapture. Indeed, presently this is underway. Given this development, the rapture could happen soon. As watchful believers, we should live as though the return of Christ is "likely to happen soon." Notwithstanding, certain events has to happen first before the rapture could materialize.

Now, let us consider events still in the future that need to come about first before the rapture.

Rapture to Occur During the Sixth Seal

The rapture event is destined to occur within the sixth seal (Revelation 6:12-17 and 7:9-17). The Seals, all seven of them, constitute a program. It is God's plan to prepare and bring His people home to heaven. The way to bring them there is through the rapture. The program started when the first seal opened. Moreover, the first seal was inaugurated in 2001.

We are now living in the period between the fourth and the fifth seal, and very soon the fifth seal will open. After a period of the fifth seal, it will be time for the opening of the sixth seal. Towards the end of the sixth seal, the rapture will occur. For further deliberation on this matter, refer to Chapter 3.

After the Judgment of America

We mention earlier, God show Dumitru Duduman this matter through one of his God-given visions. As he saw it, the rapture will only occur after Russia and China attack America. For further support, we wish to include here a vision that was given to A C Valdez, Sr. (1896-1981). He was born in California and was a Pentecostal evangelist. The Valdez family lived in Los Angeles, and they had participated in the famous Azusa Street outpouring in 1906. Below is his testimony that is self-explanatory:

Vision of A.C.Valdez, Sr.

In 1929, I was preaching in Vancouver, British Colombia. I had gone to the 6th Avenue Church that seats 1,000 people. The old building is gone. I sat down on the platform and looked down at the congregation for the Sunday morning service. There were 18 people. I had crossed the continent from Los Angeles to get to that meeting--18 people in my first service. My first thought was My Lord and my God, the nerve, asking me to come across the country to stand here in front of 18 people.

Now, that was my first thought. Now, I no sooner thought that when God spoke to my heart and said, "Son, I want you to comfort these people." They needed comfort, Brother. He gave me the capacity to comfort them. I started preaching comforting words. If I had given way to the human, Brother, I would have skinned them alive and tacked their hides up on the wall. People in a condition like that don't need a skinning; they need comfort. God helped me. He poured in the oil and the wine. He helped me to comfort those people.

They began to cry all over the place, as they needed comfort. The tears began to stream down their cheeks. They had gone through a terrible trial in that city, and the name of "Pentecost" was in the newspapers of that city, and it was not very good. The things that they had put into the newspapers were enough to keep most anybody away. I had 18 people in the inside and thousands on the outside.

God began to work, and the Spirit began to come forth. By the following Sunday, the place was well filled. The Holy Ghost began to bring them in. By the end of the third week, they had to take down the partition that separated the coat room from the main auditorium to put more seats in that auditorium that seated a thousand. It packed out. They packed the place, standing up and down the winding stairs and outside of the church building and out into the street. The glory of God came down. Souls began to get saved, and the sick were healed. We had a glorious victory over the world of flesh and the devil. The ministers were so happy. They said, "Lord, in spite of that death, you've given us victory."

Right in the middle of that victory, I stood in 6th Avenue Church one day with the power of God on me. All of a sudden the ceiling just disappeared. Now, when I say "vision," my friends, I know that some visions are what the Bible calls "night visions," like in a dream. You will find that in the Bible.

Dreams are also called "visions." Generally speaking, vision is differentiated by what you see with your eyes open, that which you see when you are not asleep. In this particular case, I was standing on my feet when all of a sudden the walls and the ceiling just faded right out. I began to see this vision, and the Lord showed me. I looked up and saw what answers to the description of an ICBM (Inter-Continental Ballistic Missile), just as real as any picture that you would see--or the real thing if you've ever seen one of those missiles. It was just as real as you would look upon one if it were right in front of you, two or three feet away!

I saw it. It was passing over a skim of clouds, not heavy clouds, but a thin skim of clouds. I was standing on the side of this mountain, a residential district. I was looking over into a bay area. It will appear like I was in Berkeley if you've ever been to Berkeley and the Berkeley hills. I was looking into the bay area toward San Francisco, the San Francisco Bay region, that direction.

I saw the freeway. I don't say that it was the Oakland freeway that is there today. I don't know where it was, my friends. I do know this, I was standing on the side of this mountain overlooking a huge metropolis, when I saw this missile directed toward the city; and suddenly, being electronically controlled, no doubt, it plummeted right down into the city and then exploded. Then I saw the fireball, which answers to the description of what I have seen in a civil defense film release of the first hydrogen bomb explosion.

This happened in 1929! The atom was not split until 1932! Yet I saw it as clear as I see you here tonight. There was a purpose in it. I have been warning people ever since that this thing is coming! As the day approaches, my friends, I feel more vibrant than ever before! I have got to bear testimony to what I saw with my eyes! I have got to warn God's people that they must live in the Spirit and walk in the Spirit and be filled with the Spirit if they want God's protection in these last days!

I saw this thing blossom out in all of its beautiful colors. Did you ever see a picture of it? It is a beautiful sight, but it is a horrible sight. All of the colors of the rainbow you can see in that big ball as it swells out. Then the pressure that it creates following the explosion, it demolishes everything before it. It leaves a crater over 300 feet deep and over 2 miles across. It is capable of destroying a huge metropolis the size of New York City in one blast. Even though there were no freeways in 1929, I saw freeways. I saw them run and jump in their cars to escape, but there was no escape! I saw the aftermath of this explosion. I saw all of the details.

The Spirit of the Lord picked me up. Like St. Paul, whether in the body or out of the body, I don't know! All I know is my friends that God took me and whisked me across that area where the bomb hit in the midst of that huge metropolis. There was nothing left. The center where it struck was molten, like molten glass. It was not, my friends until I was carried way beyond the residential area that I began to see any sign of debris.

Finally, I came to what looked similar to snow or sand drifts piled up against the fences and buildings. I saw piles or iron, like broom straw, only much finer than broom straw. It was in piles and patterns--everything completely destroyed! Finally, way, way out, beyond what I felt was the residential area. I began to find signs of human beings, only in pieces--torsos, heads, hands, arms, and legs. They were scattered around everywhere!

The Spirit of the Lord carried me out farther. I began to find signs of life. People were running. Everybody was blind. (I didn't know in 1929 that if you are 35 miles away from the explosion and you happened to be looking in that direction, you would never see again. I didn't know that at that time.) Everybody was blind, my friends. They were running and screaming and bumping up against this and that and the other, bouncing back, children blind and screaming and crying out for their parents and parents for their children. The farther I went, the more the confusion; and the cries increased.

My friends, even tonight, while I am speaking to you, I can hear those cries! I can hear those cries, children and parents screaming out for one another! It was a terrible sight to behold! If I were to live 10,000 years, I know I could just close my eyes and hear those screams and see the terror that was written all over the faces of parents and children! Indeed a terrible sight. Then, my friends, the Spirit of the Lord took me. Oh, I wonder how fast I was going. I could see the mountains and the hills just passing before me. I came sweeping down over a large valley. In the distance, I could see, as I began to approach, a body of people that looked like tens of thousands. I don't know how many were there. It was a sea of people. Long before I got there, I could see. As I came down closer, I could discern them. They had their handkerchiefs. They were wiping their tears from their eyes.

Then for the first time I began to hear heavenly anthems. I could hear the Hallelujahs, in bass and tenor and soprano and alto, voices blending together. That mass of humanity was lifted together by the heavenly music. I came right down in the midst of them. There they were; God's people. This is what I saw, friends. They were all dressed up like they were ready for the Sunday service. Their hair was parted. Nothing was disturbed. There was no soil on their shirts. They were cared for so perfectly that everything was in order, my friends. Their faces were clean. Their clothing was clean. Everything was in order! The only word you could use to describe them would be "meticulous." Meticulous! Glory to God! What a wonderful thing to be in the hands of God! I say that God is going to protect His people in these last days *if* they live in the Spirit and walk in the Spirit and keep filled with the Spirit! [2]

End of the vision.

Around the Time of the Invasion of Gog

In the vision showed to Dumitru Duduman entitled, "An Angel Revealed: America is the Mystery Babylon," the angel told him that after Russia attacks America, Russia will next invade Israel. It will be about that time that the Lord will come for His people. To recollect, refer to Chapter 12.

Preview of the Rapture

God in His great love and mercy has taken note of His people's struggle to maintain their faith in Him in these trying seasons. To encourage those who are weary and wavering, and to warn those who are backsliding, He had chosen to bless some of His servants with the preview of the rapture. This preview is meant for the body of Christ to take to heart. Provided below are visions from four godly men and women of God.

Mary K. Baxter

Mary K. Baxter is an Evangelist born in Tennessee, United States. She became a believer when she was nineteen years old. In 1976, Jesus appeared to her in bodily form, in dreams, visions, and revelations. Over a forty day period, Jesus came into her room and took her in the spirit to hell to show her the depths, degrees, levels and torments of lost souls in hell. Also, she was showed visions of heaven, the tribulation and the end times. Mary was ordained as a minister in 1983 at the Full Gospel Church of God in Taylor, Michigan. Since then, she has been sharing the message of the visions to the world. Included here is the vision of the coming rapture adapted from the book, "A Divine Revelation of Hell."

The Return of Christ

I saw the coming of the Lord. I heard His calls like the sound of a trumpet and the voice of an archangel. And the whole earth shook, and out of the graves came the righteous dead to meet their Lord in the air. For hours it seemed, I heard the horns blow, and the earth and the sea gave up their dead. The Lord Jesus Christ stood atop the clouds in vestment of fire and beheld the glorious scene.

I heard the sound of trumpets again. As I watched, those who were alive and remained on the earth ascended to meet them. I saw the redeemed as millions of points of light converging on a gathering place in the sky. There the angels gave them robes of purest white. There was great rejoicing.

It was given to the angels to keep order, and they seemed to be everywhere and giving special attention to the risen ones. A new body was given to the redeemed, and they were transformed as they passed through the air.

Great joy and happiness filled the heavens, and the angels sang, "Glory to the King of Kings!"

High in the heavens I beheld a large spiritual body—it was the body of Christ. And the body was lying on its back on a bed, and blood dripped to the earth. I knew that this was the slain body of our Lord. And then the body grew larger and larger until it filled the heavens. And going into and out of it were the millions of the redeemed.

I watched in astonishment as millions climbed up stairs to the body and filled it, beginning with the feet and continuing through the legs, the arms, the stomach, the heart and the head. And when it was full, I saw that it was filled with men and women from every nation, people and tongue on the earth. And with a mighty voice they praised the Lord.

Millions were seated before a throne, and I saw angels as they brought the books from which judgment was read. There was the mercy seat, and rewards were given to many.[3]

End of the vision.

Choo Thomas

Choo Nam Thomas was a Korean-American, born in Japan but raised in Korea. While still a teenager, she moved to America and was later married to Roger Thomas. In 1992, she became a Christian. Early 1996, she started to have a visitation from the Lord. From then until she passed away in 2013, the Lord took her to heaven seventeen times to show her many excellent things; and to hell twice. Also, she was showed the tribulation and the rapture. The Lord instructed her to record all her experiences in a book. She was to entitle her book "Heaven Is So Real." The Lord assured her the book would be a tool to lead many souls to salvation, and to prepare Christians for the rapture. Here is the rapture vision she saw:

Blessings Beyond the Blue

The first part of the vision was more like an impression rather than a visual experience. It seemed as if the whole world were excited. Earth's environment was noisy and busy. Then I began to see what all the activity was about.

The air was filled with white, moving objects. As the vision clarified, I saw people wearing white robes flying throughout the air. People were popping out of the earth everywhere and flying up into the air. The sky was literally filled with flying people, like birds in migration.

It was so unusual it was shocking. By this time I was singing loudly, and my hands were moving around like fists swinging at a punching bag. I had never felt this excited in my whole life. My body was jumping up and down because of the anointing and the shaking. I felt as if I were flying with the white-robed people I saw. The excited movement of my body and my vision-voice were so loud that I'm sure the whole house could hear me.

I had heard the rapture described before, but I had never imagined what an amazing spectacle it would be. I wondered what those who do not know Jesus would think when they observed such a scene. I was shocked and excited, but I'm sure they will be terrified.

This was the biggest surprise the Lord had ever shown me. It was the most awe-inspiring thing I'd ever seen—human beings flying through the air like birds. They soared upward with rocket-like speed. Some seemed to be soaring like kites in the wind on a clear, beautiful day.

I saw my one-year-old granddaughter. She was wearing a white robe, and her hair had grown to shoulder-length. She looked pretty grown up. At first I saw her at her house in normal clothing. Then suddenly she was wearing a white robe and flying through the air. I was dumbfounded by the vision. It certainly seemed to confirm that the Lord would be returning in the very near future.

Then I saw my daughter's ten-month-old daughter. She does not have much hair right now, but in the vision her hair was down to her shoulders, and, as my other granddaughter, she was flying through the air.

I began to cry and scream. The noise in the bedroom must have been astounding. It was a good thing that Roger was at work, for surely he would have been quite alarmed and concerned by such noise.

At first, I was not really sure if my crying stemmed from joy or sadness. My youngest granddaughter looked like she was also pretty grown up. I felt the Lord had a good reason for showing the children to me. First, I'm sure He wanted me to know that they will be with me in heaven to enjoy all eternity with Jesus. Second, I know He wanted me to see how old they will be when He returns. It is sooner than most people think.

The joyous vision changed. I saw the people who did not ascend with the others. Places on earth had been disrupted some had been turned upside down. It was noisy everywhere, and people were in an obvious state of panic. Terror was written on every face.

People were running wildly. Total pandemonium reigned. It seemed as if each person was searching for someone or something that they could not find. I began to cry like a little child as I watched people running down the streets. They were screaming and yelling. Some were trying to throw what few belongings they possessed into vehicles such as cars and boats. Thousands of boats were on the ocean. People were trying to escape.

Many men in uniforms were storming houses, ransacking them and taking the belongings they found. I noticed one family of four or five lying on the floor of a house. Most of them were on their stomach, and a pool of blood covered the floor.

Hundreds of people were fleeing on foot to the mountains. As they did, the uniformed guards fired guns at them, and several fell. Those nearest the guards were beaten with clubs and sticks.

I saw people destroying churches. A man threw a rock at a beautiful stained-glass window that showed Jesus with His lambs. The window shattered, and glass flew in all directions. I screamed more loudly.

One woman, who appeared to be looking for a lost child, was running through her house, shouting in panic and fear. She kept calling her child's name as she jumped up and down in total frustration and desperation. I wanted to help her, but there was nothing I could do. I cried and cried for her and for all the others.

Then I saw a family I know personally. The father ran into his house and rushed from room to room, calling the names of his wife and children. He found one member of his family, and they sat huddled in a corner of a room. They were holding tightly to each other and crying. I know who they are, but I am not at liberty to mention their names in this book.[4]

End of the vision.

David Jones

David Jones is Praise and Worship Leader, and a Preacher in the ministry for over 25 years. He is the founder of the Little David Ministries base in Charlotte, North Carolina. God had given David a vision of the end times which he share wherever he could. In January 2014, he was interviewed by Sid Roth on the TV program "It's Supernatural." Inserted below is a transcript of part of that interview.

The Final Day

One night in February 2012, I woke up to go to the washroom. I returned to bed but suddenly felt someone grabbed my shoulder, and I found myself being catapulted into an opened vision. I was hovering over 200 feet above the earth, and I could see the beautiful sky. People were going to and fro. I saw mothers with children going into the grocery stores. There were people pumping gas at the station and businessmen with ties going into buildings.

Then all of a sudden, a thick cloud of darkness appeared over the earth. All of a sudden, there was a sound from heaven. It was like seven claps of thunder mesh into one. The sound was so deafening it pierces the ears of all mankind. It began to penetrate their skin. When they heard it they began to shake; people began to scream.

Then all of a sudden, like someone take a razor blade and split the heaven, there comes the Son of God with all His band of angels. He was coming speedily to the earth.

People began to urinate on themselves and scream. I heard one man said, "No, no, no. Wait, wait, wait, I thought I had time." But it was too late. Another man, he looks like an Indian man, he began to say, "No, no, no, this is a dream, a dream. Wake up, wake up."

Then I heard a voice from heaven saying, "This is the Day of the Lord. It has come."

I came out of the vision, and I was shaking. I began to pray for myself because God allowed me to see such terror. We know God is a God of love, mercy, longsuffering, gentleness, kind, but there is another part of Him that mankind has not known—that is the terror of the Lord.

I began to repent for my life. I said, "Lord save me! God forgive me! Lord, I want to please You! Whatever I have done wrong, forgive me. Please count me worthy to go back with You."

I have seen the Day of the Lord. Then the Lord spoke to me and said, "I charged you now to warn all mankind." He continued to say, "I am coming, I am coming, I am coming! Whether they believe you or not, give them the warning for Me. Whether they receive you or not, give them the warning from Me." [5]

End of the vision.

Prophet David Edward Owour

God had communicated with Prophet Owour in numerous visions and dreams about the end times. God showed him hurricane, earthquake, tsunami, famine, plane crash, volcanic eruption, economic crisis, flood, and the outbreak of racial and political violence occurring in various countries. Aside from these, the Lord revealed to him the state of the church today and the urgency to put the situation in order, for His soon returns. In the early hours of April 27, 2011, he had a dream in which he received a preview of the rapture taking place.

Vision of the Rapture of the Church

I was at a meeting. I could recognize the place, the people, even the country. In that meeting, I was making the announcement on the coming of the Messiah. I was speaking about the great need for the church to prepare in absolute righteousness and holiness.

In the midst of the preaching, and it was a big meeting; I was busy talking about the nations of the earth to prepare wisely in the fear of the Lord. The time came I told the ushers in the meeting to go sit down that they also may listen to the message.

At the time the ushers had gone to sit when they had just sat down, then the glorious rapture took place. I saw some people struggling. I saw a lot of people fail to make it. I saw them remain, did not enter the kingdom of God.

I saw the glorious church, how they took off into the sky. I saw their gown very pure, whiter than white paper. They went off all the way to the cloud, and they entered into the mighty glory of the Lord. They entered, and a mighty cloud came to close up the entrance to heaven.[6]

End of the vision.

Rapture Only for Those Ready

Not everyone who calls or labels himself Christians will experience the rapture. Some have departed already from the faith (1Timothy 4:1). Within the church at large, some segments are in the state of apostasy. The Apostle Paul already alerted us when he said, "Let no one deceive you by any means; for that Day will not come unless the falling away comes first…." (2 Thessalonians 2:3). The falling away is apostasy, and apostasy must precede the rapture. These groups or people were once in the faith, but have now fallen away, and left the faith. If they left the faith, then they are no longer in the church? Not necessarily so. A local congregation can fall away, just as a whole denomination can. They have departed from the faith yet still are label as Christians. To these people, faith is no longer a dynamic relationship with Christ but has been relegated to be just a religion. The religion is labeled "Christianity," and it has a form of godliness, but they deny its power (2 Timothy 3:5).

The church is more than a building with a name on it—it is the people. Apostasy in effect is a betrayal of the people, betrayal of the One, who loved us and had given His life for us. Like Judas Iscariot, betrayal comes in three stages: [1] those who pretend to be His disciples but secretly love the things of the world (John 12:6), [2] those who secretly consort with His enemies (Matthew 26:14-16), and [3] those who openly side with His enemies (Matthew 26:47-49) [7]

Within the church at large, we find people defiled with worldliness and sins, and in extreme cases, being entangled in doctrines of demons, involvement in occult practices, and are living the abominable lifestyle. Some denominations or local congregations are conspicuous in their apostasy. Others may not be so obvious. However, within each group or congregation there is a mixture of people—some have kept themselves pure while others are defiled. To be part of the actual glorious church, one has to be pure. Christ is coming for a radiant church, a church that does not have spot or wrinkle or any such thing but is holy and without blemish (Ephesians 5:27).

The clarion call for the season we are in is to be ready for the coming of the Lord. Those who do not heed the warning will be left behind. The rapture is a very special event. Normally, one has the time to repent before death. There may be a few days opportunity, perhaps a few hours or even a few minutes to get oneself right with God. However, the rapture does not give us that luxury, not even a few minutes.

Should the rapture occur while church service is going on, how many will go and how many will not? It is not automatic that the one who is in a church meeting will be raptured. To be counted worthy for the rapture is more than just attending church service or church meeting. There is more to this. As was shown to Prophet Owour, a significant number of those attending the church meeting did not make it. As there are numerous local churches in the world, there are many scenarios. In some churches, everyone will be raptured while none in the other churches. In some, only 70% manage to go, while in others only 20%. In some congregations only the church ministers and leaders, while, in some other congregations, most of the members go up except the ministers and leaders. It is a sobering thought to ponder on.

God has been giving His Church many wake-up calls. Many view the calls lightheartedly. But a wake-up call is not a wake-up call if there is no necessity to wake-up. Some Christians who are not living right heard the wake-up call but do not understand what they need to do to wake up. The seriousness of a wake-up call is equivalent to the gravity to wake-up. How serious is it for the Church to wake-up? The Bible warned us to be ready for His return. Here again, the warning to be ready cannot be a warning if there is no need to prepped. It is meaningless to issue warning if there is no need to be all set. Some Christians have become so dull that they could not understand what to be ready means.

How should one be ready? While men look at outward appearance, God looks at the heart. To Him, readiness has to do with the condition of the heart. The heart needs to be holy, nay, to be pure for only those who are pure in heart will see God (Matthew 5:8). We are being admonished to pursue peace with all people. And we are being advised to seek holiness. We can't hope to see the Lord without fulfilling these conditions (Hebrew 12:14).

The Ten Virgins

The Lord gave us the parable of the ten virgins as a dramatic preview of the condition prevailing in His church at or about the time of the rapture. The parable is quoted here in full.

Matthew 25:1-13

1 "Then the kingdom of heaven shall be likened to ten virgins who took their lamps and went out to meet the bridegroom. **2** Now five of them were wise, and five were foolish. **3** Those who were foolish took their lamps and took no oil with them, **4** but the wise took oil in their vessels with their lamps. **5** But while the bridegroom was delayed, they all slumbered and slept. **6** And at midnight a cry was heard: "Behold, the bridegroom is coming; go out to meet him!" **7** Then all those virgins arose and trimmed their lamps. **8** And the foolish said to the wise, "Give us some of your oil, for our lamps are going out." **9** But the wise answered, saying, "No, lest there should not be enough for us and you; but go rather to those who sell, and buy for yourselves." **10** And while they went to buy, the bridegroom came, and those who were ready went in with him to the wedding, and the door was shut. **11** Afterward the other virgins came also, saying, "Lord, Lord, open to us!" **12** But he answered and said, "Assuredly, I say to you, I do not know you." **13** Watch, therefore, for you know neither the day nor the hour in which the Son of Man is coming.

The ten virgins represent the church. Of the ten, five are wise but the other five foolish. All are going to meet the Lord, the Bridegroom. They have their lamps with them. The wise ones are aware of the importance of oil and goes out to fill their lamps with it. The foolish ones are negligent and overlook this essential element. Come to think of it, what is the use of the lamp without oil?

In this context, the oil represents the Holy Spirit. Every lamp must be filled with oil for it to be useful, and every believer must be filled with His Spirit to be ready. The wise ones are diligent followers of Christ, and they treat this matter seriously. The foolish ones do not appreciate Him (Holy Spirit). We are told not to quench Him (2 Thessalonians 5:19), but instead to be filled with His presence (Ephesians 5:18). It is being filled and walking in the Spirit that we have victory over the flesh and worldliness. After that, it is the Holy Spirit who will have the final say whether one is ready to be raptured or not.

It is Him we must please and not grieve— we grieve Him to our great peril (Ephesians 4:30).

For whatever reason, the arrival of the Bridegroom is delayed. All the virgins go into slumber and sleep. The situation becomes melancholic yet it will not stay that way forever. In the meantime, notice even the wise ones are falling asleep. What is the meaning of this metaphor? To be sleeping suggests that one is not active, not actively pursuing God. There is a sense of weariness and despondency and is not this the state of affairs prevailing in the church today? Why is this so? It is due in part, to the condition of the world which is becoming more and more ungodly. People's hearts are growing in coldness towards the gospel, towards the call to repentance. Now, is falling asleep a sin? Is to be weary and despondent a sin? Not in itself, no.

Then, suddenly at midnight hour will raise a cry that the Bridegroom is coming. Everyone is to wake up and go out to meet Him speedily. All the *ten virgins wake up*, but only the wise ones were ready. It seems the wise ones slept in their readiness. Readiness is a matter of the heart, and because their hearts are pure and full of His Spirit, they are welcome into the kingdom of our Lord.

Are you in the state of readiness?

Chapter 15

70TH WEEK OF DANIEL

The Rapture is a pivotal event. Multiple millions of Christians have left the earth in a sudden collective manner. The world is in a state of shock. What will become of the inhabitants of the earth who remain? What will the governments of the world do? What will happen to Israel? What will be the scenario from this point forward?

After the rapture, the European Union will rise to be the next superpower on the world stage, filling the power vacuum created by the departure of Russia. As head of the European Union, the Antichrist will attempt to bring Israel and the Arab neighbors to the peace table, to ink a Peace Treaty lasting seven years. The Antichrist will reign as the world dictator during this period of seven years. Who is the Antichrist? Why is he from the European Union? The Antichrist will mediate a Peace Treaty between Israel and the Arab neighbors that will last seven years: why seven years? The seven years is a puzzle derived from the 70th week of Daniel.

To understand what the 70th week of Daniel refers to, let us go back to the history of Israel to the days of Prophet Daniel.

Through Prophet Jeremiah, a contemporary of Prophet Daniel, God warned the inhabitants of Judah and Jerusalem that the Babylonian would conquer Jerusalem, and the Jews would be taken captives into exile to Babylon. Following that calamity, the city of Jerusalem would be in a state of desolation for 70 years (Jeremiah 25:8-13; 29:10). Accordingly, the word of the Lord came to pass, and Daniel as a teenager was among those banished to Babylon.

In the process of time, the Medes and Persian Empire overthrew the Babylonian Empire. In the first year of the Persian King Darius reign, Prophet Daniel, who by then was in his late 70's, read the writing of Prophet Jeremiah and understood the exile will last 70 years. That awareness moved him to intercede for his people (Daniel 9:1-19).

In response to his prayer, angel Gabriel appeared to Daniel with a message from God. The message was that God had a program to deal with the Jewish people and with the city of Jerusalem which will be within a time frame of 70 weeks. The program is quoted here for easy referral:

> **Daniel 9:24-27**
> **24** "Seventy weeks are determined for your people and for your holy city, to finish the transgression, to make an end of sins, to make reconciliation for iniquity, to bring in everlasting righteousness, to seal up vision and prophecy, and to anoint the Most Holy. **25** "Know therefore and understand, that from the going forth of the command to *restore and build Jerusalem* until *Messiah the Prince*, there shall be seven weeks and sixty-two weeks; the *street shall be built again, and the wall*, even in troublesome times. **26** "And after the sixty-two weeks Messiah shall be cut off, but not for Himself, and *the people of the prince who is to come shall destroy the city and the sanctuary*. The end of it shall be with a flood, and till the end of the war desolations are determined. **27** Then he shall confirm a covenant with many for one week; but in the middle of the week He shall bring an end to sacrifice and offering. And on the wing of abominations shall be one who makes desolate, even until the consummation, which is determined, is poured out on the desolate." (Emphasis added)

What is meant by 70 "weeks"? The word week in Hebrew is *shabua* meaning "seven." The Jews have these expressions: "week of days" and "week of years." In this particular case, the 70 weeks refers to "70 weeks of years." Hence, the 70 weeks is laid out as 70 x 7 equals 490 years. The year specified here is the prophetic year. Note that each prophetic year has 360 days only unlike a solar year that has 365.24 days or a lunar year which has 354.37 days.

Now, by the end of the 70 weeks of years or 490 years, God intends to:

a. Finish the transgression
b. Make an end of sins
c. Make reconciliation for iniquity
d. Bring in everlasting righteousness
e. Seal up vision and prophecy
f. Anoint the Most High

The issues [a] to [c] above are tackled already by the Messiah's death on the cross of Calvary—the removal of sins from the nation of Israel and the world. The remaining issues of [d] to [f] will see accomplishment during the reign of the Messiah—the establishment of His millennial kingdom here on earth.[1]

When did the program of the 70 weeks of years or 490 years set in motion? Sir Robert Anderson in his book "The Coming Prince," [2] developed a chronology based upon the Jewish calendar, and on Daniel's prophetic timetable of 360 days to a year (e.g. 42 months = 1260 days). Through it he was able to determine the starting and closing date of the program. His presentation, however, was fined tune by Harold Hoehner in his book "Chronological Aspects of the Life of Christ." [3]

The program began with the command or decree to restore and build Jerusalem issued by King Artaxerxes to Nehemiah (Nehemiah 2:1-8) in his 20th year of reign. The established date of this decree was on 1st Nisan 444 BC reckoned to correspond with 5th March of the Gregorian calendar. Bear in mind that there were two other decrees issued earlier to this one:

a. Decree of King Cyrus issued in 537 BC (Ezra 1:2-4; 6:3-5); and
b. Decree of Artaxerxes given in 458 BC (Ezra 7:7-8; 11-26).

The two decrees above, however, were for the *restoration and service of the temple,* not about *rebuilding Jerusalem and its streets and walls.*

From 1st Nisan 444 BC or 5th March until the Messiah the Prince shall be 69 weeks or 483 years i.e. 7 weeks + 62 weeks equals 69 weeks (Daniel 9:25). The 7 weeks or 49 years refers to the time taken to complete rebuilding the streets and wall of the city. The following 62 weeks or 434 years will be the time lap for the appearance of the Messiah, more specifically to His last visit to Jerusalem just before His crucifixion. Hoehner had determined the triumphal entry of Jesus was on 10th Nisan which corresponded with 30th March AD 33 of the Gregorian calendar.[4]

Using the calculating method Anderson used, Hoehner arrived at his conclusion as follows:

Decree issued 444 BC	
Triumphal entry into Jerusalem AD 33	
Intervening period was 476 years, and	
Based on Solar years 476 x 365.24 days	173,855 days
Add (5th March 444 BC to 30th March AD 33)	25 days

	173,880 days
	========

Tally:	
69 weeks of prophetic years of 360 days	
i.e. 69 x 7 x 360	173,880 days
	========

Four days after Jesus the Messiah's entry into Jerusalem on Monday 30th March AD 33, He was crucified or "cut off" on Friday 3rd April AD 33 (Daniel 9:26a).[5]

After the Messiah was cut off the "people of the prince" shall come and destroy the city of Jerusalem (Daniel 9:26). History tells us that the Roman army under General Titus surrounded and finally destroyed Jerusalem in the year AD 70. So, the "people" were Romans, and the "prince" was a Roman. Pay attention that this prince is different, is not the "Messiah the Prince" who is Christ the Lord mentioned in Daniel 9:25a.

There appeared to be a significant gap between the 69th week and the 70th week. God's program for the Jewish people encountered suspension unceremoniously. Apparently, the purposes of God stipulated in verse 24 could not be completely achieved. His people rejected their own Messiah, and He has yet to establish His millennial kingdom on earth. It would take the remaining week of 7 years to see the consummation of His program.

Closing of the Church Age

The Messiah the Prince had inaugurated His kingdom in Israel. However, it was not received by the people, principally the national leaders. The rejection of Him as their Messiah meant they also rejected His kingdom. It prompted God to, without delay; open His kingdom to the Gentiles. It is true that God will eventually do that should the people of Israel at the outset believe and receive Him as their Messiah. Their misapprehension of how their Messiah should be caused them to misjudge Him. They expected Him to be from the royal family, live a regal life, and inaugurate His kingdom in a portentous manner to overthrow the shackle of the Roman Empire. Their wrong decision was a nightmare bringing untold suffering to them and their posterity. If not for their doggedness to have Jesus crucified, the Romans would not have carried it through. The acts of the Romans, representing us the Gentiles, incriminate all of us in putting the sinless One to death. Thus, all of us both Jews and Gentiles are found guilty and in need of mercy. Oh, the depth of the riches both of the wisdom and knowledge of God. How unsearchable are His judgments and His ways past finding out! (Romans 11:33).

The Church Age is the period in which God the Father opens His kingdom to welcome the Gentiles. Out of those who respond He will prepare a bride for His Son. This monumental task was assigned to the Holy Spirit, the third person of the Trinity. The Holy Spirit came *officially* to the earth on the Day of Pentecost (Acts 2:1-4). When He has done His job, He will carry the bride of Christ to heaven. It will be at the time of the rapture. Hence, the rapture will mark the *official* return of the Holy Spirit to heaven (2 Thessalonians 2:7). Does this mean that henceforth the Holy Spirit will no longer be on the earth? Yes, officially. Officially, He will not be on the earth anymore but He will carry out His work similar to the time in the Old Testament. There is more grace for the inhabitants of the earth when He is officially here; more judgment when He is not. Sinners can still be saved, by the skin of their teeth. However, they have to come through the Jews who will be entrusted for a short time to carry out global evangelism through the 144,000 Jews (Revelation 7:1-8).

God's Program For Israel Lasting 70 Weeks or 490 Years
(Daniel 9:24-27)

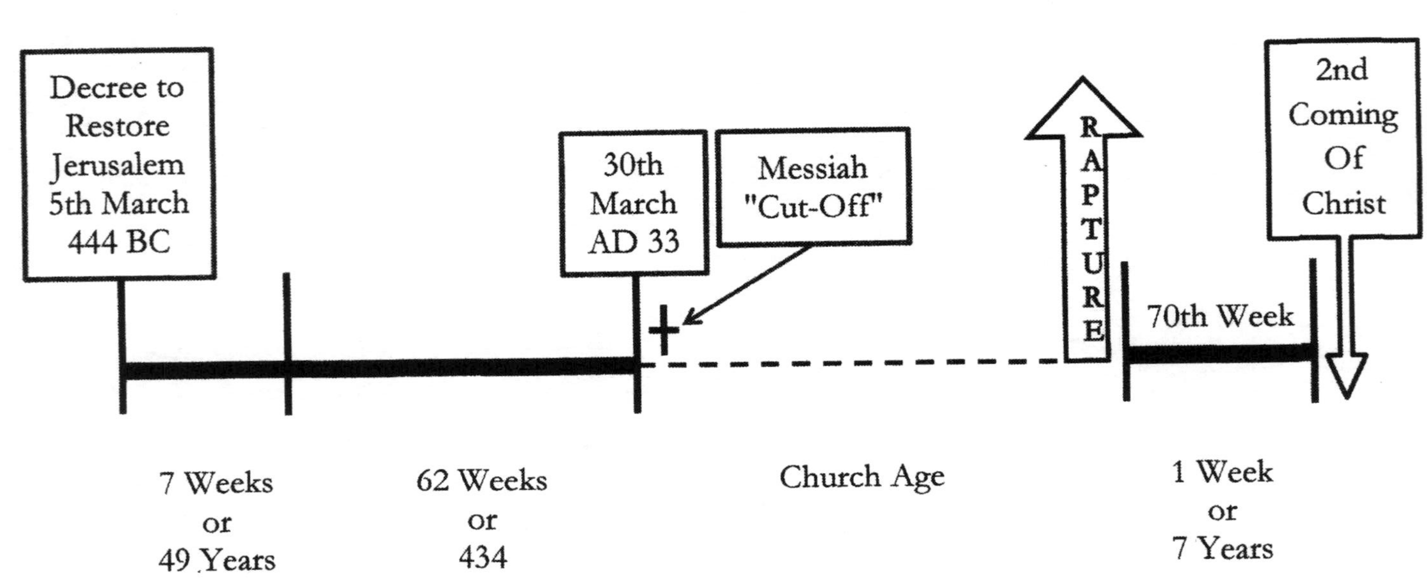

Some will raise this question: the manner in which the Holy Spirit comes to the earth and returns *officially*, does this manner also apply to the Father and the Son? The Bible seems to tell us that this applies to them as well. First, the Father Himself came to the earth. He instructed Moses to build Him a Tabernacle in the wilderness. When Moses completed in building it, the Father came to take up His residence in the building. He made Himself visible via a cloud that covered the Tabernacle (Exodus 40:34-35). Later, when the Temple was built by King Solomon to replace the Tabernacle, He transferred His presence there (1 King 8:1-11). Initially, He was happy to dwell in the midst of His people. Unfortunately, they grieved Him greatly by their heinous sins. The day came when He decided to leave the Temple and the earth because He could no longer endure their idolatrous behavior. For that occasion, He had Prophet Ezekiel to bear witness to His departure. Ezekiel was at the time exiled to Babylon. The Father took him from there and brought him in the Spirit to the Temple in Jerusalem. Ezekiel was led to view all the abominable acts and idols the children of Israel kept inside there (Ezekiel 8-11). Before He departed, He had the angels destroy in the city those who did not have contrite heart or attitude (9:3-11). The Father left, sitting on His mobile throne, carried by the cherubim (10:9-19). Thus, the Father officially came to dwell in the Tabernacle and officially left as witnessed by Ezekiel.

Secondly, officially the Son also came when He was born of the Virgin Mary (Luke 2:6-20). When He was 30 years old, He began His public ministry. After His three and half years of ministry that culminated with His death on the cross, He was taken up into heaven. On that day on the Mount of Olives, Jesus' disciples were witnesses of His official departure from the earth (Acts 1:9-11).

Finally, the Church Age will close after the rapture. God's attention will revert to His dealing with Israel, His ancient covenant people. The 70 weeks of years or 490 years program that was interrupted by the Church Age will resume.

Roman Prince is the Antichrist

When the 70th week or the last 7 years resume, the Roman prince identified as the "he" in Daniel 9:27, shall confirm or mediate a covenant with many parties for 1 week. Bible scholars agree that the covenant will be between Israel and the neighboring Arab nations.

The Roman prince is the Antichrist. Right here, the question of where the Antichrist will come from is settled. He cannot be an American President, or the Ayatollah of Iran, or the Mahdi of Saudi Arabia. This person is alive in the world just prior to the Rapture. After the Holy Spirit left the earth with the Bride of Christ in the rapture, the Antichrist will appear on the world scene. He could not reveal himself earlier because of the presence of the Holy Spirit who exerts His great power over the spirit of the Antichrist. The Bible states that the Holy Spirit is the Restrainer, who restrains him (2 Thessalonians 2:3-10).

Meaning of the Term "Antichrist"

The term "antichrist" is found only five times in the New Testament, all in the epistles of John (1 John 2:18, 22; 4:3; and 2 John 7). The Apostle John was the only Bible writer to use the name Antichrist. Other writers use other terms to describe this villainous person. From the scriptures given, it appears there are two subjects: the *spirit* of the antichrist and the *person* of the Antichrist. While the spirit remains unchanged through the ages, there were and will be many antichrists persons appearing between the times of Christ's first and second coming.

In 2 Thessalonians 2:3-4, the Antichrist is described as the "man of sin" or "son of perdition" ("the man doomed to destruction" NIV). Interestingly, Judas Iscariot was also labeled as the son of perdition by our Lord in His prayer to the Father (John 17:12). For openly revolting against Jesus, Judas Iscariot was possessed by Satan or "Satan entered him" (Luke 22:3-4; John 13:26-27). In like manner, the Antichrist will be possessed by Satan.

The prefix *anti-* can mean "against" or "in place of" (i.e.as an impostor). So, will the Antichrist be the person who is against the Christ or be an impostor of Christ when he appears? The answer is both. He will be Christ chief opponent, and will attempt to play a counterfeit role as though he is the real Christ.

Antichrist Role in Israel

The Jews will appreciate the Antichrist for his effort to mend fences between Israel and the Arab nations. They will look to him as a capable world leader—an admirable peacemaker. Through his charismatic charm, he will solicit cooperation and support from Israel. This pleasant situation will prevail for the first half of the 70th week. Sometime in the middle of the week, his true color and intent will be exposed when he demands the Jewish people worship him as a god.

The Jewish people are traveling this path to have a close encounter with this imposter because they rejected Christ when He came and continued to resist Him until today. They refuse to acknowledge the true One and will end up embracing the false one. They shall have what they want. The imposter will take them for a costly ride. In the middle of the week, the Antichrist will invade Israel and demand the Jews cease their temple sacrifice and offering. He wants them to worship him instead (Daniel 9:27; Matthew 24:15; 2 Thessalonians 2:4). This insistence will be repulsive to the Jewish people, who upon their refusal to bow to him, will face his severe wrath (Daniel 7:21, 25). Many Jews will flee the land because of the persecution (Matthew 24:16-22). He is obnoxious in character, speaking blasphemies against God (Daniel 7:8; Revelation 13:5-6). He will go as far as desecrating the rebuilt Third Temple. This state of the affair will last throughout the second half of the 70th week of Daniel (Revelation 11:2; 13:5).

In the final accounting, why will the Jews not accept the Antichrist as their Messiah? It could very well be that he is a Gentile and not a Jew. The Jews will be thinking why he is forcing them to cease temple sacrifice and offering. It is against their perennial religious belief. Their Messiah would not order them to act contrary to their religious belief, would He?

On this observation, there is another assumption that he is a Gentile. As the ruler of the revived Roman Empire, he should be a Gentile. The leaders of the previous empires, Babylonian, Medes-Persian, Greek and Roman Empires were all Gentiles.

Building the Third Temple

Since the Antichrist will compel the Jewish people to worship him as he "sits as God in the temple of God, showing himself that he is God" (2 Thessalonians 2:4), it stands to reason that the Third Temple will be built. There is currently no Temple on the Temple Mount. The Muslim Dome of the Rock and the Al-Aqsa Mosque are what occupies the site where the Third Temple should be. The Temple will be completed and fully operational by the middle of the 70th week.

From the time the Israeli took control of the old City, various groups have started working to prepare for the day when they could rebuild the Temple. Among them, the earliest organization is the Temple Mount & Land of Israel Faithful Movement (in short the "Temple Mount Faithful") founded by Gershon Salomon. He was an officer in the Israeli army who fought in the Six-Day War and was among the first batch of soldiers to enter the old City by the Eastern Gate. They immediately went up to the Temple Mount to inspect the site.

While walking with great excitement from place to place on the Temple Mount, they encountered a mysterious person. Let him relate what happened: "Suddenly a civilian appeared and presented himself as a tour guide. He was not dressed as an Arab and did not speak Arabic, but English. He asked us to allow him to guide us on the Temple Mount. When we asked him why he wanted to do this he told us that G-d sent him to show us the location of the Jewish Temple and to tell us that the G-d of Israel had returned the Temple Mount to his children Israel. He took us to the Dome of the Rock, showed us the rock, and said that this is the location of the Holy of Holies. Then he took us to the Eastern Gate and said the Messiah, the seed of David, will come from here. He said that even in the Koran it is written that G-d will redeem His chosen people Israel and will return them to their place on the Temple Mount. He said: "You can see with your own eyes that the time has come, and I am sure that Israel will soon rebuild the Temple." As we walked from place to place, he suddenly disappeared, and we did not see him anymore. He was no longer on the Temple Mount. Each of us was sure that he was an angel sent by the G-d of Israel to share with us and all the people of Israel the godly significance of this godly moment. He appeared as a human being as in the biblical times, but we were so sure that he was an angel of G-d." [6]

One of the long-term objectives, as stated on the organization website of the Temple Mount Faithful is: "Liberating the Temple Mount from Arab (Islamic) occupation. The Dome of the Rock and the Al-Aqsa mosque were placed on this Jewish or biblical holy site as a specific sign of Islamic conquest and domination. The Temple Mount can never be consecrated to the Name of G-d without removing these pagan shrines. It has been suggested that they be removed, transferred to, and rebuilt at Mecca." [7]

Another prominent group, founded in 1987 by Rabbi Yisrael Ariel is called the Temple Institute. The Institute has been laboriously reconstructing vessels and accouterments that will enable ritual service in the future Temple. Apart from the sacred vessels, other objects include the garments of the high priest, musical instruments, a massive chandelier, a small altar, and a large outdoor altar. Some of this paraphernalia, numbering over a hundred pieces, are on display in the Institute premises for visitors to view.[8] The Institute is also planning to establish a school for the priesthood. When the Third Temple opens, it will need priests who are already familiar with their work.

The Sanhedrin

The Sanhedrin was the council of seventy-one Jewish sages who constituted the Supreme Court and legislative body in Judea in the time of Christ, the Roman period. It patterned after the Council that Moses set up as God instructed him (Numbers 11:16). The president of the council was called a *nasi*, once headed by the Chief Priest but could be any respected sage. The *nasi* is a title usually translated "prince," or "captain." Assisting him was a vice-president, known as the *Av Beit Din* (father of the court), who presided over the Sanhedrin in the absence of the *nasi*. The Sanhedrin with the full seventy-one members is called the Great Sanhedrin. It presided over heavier matters of the law. There was a local Sanhedrin located in every town. It consisted of fewer numbers of sages in its council, and these handled minor local issues.

The Sanhedrin continued to function for more than four hundred years after the destruction of the Second Temple. Since then, there have been several

Orthodox attempts to re-establish it with the first known attempt in 1538. It was not successful due to disagreement among the Rabbis. Subsequent attempts in 1830, 1901, 1940 and 1949 yield the same result.

In 2004, a few Rabbis headed by Rabbi Dov Levanoni managed to bring together hundreds of the most influential and scholarly Rabbis living in Israel.[9] Out of that fruitful meeting, the modern-day Sanhedrin was formed as the sages felt the pressing need for such an institution at this time. At present, the Institution is still in a developing stage. It is because Israel has not yet achieved Halachic State status on par with its previous position. A Halachic State is a state governed by *Halakha*, the Jewish religious law that comprises the oral and written Torah.

Presently, Israel is a secular state with a democratic parliamentary system of rule. For its judiciary, it has two coexisting legal systems: the civil and the religious courts. The latter also called rabbinical court is vested with varying degrees of authority in matters related to Jewish religious life. Not unexpected, there is a conflict between the two systems. In the Israeli public space and among political parties in the Knesset, supporters of both systems are arguing and debating on the merits of their respective system for the sake of the nation. However, there is a growing support for the establishment of a Halachic State. When it is eventually formed it will be a dream comes true especially for members of the Sanhedrin.

When the Third Temple is set up, there will be a religious revival in Israel. It is a certainty that the democratic system currently dominates will be replaced by the divine religious system. The Sanhedrin will be at the forefront of the primary governing body of the nation. The Sanhedrin would have achieved an important goal, that is, to act as a vehicle to bring about Jewish unity and civil justice, and to help repair some of the deepest rifts in Israeli society.

The role of the Sanhedrin is paramount. In the days of Jesus, it was that Institution, representing the Jewish nation that tried and rejected Him as their Messiah. In the gospel account, the Institution is referred to simply as the Council (Matthew 26:59; Luke 22:66). In the very near future, the Council has to overturn its earlier decision, made nearly 2,000 years ago, to accept and welcome Jesus as their rightful Messiah.

The turnaround in the hearts of the Jewish people is what God is waiting to see. The immense task ahead requires real spiritual awakening. It will have to replace the religious revival that preceded it. The religious revival brought changes to the governmental structure, and through the Temple, worship is brought into the public sphere. This development is good but not enough. What the religious revival fail to achieve, the spiritual awakening will accomplish. The hearts of the Jewish people as a nation will be converted. As one voice, they will call out that name that they were unable to utter for two millennia: the name is Yeshua Hamashiach.

The 144,000 Jewish Evangelists

For the purpose of a genuine spiritual awakening, 144,000 Jews will be sealed and anointed. It will comprise twelve thousand from each of the twelve tribes of Israel (Revelation 7:3-4). They will be ministering within Israel and also sent out to the world to preach the everlasting gospel to every nation, tribe, tongue, and people. Their message will be simple: Fear God and give glory to Him, for the hour of His judgment has come (Revelation 14:6-7).

The Father's name will be on their foreheads (Revelation 14:1). It is a seal that will provide them supernatural protection at least until they have accomplished their task.

The Two Witnesses

God will place His two witnesses among His people. They will prophesy for 1,260 days (3.5 years) clothed in sackcloth (Revelation 11:3). Who are these two witnesses of Yeshua? Some believe they are Enoch and Elijah because both never died bodily. Enoch walked righteously with God, and God suddenly took him way (Genesis 5:24). Prophet Elijah rode on the chariot towards the sky and was not found (2 Kings 2:11-12). However, others think it more likely to be Moses and Elijah; the former represents the Law and the latter the Prophets.

God will endow them with unlimited power. They will be able to shut up heaven, so there is no rain. They will turn water into blood and to strike the earth will all kinds of plagues as often as they wish. Their testimonies will induce active persecution against them. However, the opposition will not be tolerated. Those who try to harm them will be hurt themselves, and those who try to kill them will die instead (Revelation 11:5-6). The strict rule of the law will apply. It will be "life for life, eye for eye, tooth for tooth, hand for hand, foot for foot, burn for burn, wound for wound, and stripe for stripe" (Exodus 21: 23-25). It will be the dispensation of the Law, for the period of grace had terminated when the Church Age closed.

With their ministries accomplished, the Antichrist will have victory over them. They will die, and their bodies lie on the street in Jerusalem unburied for three and a half days. The world will witness this drama and celebrate (Revelation 11:7-10).

After the three and a half days are up, a voice from heaven will summon them. The world will be in shock to see them resurrected and ascended into heaven before their eyes. In that same hour, a powerful earthquake hit the city destroying a tenth part of it and killing 7,000 people. What happened will exert at least a positive note. Those who witness the drama "were afraid and gave glory to the God of heaven." (Revelation 11:11-13).

God is a loving Father, who is "not willing that any should perish but that all should come to repentance" (2 Peter 3:9). The two witnesses are God's last effort to see that men everywhere, in Israel and elsewhere, repent and enter into eternal life.

Chapter 16

7 YEARS REIGN OF THE ANTICHRIST

In the preceding chapter, we described the role of the Antichrist in relation to Israel. Here we shall look at his broader role as the global dictator. His reign lasts 7 years; the full length of the time coincides with the period of the 70th week of Daniel. Note that this 7 years' time frame is not called the "7 years tribulation period" in this book. The phrase "7 years tribulation period" is a misnomer. This phrase inferred there is no tribulation before this time. The truth is; the Great Tribulation had just occurred prior to this period (fifth and sixth seals of Revelation 6:9-17; 7:9-17). This Great Tribulation transpires at the end of the Church Age, to purify the Church for the rapture. The other Great Tribulation is to chasten the Jews before the Messiah returns in His second coming (Matthew 24:15-29). This second Great Tribulation will break out in the middle of the 7 years when the Antichrist defiles the Jewish Temple. It will last three and half years but will be shortened somewhat. Jesus said those days would be cut short for the sake of His people. Otherwise, no one will survive (Matthew24:22).

Before particularizing the Antichrist activities, we shall first rehearse the development of his empire.

As the Roman Prince, the Antichrist comes out from the old Roman Empire, which today is the European Union, the Revived Roman Empire. We know this from the prophetic word given to Prophet Daniel. He saw the various empires rule the world starting from his day and ending with Christ second coming to set up His eternal kingdom. The message was given to him wrapped in two dreams. The first dream was given to the Babylonian king, King Nebuchadnezzar that Daniel helped to interpret. The second dream was a dream he received from God.

Nebuchadnezzar's Dream: The Metallic Man

Nebuchadnezzar was the first king of the Babylonian Empire. In the second year of his reign, he had a frightful dream. It troubled him so much he commanded all wise men, magicians, astrologers, and sorcerers to assemble in his palace. He demanded they interpret his dream. As they could not, he ordered to have them all killed. Daniel and his three companions were among those marked for death as they too were considered wise men.

Daniel was a young lad and had been in exile in Babylon for the third year up to that time. He requested the king for permission to unravel the dream. After he had sought God in prayer, he was ready to tell the king and interpret the dream. In the king's dream, there was an image of a man, a metallic man.

> **Daniel 2:31-45**
> **31** "You, O king, were watching, and behold a great image! This
> great image, whose splendor was excellent, stood before you,
> and its form was awesome. **32** This image's head was of fine
> gold, its chest and arms of silver, its belly and thighs of bronze,
> **33** its legs of iron, its feet partly of iron and partly of clay. **34**
> You watched while a stone was cut out without hands, which
> struck the image on its feet of iron and clay and broke them in
> pieces. **35** Then the iron, the clay, the bronze, the silver, and
> the gold were crushed together, and became like chaff from
> the summer threshing floors; the wind carried them away so
> that no trace of them was found. And the stone that struck
> the image became a great mountain and filled the whole earth.
> **36** "This is the dream. Now we will tell the interpretation of
> it before the king. **37** You, O king, are a king of kings. For
> the God of heaven has given you a kingdom, power, strength,
> and glory; **38** and wherever the children of men dwell, or the
> beasts of the field and the birds of the heaven, He has given
> them into your hand, and has made you ruler over them all—
> you are this head of gold. **39** But after you shall arise another
> kingdom inferior to yours; then another, a third kingdom of
> bronze, which shall rule over all the earth. **40** And the fourth

> kingdom shall be as strong as iron, inasmuch as iron breaks in pieces and shatters everything; and like iron that crushes, that kingdom will break in pieces and crush all the others. **41**
> Whereas you saw the feet and toes, partly of potter's clay and partly of iron, the kingdom shall be divided; yet the strength of the iron shall be in it, just as you saw the iron mixed with
> ceramic clay. **42** And as the toes of the feet were partly of iron and partly of clay, so the kingdom shall be partly strong and
> partly fragile. **43** As you saw iron mixed with ceramic clay, they will mingle with the seed of men, but they will not adhere to
> one another, just as iron does not mix with clay. **44** And in the
> days of these kings the God of heaven will set up a kingdom which shall never be destroyed, and the kingdom shall not be left to other people; it shall break in pieces and consume all
> these kingdoms, and it shall stand forever. **45** Inasmuch as you
> saw that the stone was cut out of the mountain without hands and that it broke in pieces the iron, the bronze, the clay, the silver, and the gold—the great God has made known to the king what will come to pass after this. The dream is certain, and its interpretation is sure."

The head of the metallic man is of gold, its chest and arms of silver, its belly and thighs of bronze, its legs of iron, and its feet and toes of iron and clay. Daniel deciphered the various metals as representing five Gentile empires. From the head down, they are the Babylonian, Medes-Persian, Greek, Roman, and Revived Roman Empires.

History confirms the truth of the interpretation. Of the five empires, four are already history. We could accurately determine their beginning and their fall. The table below shows the epoch in which they rule.

Metallic Man	Empire	Period of the Empire
Head of Gold	Babylonian	606-536 BC
Chest & Arms of Silver	Medes-Persian	536-330 BC

Belly & Thighs of Bronze	Greek	330-27 BC
Legs of Iron	Roman	27 BC – AD 476/1453
Feet & Toes of Iron & Clay	Revived Roman Empire (Union for the Mediterranean)	AD 1948 – Christ 2nd Coming

The fifth empire symbolized by the feet and toes of iron and clay is yet to manifest itself fully. We shall have more to say about this later. But Daniel saw all these Gentile kingdoms were destroyed by the God of heaven when He comes to set up His eternal kingdom. Figuratively, the kingdom of God is depicted as a stone cut out of a mountain without hands. The stone smashes against the feet of the metallic man that causes the whole image to collapse and break up into pieces.

Daniel's Dream: The Four Great Beasts

King Belshazzar succeeded King Nebuchadnezzar, and in his first year of reign, Daniel had a dream.

Daniel 7:2-25

2 Daniel spoke, saying, "I saw in my vision by night, and behold,
the four winds of heaven were stirring up the Great Sea. **3** And
four great beasts came up from the sea, each different from
the other. **4** The first was like a lion and had eagle's wings. I
watched till its wings were plucked off, and it was lifted up
from the earth and made to stand on two feet like a man, and
a man's heart was given to it. **5** And suddenly another beast, a
second, like a bear. It was raised up on one side and had three
ribs in its mouth between its teeth. And they said thus to it:
'Arise, devour much flesh!' **6** After this I looked, and there was
another, like a leopard, which had on its back four wings of a
bird. The beast also had four heads, and dominion was given to

it. **7** After this, I saw in the night visions and behold, a fourth
beast, dreadful and terrible, exceedingly strong. It had huge
iron teeth; it was devouring, breaking in pieces, and trampling
the residue with its feet. It was different from all the beasts
that were before it, and it had ten horns. **8** I was considering
the horns, and there was another horn, a little one, coming
up among them, before whom three of the first horns were
plucked out by the roots. And there, in this horn, were eyes
like the eyes of a man, and a mouth speaking pompous words.
9 "I watched till thrones were put in place, And the Ancient of
Days was seated; His garment was white as snow, And the hair
of His head was like pure wool. His throne was a fiery flame,
Its wheels a burning fire; **10** A fiery stream issued And came
forth from before Him. A thousand thousands ministered to
Him; Ten thousand times ten thousand stood before Him. The
court was seated, And the books were opened. **11** "I watched
then because of the sound of the pompous words which the
horn was speaking; I watched till the beast was slain, and its
body destroyed and given to the burning flame. **12** As for the
rest of the beasts, they had their dominion taken away, yet
their lives were prolonged for a season and a time.**13** "I was
watching in the night visions, And behold, One like the Son
of Man, Coming with the clouds of heaven! He came to the
Ancient of Days, And they brought Him near before Him.
14 Then to Him was given dominion and glory and a kingdom,
That all peoples, nations, and languages should serve Him. His
dominion is an everlasting dominion, Which shall not pass
away, And His kingdom the one Which shall not be destroyed.
15 "I, Daniel, was grieved in my spirit within my body, and the
visions of my head troubled me. **16** I came near to one of those
who stood by, and asked him the truth of all this. So he told me
and made known to me the interpretation of these things: **17**
'Those great beasts, which are four, are four kings which arise
out of the earth. **18** But the saints of the Most High shall receive
the kingdom, and possess the kingdom forever, even forever

> and ever.' **19** Then I wished to know the truth about the fourth beast, which was different from all the others, exceedingly dreadful, with its teeth of iron and its nails of bronze, which devoured, broke in pieces, and trampled the residue with its feet; **20** and the ten horns that were on its head, and the other horn which came up, before which three fell, namely, that horn which had eyes and a mouth which spoke pompous words, whose appearance was greater than his fellows. **21** I was watching; and the same horn was making war against the saints, and prevailing against them, **22** until the Ancient of Days came, and a judgment was made in favor of the saints of the Most High, and the time came for the saints to possess the kingdom. **23** "Thus he said: 'The fourth beast shall be A fourth kingdom on earth, Which shall be different from all other kingdoms, And shall devour the whole earth, Trample it and break it in pieces. **24** The ten horns are ten kings Who shall arise from this kingdom. And another shall rise after them; He shall be different from the first ones, And shall subdue three kings.**25** He shall speak pompous words against the Most High, Shall persecute the saints of the Most High, And shall intend to change times and law. Then the saints shall be given into his hand For a time and times and half a time.

In the dream, Daniel saw four great beasts arose from the sea. They are the lion, bear, leopard, and a dreadful unidentified beast. The beasts represent the five Gentile empires similar to the metallic man symbolizing those empires in Nebuchadnezzar's dream. The two dreams are complementary and also match in this manner:

Metallic Man (Daniel 2)	**Empire**	**Four Great Beasts (Daniel 7)**
Head of Gold	Babylonian	Lion
Chest & Arms of Silver	Medes-Persian	Bear

Belly & Thighs of Bronze	Greek	Leopard
Legs of Iron	Roman	Dreadful Beast
Feet & Toes of Iron & Clay	Revived Roman Empire (Union for the Mediterranean)	Ten Horns & the Little Horn

Daniel's attention began to focus on the dreadful beast (Daniel 7:19). He wished the angel to tell him more about this fourth beast (Daniel 7:23) which corresponded to the Legs of Iron of the metallic man. The beast represents the Roman Empire.

The Roman Empire commenced when Augustus became its first emperor in 27 BC, replacing nearly 500 years of the Roman Republic. Under his reign, the empire's frontiers enlarged to include Egypt, northern Spain and large parts of central Europe. For the next 100 years from the death of Augustus in AD 14, the empire reached its height under the reign of Hadrian. The extent of the empire stretched from the Middle East to northern Britain and from Egypt to Germany. Practically, the whole expanse of land bordering the Mediterranean Sea came under Rome's jurisdiction.

As there are two Legs of Iron, the Empire had two parts: Western and Eastern. In AD 284 Diocletian became emperor. The empire became too big to govern. So, he split it into two. He kept the Eastern half because of its wealth and trade. In AD 285 Diocletian appointed Maximianus to rule the Western half. In AD 306, civil war broke out in both parts of the empire. Commander Constantine took control of both regions by AD 324 and ruled it as a single empire. In AD 330, Emperor Constantine shifted the capital from Rome to the Eastern region and named the capital Constantinople in his honor (Constantinople is present day Istanbul, the capital of Turkey). At the end of the reign of Emperor Theodosius I, the Empire split again into West and East in AD 395. This time the rift was permanent.

By AD 476, the Western Roman Empire collapsed. Historians offered numerous reasons for the decline and fall of the Roman Empire. Some of the factors put forward include diseases, decadence, war, manpower shortages, and economic stagnation, loss of revenue from taxation, inept foreign policy, and even Christianity. However, there is yet another view. It postulates that the Roman Empire did not *fall* rather there was a *transformation* of the Roman world.[1] The Western Roman Empire saw its last ruler, Romulus Augustulus deposed in Rome in AD 476. But the Eastern Roman Empire continued until the Ottoman Sultan Mehmet the Conqueror overtook Constantinople in 1453. Whichever view one holds, whether the empire *fell* or went through a *transformation* process, the Bible predicts the empire will be revived. On the metallic man, the Feet and Ten Toes typify that because these parts of the body are a continuation of the legs.

How will the Roman Empire revive itself? Has it taken place already?

Revived Roman Empire

The Roman Empire was "mortally wounded" (Revelation 13:3; 17:7-8). In fulfillment of what was predicted, amazingly, it started to heal with the revival of the Western Roman Empire. It commenced with the signing of the Benelux Agreement in 1948. It was an economic agreement between Belgium, the Netherlands, and Luxemburg. In the ensuing years, the group grew into what is today known as the European Union with 28 countries joined as members. Below is a table showing the expansion of the Union.

Year	Countries Joining
Benelux Agreement June 8, 1948	Belgium, the Netherlands & Luxemburg
Treaty of Rome 1957	Italy, France, Germany (EEC)
1973	The UK, Ireland & Denmark
1981	Greece
1986	Spain & Portugal
1995	Austria, Finland & Sweden

By 2013	Bulgaria, Cyprus, Czech Republic, Estonia, Hungary, Latvia, Lithuania, Malta, Poland, Romania, Slovenia, Slovakia, Croatia
Total	28 Countries

With the former Western Roman Empire revived, what has become of the eastern part? Today, the nations of the old Eastern Roman Empire around the Mediterranean basin are members of the Mediterranean Partner Nations. It comprises 16 member states located in North Africa (Mauritania, Morocco, Algeria, Tunisia, Egypt, and Libya), Middle East (Turkey, Syria, Lebanon, Israel, Jordan and the Palestinian Authority), and the Balkans (Albania, Bosnia and Herzegovina, Montenegro, and Monaco).

In 1995, the Barcelona Process was launched to establish cooperation among this group of nations with the European Union. The association is called the Euro-Mediterranean Partnership (Euro-Med). The Secretariat is in Barcelona, Spain from which the process derives its name. On 13 July 2008, the Euro-Med expanded and was relaunched as the Union for the Mediterranean (UfM) at a summit in Paris.[2] With the establishment of this Union, the Revived Roman Empire consolidated itself. The Eastern part has now joined the Western part. It affirms the Two Feet of the metallic man place side by side each other (Daniel 2:33). The Union for the Mediterranean is the alternative term for the Revived Roman Empire.

> The Union for the Mediterranean is the alternative term for the Revived Roman Empire

How is the cooperation getting along between the Western and the Eastern Revived Roman Empire? Matter of fact, it was pristinely shown to Daniel that they will not work well together. The Western part is more advanced economically and stronger militarily than the Eastern part. The democratic system governs the Western part, which is generally of the Christian faith. On the other hand, the Eastern part is predominantly Islamic. The intransigence of the different language, culture, and religion makes cohesiveness difficult. The angel pointed out to Daniel that iron does not mix well with clay. There is strength in iron but not in clay. So, the empire will be partly strong and partly weak (Daniel 2:41-43). Note also that the mixture of iron and clay is within each foot, not one-foot iron and one-foot clay. In other words, the weakness is also felt within each part of the Revived Empire. It explains why we often witness the inability of the European Union to speak or act as one. The same goes with the Islamic Mediterranean Partner Nations.

Extending out from the Feet of the metallic man are the Ten Toes. These are ten kings (Daniel 2:44). It corresponds to the Ten Horns projected out from the head of the dreadful beast. They are also said to be ten kings (Daniel 7:24). Who are these ten kings? For clues, we need to turn to the Apostle John's vision.

The Apostle John also saw the Gentile kingdom beast. While Daniel saw the *individual* kingdom beasts, John saw the *corporate* kingdom beast (Revelation 17:3).[3] The beast that John saw had seven heads and ten horns. It "was and is not, and will ascend out of the bottomless pit and go to perdition" (Revelation 17:8). It refers to the time the Roman Empire fell and disappeared but is being revived. And the world marvels at its revival.

The *corporate* beast has seven heads that represent seven kings or empires. History tells us there are seven empires that rule that part of the world from ancient days. These empires have impacted the Jewish people one way or the other. They are Egyptian, Assyrian, Babylonian, Medes-Persian, Greek, Roman and the Revived Roman Empires. During John's time, five had fallen, one is, and the other is yet to come (Revelation 17:10). From John's perspective, living during the period of the Roman Empire, the first five empires have indeed already come and gone. The one is, was the Roman Empire. The other yet to come refers to the Revived Roman Empire.

But John was told that the seven heads are also seven mountains which the purple and scarlet woman sits (Revelation 17:4, 9). The woman is the great city (Revelation 17:18) built on seven mountains. There are dozens of cities in the world built on seven hills or mountains. The famous ones include San Francisco, Staten Island, Athens, and Rome. As the great city has influence over "people, multitudes, nations, and tongues" (Revelation 17:15), Rome would be the best choice to represent the woman. Although Rome sits on seven literal mountains, the mountains symbolize seven Gentile empires. To say it in another way, the spirit of the seven Gentile empires has made its home in Rome. One has to visit the Vatican museum to get an inkling of this impression.

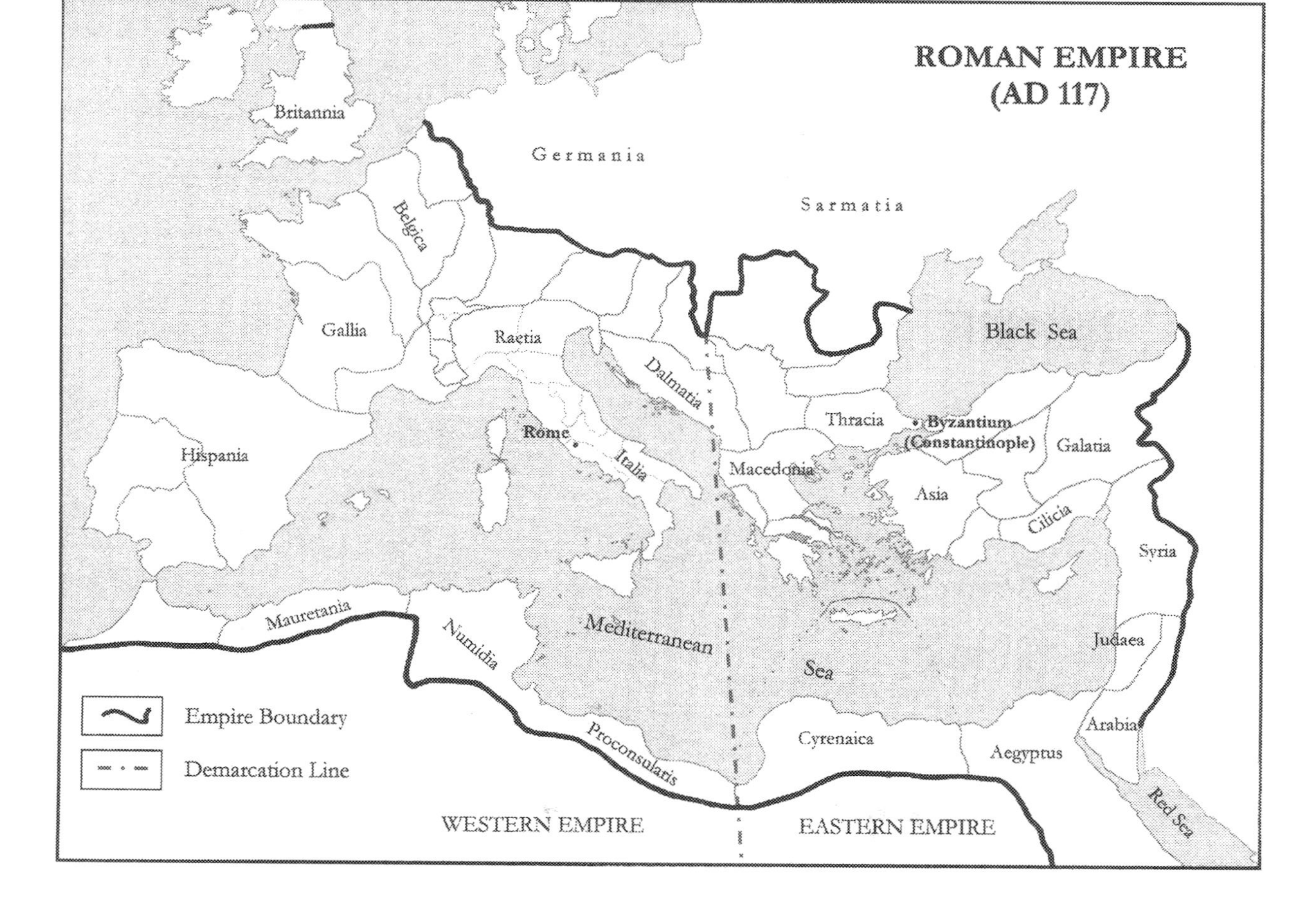
ROMAN EMPIRE
(AD 117)
Britannia
Germania
Sarmatia
Belgica
Gallia
Raetia
Black Sea
Dalmatia
Thracia
Byzantium
(Constantinople)
Galatia
Rome
Hispania
Italia
Macedonia
Asia
Cilicia
Syria
Mauretania
Numidia
Mediterranean
Sea
Judaea
Empire Boundary
Demarcation Line
Proconsularis
Cyrenaica
Aegyptus
Arabia
Red Sea
WESTERN EMPIRE
EASTERN EMPIRE

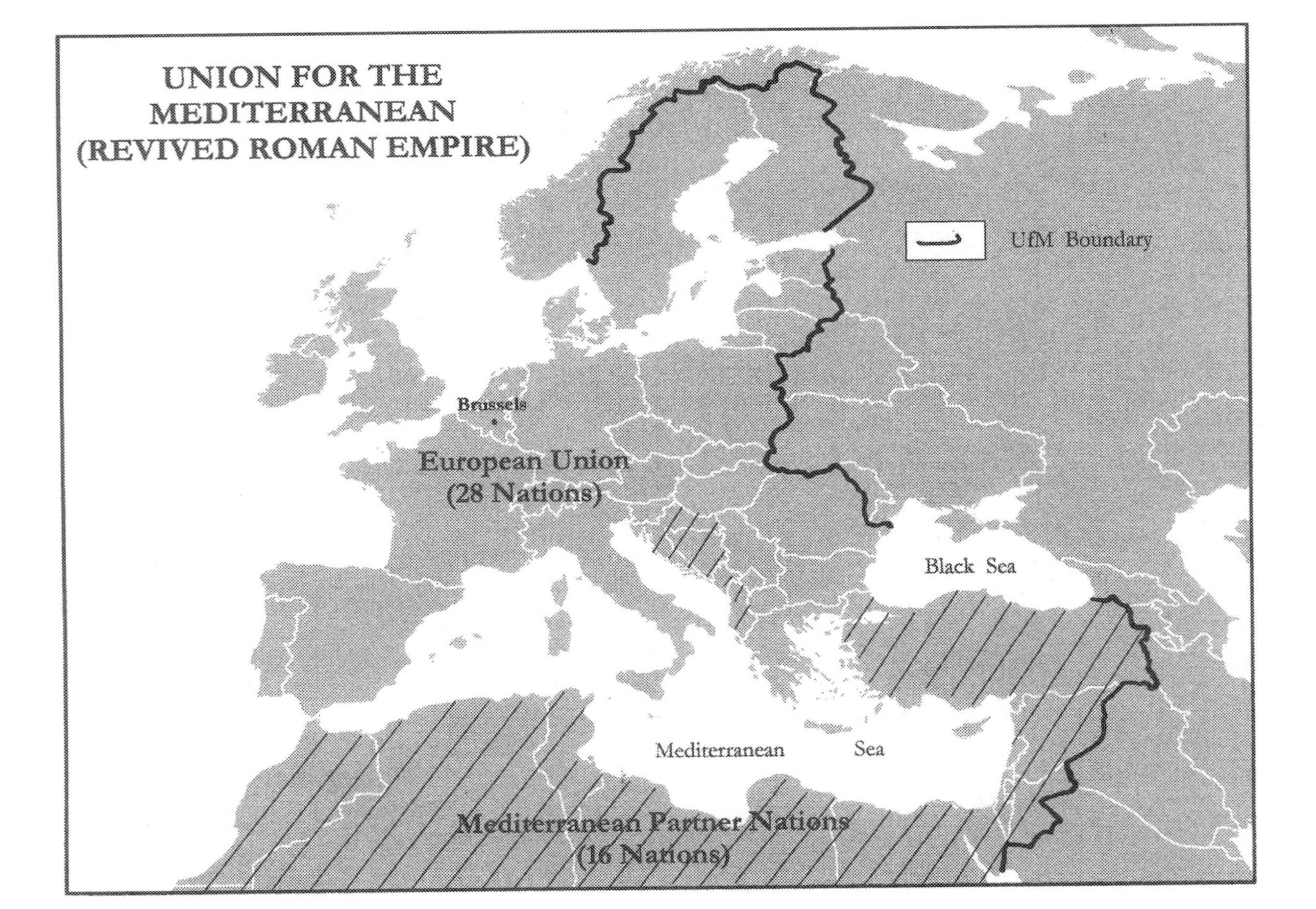
UNION FOR THE
MEDITERRANEAN
(REVIVED ROMAN EMPIRE)
UfM Boundary
Brussels
European Union
(28 Nations)
Black Sea
Mediterranean
Sea
Mediterranean Partner Nations
(16 Nations)

Returning to the question: who are the ten kings? The *corporate* kingdom beast that John also saw has ten horns representing ten kings. Because the beast is a *corporate* beast, it draws our attention to the fact that the ten kings symbolize ten kingdoms. In fact, it says that in Revelation 17:12. We seek to dispel the notion that the ten kings represent persons or ten states within the European Union or the Revived Roman Empire. No, it is much bigger. It is a global spread, not just confined to the west.

The ten kings are ten kingdoms. Interestingly, the globalist, guided by their vision of the New World Order, planned the division of the world into ten regions. Their agenda began to surface in the seventies. A document purported to be written by one of their organizations came to light espousing ways to manage and control the world and its resources. While their goal remains, the strategy is going through stages of adaptation. It takes a lot of time and effort— prodding, coercion, and regime change—to see their vision come true. Their agenda is no longer a secret as it is now public knowledge. Countries of the world are grouped into ten regions according to their proximity to each other. The ten regions (or kingdoms) are as follows:

1) America, Canada & Mexico
2) South America
3) Western Europe
4) Eastern Europe
5) North Africa & the Middle East
6) Central & Southern Africa
7) South Asia
8) Central Asia
9) Japan
10) Australia, New Zealand & the Oceania

Nations within each region are driven to cooperate among themselves through some multilateral trade agreements, or economic and political cooperation agreements. The President or Chairman of each regional pact will be the "king" as indicated by the Toes (Daniel 2:41-44), and Horns (Daniel 7:24; Revelation 17:12). The ten regions that these "kings" preside over are what the Bible called "kingdoms." As the Ten Toes are a mixture of iron and clay, so these "kingdoms" are not cohesive. They are partly strong and partly fragile.

Are these ten "kingdoms" already established? Yes, they are already up and running. Look at the numerous legal, financial, technical, economic and political cooperation agreements in existence these days. All the regions of the world have formulated agreements among themselves, and with the European Union. Many of the world's critical organizations have their headquarters there. To name a few, they are the World Trade Organization (WTO), United Nations (Geneva), World Court, International Labor Organization (ILO), and the International Telecommunication Union.

The conclusion is, we are the generation that is living in the days of the Revival Roman Empire. Soon, the Little Horn, the Antichrist will arise from this Empire.

Antichrist as the World Dictator

The ten kings are ten kingdoms. In Daniel's dream, the ten kingdoms are the ten horns of the fourth beast (Daniel 7:7). Daniel saw that a Little Horn appeared from among the ten horns. Who is the Little Horn? He is none other than the Antichrist. When he arises, three of the horns were "plucked out by the roots" (Daniel 7:8, 24). What happens to these horns? We surmised that physical destruction came upon these three kingdoms, or their vast population decimated or both. According to what is being expounded in this book, we believe it is the result of the Third World War. And the three regions could likely be America (North America), Russia (Eastern Europe), and one other region.

As the horns refer to kingdoms, the Little Horn should be a little kingdom. It means that the Antichrist is himself a kingdom. The angel explained it to John this way. Remember, the beast that John saw is a *corporate* beast. The angel said, "The beast that was, and is not is himself also the eighth (head), and is of the seven (head)" (Revelation 17:11). "The beast that was" refers to the Roman Empire (sixth head). It fell and came back as the eighth head or empire—the Antichrist Empire. But it is from the seventh head or Revived Roman Empire. So plainly, the Antichrist Empire will rise above the Revived

Roman Empire. With the Revived Roman Empire as its base and Brussels as its headquarters, the Antichrist will institute his power and authority to dictate the world. When he appears, the ten kingdoms will pledge their "power and authority" to him (Revelation 17:13).

Unbelievable as it may sound, the Antichrist himself cannot rule the world alone. He has to work through the ten kingdoms. With the ten kingdoms, he establishes the New World Order. It is a dictatorial system of government. He will not tolerate religious dissent. The post-rapture saints will not worship him. For this reason, he launches a war against them. These saints are believers left behind after the rapture but would include new believers as well. God will allow him to have victory over them (Daniel 7:21, 25; Revelation 13:7).

> The world refuses the true Christ; God will give them the Antichrist

At some point during the Antichrist reign, the ten kingdoms will "hate the harlot, make her desolate and naked, eat her flesh and burn her with fire" (Revelation 17:16-17). The harlot is the city of Rome.

The Antichrist is hubris without limit. He dares to speak pompous words, to blasphemy against the Most High (Daniel 7:25; Revelation 13:6). He manages to inveigle the world to worship him (Revelation 13:4, 8). The world refuses the real Christ. Therefore, God will give them the Antichrist.

Antichrist's Assistant: The False Prophet

Assisting the Antichrist is the false prophet. The false prophet is the beast who had "two horns like a lamb and spoke like a dragon" (Revelation 13:11). He seems to exercise the same authority as the Antichrist and persuade the world to worship the Antichrist (Revelation 13:12). Through his ability to perform signs and wonders, he deceives the inhabitants of the earth to make an image of the beast. The image of the beast could speak (Revelation 13: 14-15). Whatever the system it is, it could project the voice of the Antichrist to the zombified public.

On behalf of the Antichrist, the false prophet causes everyone to receive a mark on their right hand or their foreheads (Revelation 13:16-18). The mark is a tiny electronic chip. It enables a person to buy or sell. It is a system to replace paper money, credit or debit cards. It could be inserted into the first web space, the loose skin between the thumb and the index finger of the right hand or on the forehead. The system is called 666, a number representing the beast and a man. In biblical numerology, the number 6 represents Man. God created man on the sixth day. Six days we work but rest on the seventh day. The number 6 is repeated three times. Three is the number of divinities. God is a trinity. Thus, the mysterious number 666 means: Man attempts to be God.

God warns those who are alive during the reign of the Antichrist not to take the mark 666. He will not forgive anyone who yields himself to the system. BE WARNED.

> **Revelation 14:9-11**
> **9** Then a third angel followed them, saying with a loud voice,
> "If anyone worships the beast and his image, and receives
> his mark on his forehead or on his hand, **10** he himself shall
> also drink of the wine of the wrath of God, which is poured
> out full strength into the cup of His indignation. He shall be
> tormented with fire and brimstone in the presence of the holy
> angels and in the presence of the Lamb. **11** And the smoke
> of their torment ascends forever and ever, and they have no
> rest day or night, who worship the beast and his image, and
> whoever receives the mark of his name."

Will there be people who will not bow to the Antichrist? Yes there will be, read this:

> **Revelation 15:2-3**
> **2** And I saw something like a sea of glass mingled with fire,
> and those who have the victory over the beast, over his image
> and over his mark and over the number of his name, standing
> on the sea of glass, having harps of God. **3** They sing the song
> of Moses, the servant of God, and the song of the Lamb,
> saying: "Great and marvelous are Your works, Lord God
> Almighty! Just and true are Your ways, O King of the saints!

Those who will not take the mark or submit to the Antichrist system will not be able to buy or sell. Many will undergo beheading for their uncompromising stand (Revelation 20:4).

The Satanic Trinity

God is the creator. Satan is an imitator. The real God is a triune God: Father, Son, and Holy Spirit. Satan wants to imitate. The Bible says, "Three unclean spirits like frogs comes out of the mouth of the dragon, out of the mouth of the beast, and out of the mouth of the false prophet" (Revelation 16:13). The dragon is Satan, the Beast is the Antichrist, and together with the false prophet they form an unholy alliance.

The whole world worships the Antichrist. On behalf of the world, he challenges the Most High in heaven. He and the false prophet will mobilize the nations to fight against Christ and His people in Jerusalem at the end of his 7 years reign. The Bible calls that great battle, the Battle of Armageddon (Revelation 16:14, 16). Christ will defeat His enemies upon His glorious return to earth.

The beast (Antichrist) and the false prophet will be captured and cast alive into the lake of fire (Revelation 19:20).

Chapter 17

7 TRUMPETS AND 7 BOWLS JUDGMENT

The Seven Seals comprise two parts: (i) the first six seals, and (ii) the 7th seal. The first six seals are to prepare the Church for the rapture. After the rapture of the Church, divine judgment on the world commences with the opening of the 7th seal. Within the 7th seal is 7 trumpets judgment. And contain within the last trumpet, that is, the 7th trumpet are 7 bowls judgment. Apparently, these series of fourteen plagues are arranged in a telescopic manner. They will be poured out throughout the length of the 7 years reign of the Antichrist.

The 7 trumpets are so-called because they serve the purpose of warning the people of the earth to repent.

7 Trumpets Judgment

At the opening of the 7th seal, there was silence in heaven for about half an hour (Revelation 8:1). Standing before the throne of God are seven angels with seven trumpets ready to sound. The sounding of each trumpet, herald the outpouring of the wrath of God on the earth (Revelation 8-11).

First Trumpet Sounded: Hail and fire rain down on the earth burns away one-third of the earth's trees, and all green grass.

Second Trumpet Sounded: Something like a mountain burning with fire thrown into the sea. A third of the sea became blood killing a third of the sea creatures. Also, a third of the world's ships destroyed.

Third Trumpet Sounded: A star (asteroid or comet) named Wormwood burning like a torch falls to the earth causing a third of the rivers and water springs to be bitter or undrinkable. Many died from drinking the water.

Fourth Trumpet Sounded: The sun, moon and stars are stricken causing one-third of their luminance to be black-out. On the earth, a third of the day did not shine. Woe, woe, woe to the inhabitants of the world for the remaining trumpets are about to sound!

Fifth Trumpet Sounded (First Woe): A star (an angel) was given the key to the bottomless pit. When he opened the pit, smoke like a great furnace gush out that darkened the sun and air over the earth. Out of this cloud of smoke came locusts of demons. Their leader's name is Abaddon in Hebrew but Apollyon in Greek. The locusts shaped like horses prepared for battle. On their heads crowns of something like gold, and their faces were like the faces of men. They had hair like women's hair, and their teeth were like lions' teeth. And they had breastplates like breastplates of iron, and the sound of their wings was like the sound of chariots with many horses running into battle. They had tails like scorpions, and there were stings in their tails. Power was given to them to hurt the inhabitants of the earth for five months. They were not allowed to kill. During these five months, people desire to die but will not be able to. These locust demons do not have power over God's people, those who have the seal of God on their foreheads.

Sixth Trumpet Sounded (Second Woe): The four angels guarding the crossroad between the West and the East at the River Euphrates were ordered to stand down. It paved the way for the movement of an army of 200 million to start off killing a third of mankind in battle. The multitude was killed by three plagues: by fire, smoke and brimstone. Those not killed did not repent from worshipping demons. And from worshipping idols of gold, silver, brass, stone, and wood. They also did not repent of their crimes.

Seventh Trumpet Sounded (Third Woe): When the seventh trumpet sounded, there was a loud voice in heaven saying, "The kingdom of this world have become the kingdom of our Lord and His Christ, and He shall reign forever!"

This declaration indicates the immediacy of the second coming of Christ to set up His kingdom. The time has come for the stone cut out of the mountain without hands to strike the feet of the metallic man. It will break the feet of the iron and clay kingdom of the Antichrist into pieces (Daniel 2:34, 44-45).

7 Bowls Judgment

The 7 bowls are called the seven last plagues because they represent seven full cups of God's vengeance that He will pour out upon His enemies.

At this juncture, the scene in heaven changed. The Apostle John saw the Temple of God open and there is the Ark of the Covenant in it (Revelation 11:19). There were other scenes shown to John. But skipping over the parenthesis in Revelation chapters 12, 13, and 14, the Temple scene was repeated in chapter 15:5-8. Here John described what he saw. He saw one of the four living creatures gave to a group of seven angels, seven golden bowls (some translated as "vials") [1] full of the wrath of God. These seven angels were ordered to go out of the Heavenly Temple and pour the wrath of God on the earth (Revelation 15 &16).

First Bowl Outpouring: The wrath of God causes those who had the mark of the beast and who worship his image to suffer foul and loathsome sore on their bodies.

Second Bowl Outpouring: The angel pours his bowl on the sea, and the sea became blood. Every living creature in the sea died.

Third Bowl Outpouring: The rivers and springs of water became blood.

Fourth Bowl Outpouring: The angel pours out his bowl on the sun. He was given the power to scorch people with fire. People blaspheme God because of these plagues and refuse to repent of their sins.

Fifth Bowl Outpouring: This bowl was poured on the throne of the beast and his kingdom became full of darkness. Everyone was in pain but refuses to repent.

Sixth Bowl Outpouring: The River Euphrates was dried up by this judgment. The way was prepared for the kings of the east to be in battle. Three unclean spirits like frogs coming out of the mouth of the dragon, the mouth of the beast, and the mouth of the false prophet. These demons mobilize the world to gather in Israel. The world is compelled to gather in the place called Armageddon for the largest battle ever against Christ.

Seventh Bowl Outpouring: When the seventh angel pours out his bowl into the air, a loud voice from the Temple says, "It is done!" There were noises, thundering, and lightning. A very powerful earthquake rocks the earth. An earthquake, so mighty the world have not witnessed before since creation.

By the time of the seventh bowl outpouring of the wrath of God, nations of the world will lay in ruins. The world's physical infrastructure severely damaged. The planet's natural ecosystems so severely degraded it will not be able to sustain human life. Human extinction is all too possible. In the light of this, Jesus said to his disciples that "unless those days were shortened, no flesh would be saved. But for the sake of the elect those days will be shortened" (Matthew 24:22). This statement meant He will come a little sooner than planned.

Chapter 18

SECOND COMING OF CHRIST

A few days before His crucifixion, Jesus was in Jerusalem visiting the Temple. A large crowd gathered around Him. He warned them that the kingdom of God would be taken away from them and given to other nations. The Scribes and Pharisees were present. He gave them a scathing rebuke for rejecting the prophets sent to them. Then, addressing the city of Jerusalem, He said, "O Jerusalem, Jerusalem, the one who kills the prophets and stones those who are sent to her! How often I wanted to gather your children together as a hen gathers her chicks under her wings, but you were not willing." He went on to say, "See! Your house is left to you desolate. For I say to you, you shall see Me no more till you say, "Blessed is He who comes in the name of the Lord!" (Matthew 23:37-39).

The Jews will cry out "Blessed is He who comes in the name of the Lord!" It will entail a national repentance. No more will there be any mistaken identity; no longer any illusion of who He is. The one they are desperate to see is Yeshua. His plan for the Jews in the last two millennia is precise to bring them to this point of decision. It is said as soon as Zion is in labor she will give birth to her children. A unique fountain of grace will open for the house of David and to the inhabitants of Jerusalem to remove sin and uncleanness. Prophet Zechariah of old saw this wonderful day of great mercy and favor poured upon his people:

Zechariah 12:10-11

10 "And I will pour on the house of David and on the inhabitants of Jerusalem the Spirit of grace and supplication; then they will look on Me whom they pierced. Yes, they will

> mourn for Him as one mourns for his only son, and grieve for Him as one grieves for a firstborn. **11** In that day, there shall be a great mourning in Jerusalem, like the mourning at Hadad Rimmon in the *plain of Megiddo*." (Emphasis added)

> Each Jew will say to Yeshua, "The Lord is my God"

In the meantime, at the plain of Megiddo located some 60 miles north of Jerusalem the Battle of Armageddon is raging. All the nations have sent their armies to conduct the final battle against Israel and her Messiah. In this fight, two-third of the population in Israel will perish. The remaining one-third preserved through the fire, to refine them as silver and gold is refined. Then, Yeshua will address them saying, "You are My people." And *each of them* will reply, "The Lord is my God" (Zechariah 13:8-9 paraphrase).[1]

In Jerusalem, the city will succumb to the combined assault of the foreign powers. Houses will be rifled; the women ravished. Half the city will be overthrown. But the remnant of God's people will be preserved in this very stressful environment (Zechariah 14:1-2).

For what they are doing to His people and His land, Yeshua will recompense the invaders. He will hit them with nuclear bombs or chemical weapons. Their flesh will dissolve while they stand on their feet. Their eyes will dissolve in their sockets, and tongues dissolve in their mouths (Zechariah 14:12).

Behold He Comes

The second coming of Christ is also termed His Glorious Appearing. It is an event the Bible has much to say. Consider some scriptural statistics.

a. Jesus' return is explicitly referred to 1,845 times in the Bible—1,527 times in the Old Testament, and 318 times in the New Testament.
b. The second coming is mentioned in 23 of the 27 New Testament books.
c. Enoch who lived only seven generations after Adam and is considered the first prophet of the Bible. He prophesied about this event

(Jude 14). Therefore, the first prophecy of the Bible concerns the second coming.

d. The final prophecy of the Bible deals with the second coming (Revelation 22:20).
e. Jesus Himself refers to His return twenty-one times.[2]

The Event of His Return

Jesus will return physically or bodily to the earth. Unlike His first coming which is discreet, this time it will be openly and indubitably. Below is the going on about His return.

Descend from heaven on a white horse. The Lord will ride on a white horse coming out of heaven to the earth. He is called Faithful and True. His eyes are as flames of fire, and He has many crowns on His head. His white robe dipped in blood. He, who is called the Word of God; out of His mouth goes a sharp sword with which He judged the nations. Written on His robe and thigh is the title: King of kings and Lord of lords (Revelation 19:11-13; 15).

The saints will come with Him. Accompanying His descent from heaven are the first resurrected saints. These are those who participated in the rapture seven years earlier. As part of the armies of heaven, they followed the Lord on white horses. They are clothed in fine linen, white and clean. Their impeccable garments depict their righteous acts (Zechariah 14:5; Revelation 19:8 & 14).

Touchdown on Mount of Olives. The feet of Jesus will land on the Mount of Olives overlooking the Kidron Valley on the Eastern side of the Temple Mount. A powerful earthquake will split the Mount of Olives into two from the East to the West. Half the mountain will move north, and the other half move south. The chasm will create an enormous valley running from east to west. Very likely, it will stretch from the northern tip of the Dead Sea to the city of Ashdod by the Mediterranean Sea (Zechariah 14:4). It is obvious the split will significantly affect the Temple Mount and the city of Jerusalem.

The Dead Sea comes alive. Somewhere on the northern side of the rift, fresh water from the subterranean will flow out from the site of the future Millennium Temple. The water will flow in two courses. Part of the water will flow south into the newly created valley. From there it continues to flow westward into the Mediterranean Sea. The water will flow all year round, in both summer and winter (Zechariah 14:8).

The other river course will channel the water eastward, down the valley, and enters the Dead Sea. [3] The flowing fresh water will heal the salt water of the Dead Sea on contact. Fishes will begin to live and thrive. Fishermen will spread their nets to catch the abundant supply. The fishes will be similar to the fishes found in the Mediterranean Sea. Only the northern and center part of the Dead Sea will experience rejuvenation, the southern side will be swamps and marshes. These will not heal but be given over to salt contamination. Along the banks of the river that flows into the Dead Sea, all kinds of fruit trees will grow. The fruits will be for food, and their leaves for medicine (Ezekiel 47:1-12).

When all these come to pass, the Dead Sea will no longer be dead. Perhaps, time to change its name?

A 24-hours daylight. When the Lord returns, there will be a supernatural phenomenon in the sky. The solar cycle of day and night will be suspended, possibly for 24-hours. There will be a supernatural light, lighting up the whole world (Zechariah 14:6-7).

His Millennium Kingdom

Soon after the Lord's return, He will set up His millennium kingdom. Millennium (Latin *mille* = thousand, and *annum* = year), or one thousand years of Christ reign (Revelation 20:1-6). His kingdom administrative center will be in Jerusalem.

With regards the spiritual aspect, the fourth Temple will be built on a site a few miles to the north of Jerusalem. Prophet Ezekiel was given the details of the Temple (Ezekiel 40-48). The Lord will require the nations that exist at that time, to visit the Temple and to take part in His feasts. Those not willing to observe the feasts such as the Feast of Tabernacle will face judgment. Rain will be withheld, and plagues will strike families and nations who disobey (Zechariah 14:16-19).

Then, it is accomplished. The 70 weeks of years or 490 years of God's program for the Jewish people will conclude. The Lord would have:

- Finish the transgression
- Make an end of sins
- Make reconciliation for iniquity
- Bring in everlasting righteousness
- Seal up vision and prophecy
- Anoint the Most High

NOTES

Chapter 1 – Opening of the Seals

1. Prophet David Edward Owour, https://www. repentandprepare theway.org
2. Extract from an interview Prophet Owour gave to a journalist, February 18, 2011, http://www.youtube.com/watch?v=7RGRG-2owKE.

Chapter 2 – The Four Horses of the Apocalypse

1. Apocalypse is a transliteration of the Greek word *apokalypsis* meaning "unveiling" or "revelation." The modern English dictionary defines the word to mean "the destruction of the world" or "the end of the world." While the world would be recreated in the distant future, it will not cease to exist, as it is clearly taught in the Bible.
2. The rider on this white horse is an angel. Therefore, it could not be the same as the white horse mentioned in Revelation 19:11, whom the rider is Jesus Christ.
3. AE911Truth.Org, Architects & Engineers for 9/11 Truth is an organization of architects, engineers and affiliates at the forefront dispelling misinformation and disinformation of the official story of what happened on September 11 with scientific facts and forensic evidence.
4. Prophet David Edward Owour, https://www. repentandprepare theway.org
5. Video clip documenting the announcement of Prophet Owour's vision of the black horse and subsequent sighting of the horse flying over the sky in Jeddah, Saudi Arabia on November 26, 2014 which was witnessed by several bystanders, https://www.youtube.com/watch?v=v4TDn0y4Ymk (accessed December 10, 2014).
6. Warrior angels sent to destroy the twin cities of Sodom and Gomorrah due to their abominable sins of homosexuality (Genesis 19:12-14). They were sent to punish King David for his great sin. The warrior angels had

killed 70,000 men of the children of Israel before they stopped in response to King David's repentance (2 Samuel 24:15-17). In the days of King Hezekiah of Judah, the Assyrian army lead by King Sennacherib went up and surrounded Jerusalem with the intent to subjugate it. In response, God sent His warrior angels, and they annihilated the whole camp of the Assyrians of 185,000 soldiers (2 Kings 19:35-36).

7. In referring to the vast population of human beings killed, the phrase "a third of mankind" was used (Revelation 9:15, 18). Elsewhere, the phrase "a third of the trees were burned up" (Revelation.8:7) refers to a third part of earth vegetation destroyed, "a third of the ships were destroyed" (Revelation 8:9) refers to the number of ships destroyed, or "a third of the sun was struck" (Revelation 8:12) refers to a third part of the sun surface being damaged, thus, no longer gives out light.
8. Video clip documenting the announcement of Prophet Owour's vision of the pale horse and subsequent sighting of the horse moving among a crowd of protestors in Tahrir Square, Cairo, Egypt, April 6, 2011, https://www.youtube.com/ watch?v= P4roQWBVdr0 (accessed December 11, 2013).
9. Jessica Rettig, "Death Toll of 'Arab Spring'," November 8, 2011, http://www.usnews.com/news/slideshows/death-toll-of-arab-spring (accessed December 5, 2014).
10. "The War on Terror in Numbers," January 6, 2015, http://owni.eu/2011/05/05/the-war-on-terror-in-numbers/ (accessed January 6, 2015).
11. The video clip showing a black horse flying over the sky in Jeddah, Saudi Arabia captured on a camera by a witness on November 26, 2014, https://www.youtube.com/watch?v =dOVduROwRrk (accessed December 10, 2014).
12. The video clip showing MSNBC cameraman recorded a pale horse among the protesting crowd in Tahrir Square, Cairo, Egypt on April 6, 2011, https://www.youtube.com/watch?v= mLNtDqDpxzI (accessed December 11, 2013).
13. "Ebola Situation Report - January 14, 2015," http://www.who.int/csr/disease/ebola/situation-reports/en/ (accessed January 15, 2015).
14. The list is an adaptation from the chart appearing in the website, "Lions go global: Deepening Africa's ties to the United States," August, 2014, http://www.mckinsey.com//globalization/ lions_go_global_deepening_africas_ties_to_the_united_states, (accessed January 9, 2015).

Chapter 3 – Living Between the Seals

1. Hippolytus, *Hippolytus on the Twelve Apostles*; Christian Classics Ethereal Library.
2. Ibid.
3. Michael W. Holmes, ed., *The Apostolic Fathers: Greek Texts and English Translations*, 3rd ed., (Grand Rapids: Baker Academic, 2007), 323.
4. One of those organizations who did a study on the subject of martyrdom was Gordon-Conwell Theological Seminary as published in "Martyrology: The demographics of Christian martyrdom, AD 33–AD 2001" in 2002.
5. "Coptic Church confirms 21 Egyptian Christians dead after ISIS issues said beheading video," February 16, 2015, http://www. jpost.com/Middle-East/Coptic-Church-confirms-21-Egyptian-Christians-dead-after-ISIS-issues-said-beheading-video-391139 (accessed February 18, 2015).

Chapter 4 – The Jews

1. Biological anthropologists and some Jewish theologians say the Jews are not a race. They prefer to call it "household." They point to the fact that there are Caucasian Jews, Black Jews, and Oriental Jews. In the genealogy of Jesus, four non-Jewish women were named—Tamar, Rahab, Ruth and Bathsheba (Matthew 1:1-17). It is a fact, intermarriage of races happened in all racial groups. As it did not thoroughly dilute the Jewish race, we still stick to the view that the Jews are a race.
2. See Raymond F. Surburg, *Introduction to the Intertestamental Period*, (St. Louis, MI: Concordia Publishing House, 1975).
3. William Whiston, trans., *Josephus: The Complete Works* (Nashville, TN: Thomas Nelson Publishers, 1998), 368.
4. Ibid., 388-9.
5. Ibid., 393.
6. There is general agreement among Bible scholars that the boundaries of the land promised to Abraham: [1] On the Northern part, should stretch from the Mediterranean coast to the land of present-day Lebanon and Syria. It reaches even as far as the Northwest section of the Euphrates River. [2] On the Eastern border, the land should be along the Jordan

River, and include the area of what is today called the Golan Heights. [3] On the Southern border, the land should include the Negev wilderness and meets the Mediterranean Sea at the Wadi or River of Egypt. [4] On the Western border, the land should include the Wadi of Egypt along the Mediterranean coast up to Lebo Hamath in the North.

7. J. Dwight Pentecost, *Things To Come* (Dunham Publishing Company, 1958; reprint, Grand Rapids, MI: Zondervan, 1964), 97.

Chapter 5 – Have the Christians Replaced the Jews? (Replacement Theology)

1. They are called Parties rather than Sects as all of them kept their reverence for the Jerusalem Temple, despite differing interpretation on other issues. On the other hand, the Qumran community and the Samaritans could rightly be called Sects as they do not recognize the legitimacy of the Temple. See Richard Bauckham, *The Jewish World around the New Testament*, (Grand Rapids, MI: Baker Academic, 2008), 175-192.
2. William Whiston, trans., *Josephus: The Complete Works* (Nashville, TN: Thomas Nelson Publishers, 1998), 898.
3. Eusebius, *Church History* 5:631; Christian Classics Ethereal Library.
4. Origen, *Against Celsus* 433; Christian Classics Ethereal Library.
5. Cyprian, *On the Lord's Prayer* 450; Christian Classics Ethereal Library.
6. John Chrysostom, "Eight Orations Against Judaizing Christians" (387-388), http://www.ccjr.us/dialogika-resources/primary-texts-from-the-history-of-the-relationship/247-chrysostom (accessed on March 2, 2015).
7. Ibid.
8. Ibid.
9. Ibid.
10. Ibid.
11. Ibid.
12. August C. Krey, *The First Crusade* (USA: Princeton University Press, 1921), 249-261.
13. Martin Luther, *The Jews and Their Lies* (Germany, 1543), trans. (Los Angeles, CA: Christian Nationalist Crusade, 1948), 54.

14. "Modern Jewish History: The Pale of Settlement," http://www.jewishvirtuallibrary.org/jsource/History/pale.html (accessed March 10, 2015).
15. "Jewish Population of Europe in 1933: Population Data by Country," http://www.ushmm.org/wlc/en/article.php?ModuleId=10005161 (accessed March 12, 2015).
16. Derek Prince, *The Last Word on the Middle East* (Eastbourne: Kingsway Publications, 1982), 29.
17. Raul Hilberg, *Holocaust*, Microsoft "Encarta" 98 Encyclopedia (1993-1997), Microsoft Corporation.
18. Berenbaum, Michael, "Holocaust: The Events." *Encyclopaedia Judaica*. Ed. Michael Berenbaum and Fred Skolnik. 2nd ed. Vol. 9. (Detroit: Macmillan Reference USA, 2000), 325-343, *Gale Virtual Reference Library*, 14 March 2015.
19. Austin Flannery, gen. ed., *Declaration on the Relation of the Church to Non-Christian Religions*, Vatican Council II, new and rev. ed. (New York: Costello Publishing Company, 1992), 741.

Chapter 6 – Jewish Global Influence

1. "Selected Indicators of World Jewry," http://jppi.org.il/uploads/Selected%20Indicators%20of%20World%20Jewry.pdf (accessed March 20, 2015).
2. Ricardo Fuentes-Nieva and Nick Galasso, "Working for the Few," January 20, 2014, https://www.oxfam.org/sites/www.oxfam.org/files/bp-working-for-few-political-capture-economic-inequality-200114-summ-en.pdf (accessed March 20, 2015).
3. "Forbes Ranking of Billionaires: the world's richest Jews," April 12, 2013, http://www.forbes.co.il/news/new.aspx?pn6Vq= J&0r9VQ=IEII (accessed March 21, 2015).
4. "Our Group," http://www.rothschild.com/about_rothschild/our_group/ (accessed March 25, 2015).
5. Niall Ferguson, *The House of Rothschild: Money's Prophets, 1798-1848* (New York: Penguin Books, 1999), 45.

6. Niall Ferguson, *The House of Rothschild: The World's Banker, 1849-1999* (New York: Penguin Books, 2000), 79-80.
7. Theodor Herzl, *The Jewish State,* reprint, (USA, Digireads.com Publishing, 2011), 44.
8. Frederic Morton, *The Rothschilds: A Family Portrait* (New York: Diversion Books, 2014), 16.
9. "Jewish Population in the United States, Nationally," https:// www.jewishvirtuallibrary.org/jsource/US-Israel/usjewpop1.html (accessed March 25, 2015).
10. Tani Goldstein, "How did American Jews get so rich?" October 26, 2011, http://www.ynetnews.com/articles/0,7340,L-4099803,00.html (accessed June 8, 2015).
11. "A Portrait of Jewish Americans," October 1, 2013, http://www.pewforum.org/2013/10/01/jewish-american-beliefs-attitudes-culture-survey/
12. See G. Edward Griffin, *The Creature from Jekyll Island*, 3rd. ed. (California: American Media, 1998).
13. Yueh-Yun C. O'Brien, "Reserve Requirement Systems in OECD Countries," July 23, 2007, http://www.federalreserve.gov/pubs/feds 2007/200754/index.html (accessed March 29, 2015).
14. Alison Weir, "Introduction to the Israel Lobby," August 2014, http://www.ifamericansknew.org/us_ints/introlobby.html
15. Michael Snyder, "Who Owns The Media?" October 4, 2010, http://theeconomiccollapseblog.com/archives/who-owns-the-media-the-6-monolithic-corporations-that-control-almost-everything-we-watch-hear-and-read
16. Donald Neff, "An Updated List of Vetoes Cast by the United States to Shield Israel from Criticism by the U.N. Security Council," http://www.wrmea.org/2005-may-june/an-updated-list-of-vetoes-cast-by-the-united-states-to-shield-israel-from-criticism-by-the-u.n.-security-council.html

Chapter 7 – The Shemitah

1. Jonathan Cahn, *The Mystery of the Shemitah* (Lake Mary, FL: FrontLine, 2014), 30.

2. D. James Kennedy, *What If America Were A Christian Nation Again?* (Nashville, TN: Thomas Nelson Publishers, 2003), 31.
3. Phillip Swagel, "Why Lehman Wasn't Rescued," September 13, 2013, http://economix.blogs.nytimes.com/2013/09/13/why-lehman-wasnt-rescued/?_r=0 (accessed April 10, 2015).
4. Alexandra Twin, "Stocks crushed," September 29, 2008, http:// money.cnn.com/2008/09/29/markets/markets_newyork/ (accessed April 11, 2015).
5. Buck Stephens, "September 13, 2015 – Part 1: A Reoccuring Dream," https://drive.google.com/file/d/0BwlPj3R-8rUFaktaVlYzZTBrMjA/edit?pli=1 (accessed April 12, 2015).
6. Jonathan Cahn, *The Mystery of the Shemitah* (Lake Mary, FL: FrontLine, 2014), 262.

Chapter 8 – The Blood Moons

1. Mark Biltz, "Blood Moon Videos & Teaching," http://elshaddaiministries.us/eclipses.php (accessed April 14, 2015).
2. "Eclipses During 2014 & 2015," http://eclipse.gsfc.nasa.gov/OH/OH2014.html (accessed April 16,2015).
3. John Hagee, "Blood Moons," https://www.youtube.com/watch?v=mAy_4vgua4s (accessed March 4, 2015).

Chapter 9 – America

1. Jonathan Edwards, http://www.theopedia.com/Jonathan_ Edwards
2. George Whitefield, http://www.theopedia.com/ George_ Whitefield
3. Charles Finney, http://www.theopedia.com/Charles_Finney
4. Daniel H. Bays, "The Foreign Missionary Movement in the 19th and early 20th Centuries," http://nationalhumanitiescenter.org/tserve/nineteen/nkeyinfo/fmmovementc.htm
5. "America's Changing Religious Landscape," May 12, 2015, http://www.pewforum.org/2015/05/12/americas-changing-religious-landscape/

6. Sean M. Lynn-Jones, "Why the United States Should Spread Democracy," March 1998, http://belfercenter.ksg.harvard.edu/publication/2830/why_the_united_states_should_spread_democracy.html
7. Ibid.
8. Ibid.
9. "Nuclear weapons and Israel," https://en.wikipedia.org/wiki/Nuclear_weapons_and_Israel
10. "Security Council Resolution 242 (1967) of 22 November 1967," http://unispal.un.org/unispal.nsf/0/7D35E1F729DF491C85256EE700686136
11. Ahuva Balofsky, "Jewish Population in Judea & Samaria Growing Significantly," January 5, 2015, http://www.breakingisraelnews. com/26966/jewish-population-in-judea-and-samaria-growing-significantly/#KPu0qmi4KYTeKyql.97
12. Barak Ravid, "U.S.: It will be hard to support Israel in UN if it steps back from a two-state solution," April 27, 2015, http://www. haaretz.com/news/diplomacy-defense/.premium-1.653819

Chapter 10 – Moral Decline & Changing of God's Law

1. Kevin J. Conner, *What Do You Mean? I Am Not Under Law I Am Under Grace*, (Vermont, Australia: KJC Resources, 2009), 9-10.
2. Ibid.
3. Ibid., 41.
4. Michael Snyder, "100 Facts About The Moral Collapse Of America That Are Almost Too Crazy To Believe," April 9, 2014, http://thetruthwins.com/archives/100-facts-about-the-moral-collapse-of-america-that-are-almost-too-crazy-to-believe (accessed June 29, 2015).
5. James Bailey, "TD Hale's Dreams Tell the Future of America," January 16, 2013, http://z3news.com/w/td-hale-prophetic-dreams-tell-the-future-of-america/(accessed March 5, 2013).
6. James Bailey, "TD Hale's 4th Prophetic Dream: Rain of Fire Coming to America," January 10, 2013, http://z3news.com/w/td-hale-4th-prophetic-dream/ (accessed March 5, 2013).
7. Brian Resnick, Lauren Fox and Dustin Volz, "Why Four Justices Were Against the Supreme Court's Huge Gay-Marriage Decision," June 26,

2015, http://www.nationaljournal.com/domesticpolicy/marriage-same-sex-gay-supreme-court-dissent-20150626 (accessed June 27, 2015).

8. "Franklin Graham releases statement on same-sex marriage decision," June 27, 2015, http://www.foxcarolina.com/story/ 29417405/franklin-graham-releases-statement-on-same-sex-marriage-decision
9. Paul Strand, "Supreme Court Extends Same-Sex Marriage Nationwide," June 27, 2015, http://www.cbn.com/cbnnews/us/ 2015/June/Supreme-Court-Extends-Same-Sex-Marriage-Nationwide/

Chapter 11 – Economic Decline & Collapse of the USD

1. Michael Snyder, "40 Statistics About The Fall Of The U.S. Economy That Are Almost Too Crazy To Believe," May 26, 2013, http://theeconomiccollapseblog.com/archives/40-statistics-about-the-fall-of-the-u-s-economy-that-are-almost-too-crazy-to-believe (accessed July 3, 2015).
2. Pastor Shane Warren interviewed by Sid Roth, http://www. youtube.com/watch?v =8714512Q4rY (accessed July 4, 2015).

Chapter 12 – Coming Judgment of America

1. Other prophets or servants of the Lord who were shown details of the coming judgment include A.C.Valdez, A.A.Allen, Daisy Osborn, Zelma Kirkpatrick, Nita Johnson, David Wilkerson, Henry Gruver, David E. Taylor, Shane Warren, T D Hale and Mary K. Baxter.
2. See Dumitru Duduman, *Through the Fire Without Burning* (Titusville, FL: Christ Is Creator Ministries, 1991).
3. Ibid., 141-146.
4. Dumitru Duduman, "Russia and China Strikes," http://www. handofhelp.com/vision_36.php
5. Dumitru Duduman, "The Bear Awakes," http://www. handofhelp.com/vision_44.php
6. "Brief introduction to the Shanghai Cooperation Organisation," http://www.sectsco.org/EN123/brief.asp (accessed February 12, 2015).

7. "Aegis Ballistic Missile Defence (BMD) System, United States of America," http://www.naval-technology.com/projects/aegis-ballistic-missile-defence-bmd-us/ (accessed April 10, 2015).
8. "US Awards $600 Million for NATO's Ballistic Missile Defense Kill Vehicle." http://sputniknews.com/military/20150504/ 1021707775.html (accessed May 4, 2015).
9. During the Cold War, the Cuban Missile Crisis in 1962 nearly led to a thermonuclear war between the U.S. and the Soviet Union. A year earlier, the U.S. attempted to overthrow the Castro regime in Cuba which failed. The U.S. decided to place Jupiter ballistic missiles in Italy and Turkey against the USSR. Soviet leader Nikita Khrushchev decided to agree to Cuba's request to place nuclear missiles in Cuba to deter future U.S. harassment. President Kennedy ordered Khrushchev to remove the missiles from Cuba, which is just 90 miles from Florida. Otherwise, there will be a war. After 13 days of tense negotiation, both sides backed down and removed their respective missiles.
10. "China able to attack Taiwan by 2020: report," October 9, 2013, http://www.taipeitimes.com/News/front/archives/2013/10/09/2003574061 (accessed April 30, 2015).
11. The sun creates a solar storm that releases an enormous amount of energy. If the scorching electrified gasses (coronal mass ejection) directly hit the earth, it could "burn" or damage the sensitive microchips used in any electronic devices.
12. A nuclear explosion releases electrons. When the earth magnetic field traps them, they give rise to an oscillating electric current. The current in turn radiated electromagnetic field called an electromagnetic pulse. Should a nuclear bomb explodes, say, 200 miles above the U.S., the electromagnetic pulse could hit the whole continental U.S. permanently disabling all microchips used in equipment.

Chapter 13 – Coming Russian Invasion of Israel

1. Ari Yashar, "Israel Among Ten Most Powerful Nations In World," January 24, 2014, http://www.israelnationalnews.com/News/News.aspx/176683#.VUhMaPmqqko

2. "The World Fact Book," https://www.cia.gov/ library/ publications/the-world-factbook/geos/is.html (accessed May 2, 2015).

Chapter 14 – Rapture

1. Tim LaHaye and Jerry B Jenkins, *Are We Living in the End Times?* (Wheaton, IL: Tyndale House Publishers, 1999), 98.
2. A.C.Valdez, Sr., "Vision by A. C. Valdez, Sr." http://healingandrevival.com/ValdezSrVision.pdf
3. Mary K. Baxter, *A Divine Revelation of Hell* (Fort Washington, MD: Whitaker House, 1993), 199-200.
4. Choo Thomas, *Heaven Is So Real* (Lake Mary, FL: Creation House Press, 2004; reprint, Malaysia: Divine Cultivations Sdn. Bhd., 2004), 139-141.
5. David Jones, "The Final Day," http://littledavidministries.org/videos
6. Prophet David Edward Owour, "Mighty Vision of the Rapture of the Church," June 22, 2013, https://www.youtube.com/ watch?v= hjwWu7K69sA
7. Anna Rountree, *Heaven Awaits the Bride* (Lake Mary, FL: Charisma House, 2007), 47.

Chapter 15 – 70th Week of Daniel

1. J. Dwight Pentecost, *Things to Come* (Dunham Publishing Company, 1958; reprint, Grand Rapids, MI: Zondervan, 1964), 241.
2. See Sir Robert Anderson, *The Coming Prince* (Grand Rapid, MI: Kregel Publications; reprint, Kregel Classics, 1957).
3. See Harold W. Hoehner, *Chronological Aspects of the Life of Christ* (Grand Rapid, MI: Zondervan, 1977).
4. Tim LaHaye and Thomas Ice, *The End Times Controversy* (Eugene, OR: Harvest House Publishers, 2003), 328-331.
5. Ibid.
6. Gershon Salomon, "The Personal Experiences of Gershon Salomon During the 1967 Six Day War," http://www. templemountfaithful.org/articles/gershon-salomon-and-the-1967-six-day-war.php (assessed May 20, 2015).

7. "Objectives of the Temple Mount Faithful," http://www. temple mountfaithful.org/objectives.php
8. "Sacred Vessels and Vestments," https://www.templeinstitute.org/vessels_gallery.htm (assessed May 24, 2015).
9. "The Sanhedrin Initiative," http://www.thesanhedrin.org/en/ index.php?title=The_Sanhedrin_Initiative (assessed May 26, 2015).

Chapter 16 – 7 Years Reign of the Antichrist

1. Stephen P. Kershaw, *A Brief History of the Roman Empire* (London, UK: Constable & Robinson Ltd., 2013), 383.
2. "History," http://ufmsecretariat.org/history/ (assessed May 29, 2015).
3. What is meant by *corporate*? In another scene in John's vision, he saw the corporate empire beast with seven heads and ten horns (Revelation 13:1-3). The beast showed traces of past empires in its body. Notice it was like a leopard (Greek empire), had feet like a bear (Medes-Persian empire), and mouth like a lion (Babylonian empire). One of its head was "mortally wounded" but it began to heal. The seven heads represents the seven world empires. We believe the one wounded was the Roman Empire. It was healed, meaning it revived.

Chapter 17 – 7 Trumpets and 7 Bowls Judgment

1. The Greek word *phiale* should better translate as "bowl" than "vial." The vessel is more like a saucer than a test tube. See Robert G. Gromacki, *New Testament Survey* (Grand Rapids, MI: Baker Book House, 1974), 408.

Chapter 18 – Second Coming of Christ

1. Interesting to note is that the Lord requires each Israeli to acknowledge Him personally as his or her Messiah. Salvation is an individual matter. Notwithstanding, the goal is for Israel's national repentance and salvation.
2. Mark Hitchcock, *101 Answer to the Most Asked Questions about the End Times* (Sisters, OR: Multnomah Publishers, 2001), 200.

3. The water surface of the Dead Sea (Salt Sea) is 429 m (1,407 feet) below sea level, that is, below the water surface of the Mediterranean Sea. The Dead Sea itself is 304 m (997 feet) deep, the deepest hypersaline lake in the world. It is also one of the world's saltiest bodies of water. No fish could live in such water.

To contact the author or for more information

Visit the Website:
EndTimeScenario.com

Or Email:
etscenario@gmail.com

Or Write to:
P. O. Box 3
Pejabat Pos Jelutong
11600 Penang
Malaysia